Alternate States of Consciousness

By the same author:
FRONTIERS OF REALITY
GODS*SPIRITS*COSMIC GUARDIANS
VISIONS*APPARITIONS*ALIEN VISITORS

Alternate States of Consciousness

Unself, Otherself, and Superself

HILARY EVANS

THE AQUARIAN PRESS

First published 1989

British Library Cataloguing in Publication Data

Evans, Hilary
Alternate states of consciousness.
1. Man. Consciousness
I. Title
153

ISBN 0-85030-802-X

The Aquarian Press is part of the Thorsons Publishing Group, Wellingborough, Northamptonshire, NN8 2RQ, England.

Printed in Great Britain by Biddles Limited, Guildford, Surrey

1 3 5 7 9 10 8 6 4 2

Contents

Preface

This book is written out of ignorance. I found myself talking a lot about alternate states, without really knowing what they are. But when I tried to find out, I found that others are hardly less ignorant than I am. There is no consensus of agreement even as to whether alternate states exist, let alone what they are, what causes them or what purpose they serve.

This was so discouraging that I came close to abandoning the attempt; but then I thought, at least I can inquire what seems to be known about alternate states, however tentatively and provisionally; and perhaps others equally puzzled will find the inquiry helpful.

But it is important we bear in mind that what follows is only an inquiry, and only rarely will the material be other than speculative. We shall find patches of firm ground here and there, because there are things we know to be historical fact. But most of our path will be doubtful going, even treacherous, because even though we may know something to be historical fact, we don't necessarily know what kind of fact it is.

And that is not all. One of the reasons why alternate states are so incompletely understood is that the subject is so vast and so complex. The enigmas of dreaming, of hypnosis, of multiple personality have each generated a library of case histories and theories; I haven't read them all, nobody has; inevitably I am not going to do justice to them in a brief survey. All I can hope to do is to get them into some sort of helpful perspective.

To do this, I shall have to refrain from going into some questions as deeply as they — and you — deserve; I shall have to make assumptions in matters which should really be discussed at length; I shall have to ask you to make do with a single example where really I ought to offer you several to prove to you that something is truly taking place; and I shall have to over-simplify the accounts of the alternate states themselves to a degree which you may feel amounts to outright distortion. But were I to take into account every nuance and complexity of, say, hypnosis, our hope of achieving a graspable perspective would vanish. I can only say that I have tried to make as few assumptions as possible, and to maintain a fair balance between the different ways in which these experiences can be interpreted.

One further shortcoming: the definition of alternate states being so uncertain, it is evident that at the time when most of my case histories were recorded, there were even fewer reliable yardsticks by which to evaluate them than exist today. Even when they are correctly reported, the questions we would like to ask were generally not asked, so that our knowledge of them is incomplete. Inevitably, therefore, our interpretation of what happened, say, to a bunch of nuns in sixteenth-century Flanders, or to an amnesia subject in nineteenth-century America, must be, ultimately, no more than an educated guess.

Terminology

In a field of study where there is so little consensus of opinion, it is not surprising that terminology is used loosely and sometimes arbitrarily. Since nobody knows what hypnosis is, each will use the term in accordance with his own ideas.

For this reason, I have used as few technical terms as possible, and it will be helpful if I indicate here at the start the terms I do use, and what I mean by them:

* The two basic concepts are 'usual state of consciousness' (USC) and 'alternate state of consciousness' (ASC). By

'usual' I mean the everyday conscious state in which we perceive our surroundings more or less as (it seems) everyone sees them, and are more or less in control of our thoughts and actions. By 'alternate' I mean any state in which significant changes take place in our perception and behaviour. I use 'alternate', as including both spontaneous states and those which are entered by choice; I avoid 'altered' because it seems to suggest a deliberate change from one state to another, which is true of cases like spirit trance or drug taking, but not of, say, somnambulism.

★   I use (though as rarely as I can help) the term *'psychic'*, as a convenient label for any process which seems to go beyond currently accepted ideas about what the mind can do — telepathy, clairvoyance and so on. However, I do not wish to imply that this happens by 'supernatural' means, simply that science is currently unable to explain how it happens.

★   There are two other terms we shall need so frequently that it seems practical to employ the accepted abbreviations: 'OBE' = *out-of-body experience*, and 'NDE' = *near-death experience*. I use these terms with no prejudgement as to whether these experiences are what they seem to be.

For definitions of mental disorders (though I am not sure that 'disorder' is always the right term) I have relied on the World Health Organization's admirable glossary and guide which, though it confines itself to the clinical aspects, at least offers some kind of solid ground in this uncertain terrain.

Notably, the WHO has not only not discarded the convenient label 'hysteria' for certain conditions, as so many have, but actually recognises the possibility that hysteria may offer 'psychological advantage or symbolic value' — a crucial point, as we shall find.

SPR refers to the Society for Psychical Research; *JSPR* to its *Journal* and *PSPR* to its *Proceedings*. PF refers to the *Proceedings* of the Parapsychology Foundation, New York.

A reference such as (#5.3) indicates that the case is more fully narrated in Chapter 5.3.

One final note: when making general comments I use the terms 'he' and 'him' in order to save the text from becoming laboured.

Case histories

Readers with a knowledge of the subject will recognise many familiar friends among the cases, for I have used whatever examples seemed to make the point best, and often — obviously — it is the best-known cases which do this.

You will notice, in particular, how frequently I make reference to the work of Pierre Janet: my debt to this too frequently overlooked researcher is equalled only by my admiration. I hope this book will remind others what a store of insight he has left us. (In these pages, 'Janet' = Pierre Janet; his brother Jules, who also contributed to psychology, is specifically named.)

When quoting cases, I have taken occasional liberties with the original texts. I have shorn some words from verbose ancient authors; I have telescoped sentences from separate paragraphs; when they designate their subjects by initials I have bestowed names on them — Podmore's 'Miss A.B.' becomes 'Ann Brown', Bramwell's 'Mary W--d' becomes 'Mary Wood'; and so on. All such changes are in the cause of greater comprehension and ease of access: to make my authorities' intentions clearer, not to distort them.

Finally, I am the first to acknowledge that this book is made up almost wholly of other people's experiences and findings. If there is anything original in it, it lies in bringing them together, arranging them helpfully, and drawing what I hope are useful conclusions.

If those conclusions are to be truly useful, they must be founded on a recognition that in the present state of ignorance about ASCs, we have no right to take anything for granted. Many people will tell us stories about their experiences; while we must believe that they had the experiences, we must question whether they are what they seem to be. Many other people will offer us explanations; while we must give them a fair hearing, we must question whether their findings are as valid as they claim.

In the course of the pages that follow, you will find me from time to time questioning the opinions of people vastly more qualified than myself, often who have had first-hand experience where I have not. But I do so in the light of other people's findings, which frequently were not available to the original author. Similarly, I recognise that my ideas, in their turn, are liable to be disputed; if so, they will have served their purpose, in helping to illuminate these shadowy sidestreets of human behaviour.

We are a long way from saying the last word on alternate states: as Janet says, 'l' on peut décomposer la conscience à l'infini' — one can go on taking consciousness apart for ever... (1889).

1 From self to otherself

A man in his time plays many parts. Even the most normal
and healthy of us know there are days when we are 'one
degree under', others when we are 'walking on air'. And
we know that others, if not ourselves, have higher highs
and lower lows: when, at one end of the scale, self seems to
diminish to unself and the individual hardly seems to exist
at all, to the point where even ordinary everyday life seems
an unattainable blessing; and when, at the other, self is
lifted to superself status, bestowing insights and experiences which make everyday existence seem trivial and
humdrum.

Compare two of Pierre Janet's patients:

> Berthe: I just can't understand what's going on. My work
> seems strange to me, as if it's not me who's doing it, but my
> hands. They do the work pretty well, but as if they're nothing
> to do with me at all. When it's finished, I don't recognise my
> handiwork at all. I can see it's well done, but if someone were
> to say to me, It wasn't you who did it, I'd answer, You're
> right, it wasn't me! I don't understand my thoughts, they ar-
> rive by themselves, as if they were written on a huge roller
> which unrolls in front of me. I'm nothing but a puppet with
> someone else holding the strings. (1911, p.127)

> Madeleine: No, the state I enter isn't sleep: sleep is a kind of
> suspension of the life of the spirit, whereas mine is just the op-
> posite. It's as though I'm dead to everything around me; my

body remains here on its own, while my spirit and my heart soar over immense horizons into which they plunge and lose themselves in delight. I feel myself lifted up above material things, I'm in another world, I have another life where impressions succeed one another like flowers in a huge garden… Often God will stoop towards me, raise me from the dust where I lie, treating me like a child, like a bride, bestowing on me ineffable sensations… Heart against heart with the object of my love, my mouth is filled with delights, my whole being is plunged in a sublime intoxication, truly it's the divine kiss which I feel… The divine kiss, how sweet it is! No earthly pleasure can be compared to it! Ah, if only I could describe what I feel… I have just spent a night of love and madness, yes, it's true, God makes me mad with love! (1926, pp.68f)

Though much has been written on the subject of alternate states, they remain enigmatic in almost every possible way. Our inquiry will show there is no aspect of them which is not open to question — including the question, Do they exist at all? The 1987 *Oxford companion to the mind*, for instance, an authoritative publication if ever there was one, does indeed contain an index entry for 'altered states', but merely refers us to hypnosis and out-of-body experiences: it offers no general discussion of alternate states as such.

Yet it is clear, not only that we undergo alterations in our behaviour, but that they are often alterations in *kind*: often, they alter us so much that we seem to become different persons. If only as a label for such manifest alterations of behaviour, we need some such concept as ASCs.

But how much further can we take the concept? Even if we accept that ASCs exist, we shall need to ask, Are they all the 'same kind of thing', variations on a single theme, which can usefully be studied together as a category? Or is sleep, say, something altogether different from panic or the effects of food poisoning? And even if ASCs can be treated as a category, should we regard them as a series of separate states, clearly defined each with its own characteristics? Or as clusters of individual mental and physical processes which can be brought together in any number of different ways?

Put like that, these seem abstract questions: but the puzzles of human behaviour to which they relate are real enough. Are some of us possessed by devils which must be evicted by exorcism? How do unconscious people drive a car through busy traffic? Can we control our dreams? Do thunderstorms and the phases of the moon affect our behaviour? Can hypnosis help us remember previous lives? Can drugs bestow on us experiences to compare with the ecstasies of the saints?

Above all, when these things happen to someone we know — or even to ourselves — what should we think of them? Are they 'normal' or 'abnormal'? Pathological or purposeful? Should we seek them or avoid them?

Subjective and objective

If an individual sits in huddled silence, refusing all invitations to communicate, is it because he *can't* or because he *won't*? If he can't, who or what is stopping him? And if he won't, who or what has decided so?

Such questions bring us up against the fundamental difficulty with alternate states: how can we make a connection between what we, from the *outside*, see happening to someone, and what he, from the *inside*, feels happening to himself? Even if he is able to describe his state, either at the time or later, we can't be sure how accurate his description is. And how can we extract, from his *subjective* account, *objective* criteria which will enable us to say, *this* and *this* are what constitute such-and-such a state, so when we come across those criteria in another person's case, we shall know what is happening to him?

Moreover, there are many states in which the individual just isn't able to tell us what it's like to be in that state: sleepwalkers can't tell us what is happening to them for the simple reason that they are asleep. Or the individual can't reply for the equally irrefutable reason that his place — so he tells us — has been taken by someone else. We might be prepared to accept a medium's account of spirit trance, but we would surely hesitate when the explanation is offered by a being who claims to be the spirit of a deceased Red Indian or a one-time priest of Atlantis.

Despite these difficulties, many studies of ASCs have of course been made. The literatures of dreaming and of hypnosis are vast, and there are many specific studies, ranging from subjective accounts of hallucinogenic drug taking to analytical comparisons of 'fantasy-prone' subjects. Unfortunately — though understandably — these tend to be based on experiments conducted under clinical conditions, rather than people's spontaneous real-life experiences.

We must of course applaud any attempt to set these subjective experiences in an objective perspective; but the difficulties verge on the insuperable. Consider, for instance, the attempt which, more than any other, has seemed to provide some kind of yardstick: the concept of *brainwaves*.

Starting from the fact that the brain operates, fundamentally, by electricity, German scientist Hans Berger, back in the 1920s, developed a method of measuring the strength and frequency of changes in electric potential occurring in the brain, thus providing a rough indication of the brain's electrical activity.

I say 'rough' because there is no consensus as to how brainwaves correlate with real states. As developed, electroencephalography (EEG) is used to classify levels of brainwave output (measured in Hertz = cycles per second) as:

BETA	30–12 Hz	awake, but tending to nervous and anxious
ALPHA	11–9 Hz	awake, relaxed
THETA	8–4 Hz	asleep, or in creative, concentrating mood
DELTA	3–0 Hz	deep sleep, trance

(Beta and alpha states constitute different levels of the USC: theta and delta comprise the ASCs.)

That sounds splendid in principle, but how does it work out in practice? I have just consulted four separate authorities on the subject, and found that each offers substantially different values for all four levels!

If this widely respected yardstick provides us with so uncertain a measure, it is clear we must be prepared for similar uncertainty at every step of our inquiry.

The one aspect of alternate states that is *not* in dispute is that, whatever they are, people have them. Either because of the state of the weather, or because they are driving alone at night, or because they've taken drugs, or because of personal disaster, something causes them to act in ways which are sometimes strikingly different from their normal behaviour.

If we approach these experiences with pre-formed beliefs, we will get answers — of a sort — to the questions raised earlier. If we believe in reincarnation, we will accept at face value the ability of hypnosis to reveal previous lives. If we believe in the Devil, we will accept at face value that people are possessed by him. If we believe that the dead seek to communicate with the living, we will accept at face value the messages from beyond the grave brought us by spirit mediums.

If you hold such beliefs, and are happy with such face-value explanations, you may as well stop reading here and now. For as our inquiry proceeds, we shall find that the world of ASCs is a looking-glass land, where nothing is necessarily what it seems to be — where 'normal' and 'abnormal' become relative terms, and where, as Alice found in her Wonderland, things mean what we — or our subconscious selves — want them to mean.

Conscious and subconscious

One of the many paradoxes of the ASC is that the individual who is in one is often capable of a fair amount of activity, even though he is not consciously aware of his surroundings or in control of his actions. This may range from the awareness of sounds while asleep, to the almost totally lifelike behaviour of an amnesia victim.

The implication is that each individual possesses a second self which is capable of playing an active part independently of his conscious self. Indeed, we shall find that unless we are prepared to make some such assumption, at least as a provisional hypothesis, our inquiry is unlikely to make much progress.

Many researchers have offered suggestions as to what form this active subconscious self might take, and a book could be devoted to setting them out and comparing them. Because there is no way we can determine which if any of them is valid, we should hold any hypothesis as loosely and as provisionally as we can.

At this stage it may be helpful if I state my own position in this matter.

I think that each of us possesses a subconscious self of immense insight and capability, autonomous inasmuch as it has ultimate control over our behaviour and actions, and functioning continually, even if most of the time it functions inconspicuously.

Because the most unequivocal evidence we have that such an entity exists is our dreams — since the very fact that we dream implies a mind that produces them — I have labelled this secondary self the 'producer', though this should be seen simply as a convenient label, implying no specific attributes.

Nevertheless, I would be disingenuous if I pretended I don't think it has specific attributes. I see the producer as highly creative; manifestly concerned for our well-being; and possessing many capabilities not possessed by our conscious minds, such as access to information hidden from us in our usual state.

I can understand that many will find this concept naive; also that many will question my right to assume so much at the outset of the inquiry. Again, I say that this inquiry won't get very far unless we assume, not necessarily my producer, but at any rate something of the sort.

I take comfort from the fact that many others have also felt this necessity. Socrates took his daemon for granted, without troubling too much as to its nature; and in an age which took nothing for granted, yet long before psychologists were producing evidence for the subconscious mind, the astronomer Sir John Herschel, seeking to account for certain geometrical images which came into his mind, said in 1816: 'It would almost seem that in such cases we have evidence of a *thought*, an intelligence, working within our own organisation, distinct from that of our own personality.'

Pathological or purposeful?
A great many ASCs come to our attention only when their subjects wind up in the wards of a mental hospital or in a psychiatrist's consulting room. This has contributed to en-

courage the idea, not entirely dissipated even today, that *all* ASCs are morbid. Until the eighteenth century, they were liable to be ascribed to the Devil, controlling our minds for his sinister purposes; the exceptions were the raptures and ecstasies of the saints, evidently a heavenly privilege. Even in the Middle Ages there were some who offered an alternative explanation, but the idea persisted — and does so to this day — that the great majority of ASCs are pathological states, requiring treatment.

So long as it was supposed that they were symptoms of an organic malady, this was a reasonable inference. It was the demonstration by doctors such as Janet that many states had a psychological rather than a physiological origin which changed the picture. Gradually it has come to be understood that far from ASCs being symptoms of mental derangement, mental patients are actually *less* liable to experience them, for the simple reason that they are already there! Psychiatric patients are already at one remove from reality, displaying the same suggestibility and tendency to role-playing as the ASC subject — in a sense, they are in a chronic ASC.

Speaking of mind control, British psychologist William Sargant explains that the tendency to be overcome by stress to the point of abnormal behaviour 'is particularly true, not of the insane, but of the sane, not of the severely mentally ill but of normal, ordinary, average people, who make the best possible material [because] a normal person is responsive to other people and is reasonably open to their influence' (1973, p.195), whereas those who are truly mentally ill are so wrapt up in their own preoccupations that they are impervious to any outside influences except those which they perceive to be of immediate concern to themselves.

Today we recognise that a person can be taken out of his USC into an ASC by a bewilderingly diverse range of factors and circumstances, some of them physiological and some psychological, some emanating from within himself, some from outside. We shall also see that they can make his condition *better* than before, or *worse*, or simply *different*.

As a framework for our inquiry, therefore, we can draw up a rough-and-ready classification scheme as follows:

1   The USC.

2   'Unself' states, in which consciousness is reduced to below an acceptable level of awareness and control; where the individual is reduced either to a robot or to a zombie, or loses the capacity to act altogether. We shall see that hysteria and many mental disorders display this kind of behaviour.

   We can safely classify most such states as malfunctions, some of them specifically pathological, resulting from some organic trouble, others which are well-meant efforts on the part of the subconscious to achieve something, but which have gone wrong. However, as we shall see, the subtleties of ASC behaviour are so infinite that even the most negative-seeming state may turn out to have been chosen by the producer for some positive purpose.

3   'Otherself' states, characterised by depersonalisation — where the individual starts to behave so differently that it is as though he has become another person. We shall see examples in cases of amnesia, multiple personality and ostensible possession by demons and other entities. Though such cases frequently degenerate into disorders demanding treatment, we can generally see that they started out as purposeful quests to resolve a crisis situation.

4   'Superself' states, in which the individual rises above the limits of his usual self, experiences enhanced powers, and enjoys unwonted insights and self-awareness. Such are the raptures of saints and mystics, but comparable experiences may result from drugs or even simply from a spontaneous mood.

5   Paradoxical states, in which the changes are ambiguous. Overall the individual displays a diminished response to reality, but this seems to be compensated for by an enhancement in certain specific directions. The most striking example is hypnosis, which generally renders the subject unfit for everyday activities, but enables him to do things he could not do in his USC.

   Among the many paradoxical features of these states

is, for instance, the fact that local abilities — enhanced powers of hearing, say — manifest even in states normally thought of as pathological, such as hysteria.

Internal or external?

Should we look on the ASC as a state in which the body/mind system switches itself into a different operating mode, in which it is able to employ faculties which are usually latent, calling on resources normally kept in reserve? Or as one in which it opens a channel whereby some external agency can intervene, take control, and bestow those exceptional powers? Consider this case:

> A Dr Holbrook, of New York, writes to the SPR in 1884 that as a young man he had been so ill that he despaired of being able to pursue his career: 'In this depressed condition I fell into a sleep which was not very profound, and the following circumstances appeared to take place. My sister, who had been dead more than twenty years, and whom I had almost forgotten, came to my bedside, and said, ''Do not worry about your health, we have come to cure you; there is much yet for you to do in the world.'' Then she vanished, and my brain seemed to be electrified as if by a shock from a battery, only it was not painful, but delicious. The shock spread downwards, and over the chest and lungs it was very strong. From here it extended to the extremities, where it appeared like a delightful glow. I awoke almost immediately and found myself well. Since then I have never had an attack of the disease. The form of my sister was indistinct, but the voice was very plain.' (*PSPR*, 8, p.374)

In the eyes of many, such a case is evidence of otherworldly intervention. Maybe it is: I know of no way of disproving that this is what happened, nor do I particularly want to. At the same time, I have to recognise that there exists an alternative explanation: that it may have been Holbrook's subconscious self which staged the experience, to help his conscious self overcome a disability which was probably of psychosomatic origin.

If so, why did his subconscious self go to the trouble of presenting it in so dramatic a form? Because if he had suspected it was, as it were, nothing but himself curing himself, he would have doubted its effectiveness; whereas

when it came seemingly backed by his dead sister's authority, it carried a conviction that swept aside all doubt.

Compared with the face-value interpretation, that may
seem devious and complicated; but in the course of this inquiry we shall come across many scenarios as far-fetched as
that. The subconscious self acts in mysterious ways to perform its wonders.

Fortunately it does not make too much difference to our inquiry whether or not we believe that external intervention
occurs. At the beginning of the twentieth century F. W. H.
Myers, at the outset of his monumental inquiry into human
personality, thought it right to declare his own belief: 'I
believe that there is another break, at a point much further
advanced, where some external intelligence begins in some
way to possess the organism and to replace for a time the ordinary intellectual activity by an activity of its own.'

I had better be equally honest, and warn you that I do not
share his view. While I do not rule out the possibility of external intervention in human behaviour, I see no reason to
suppose it plays a part within the scope of our present
inquiry.

However, just as Myers, having stated his belief, thought
it only right to set it aside during the course of his inquiry,
so shall I, and so, I suggest, should you.

External agents may or may not be responsible for some
of the phenomena we shall be examining. Some kind of a
supreme deity may be manifesting in states of ecstasy,
some kind of evil power may be present in states of possession. But it is best we do not assume either that they do or
that they don't, until we have looked closely at *what*, in fact,
is happening in these states, and *how* it happens, and *why*.

2   Usual states

The term 'alternate state' implies a 'usual' state, but is there any such thing?

Most people, in practice, behave as though there is. If not at the time, at least subsequently, we know when we are or are not behaving normally, or when the world around us does or does not seem normal.

More substantially, there is the fact that people don't usually stay for long in ASCs, but come back to a state which they feel to be usual: nor do they often shift from one ASC to another, but similarly return to the USC. If we have been asleep, we awaken; if we have been drunk, we sober up; a spirit medium comes out of trance and becomes a housewife again; a hypnosis patient, if not brought out of trance by the hypnotist, will fall asleep and wake in the normal way. So the USC seems to be a kind of equilibrium, from which all ASCs are more or less temporary departures. To make an analogy with chemistry, the USC is a *stable* state, ASCs are *unstable*.

This does not mean that, in their usual state, people will always behave in precisely the same way: but in general terms they will be aware of what they are doing, be in touch with reality and in control of their actions.

However, as soon as we put it like that, we realise that USCs vary greatly from one person to another. There are some people who seem to be always in command of the situation, others who live from moment to moment, taking things as they come. A streetwise city-dweller lives in a world made up primarily of here-and-now facts, a poet/artist/mystic like Blake or Van Gogh inhabits a world which is only remotely related to the everyday reality of you and me. Usual states are just as *subjective* as alternate states.

To further complicate matters, there are ASCs which cannot easily be recognised as such, because to all appearances the individual is behaving no differently from someone in a USC. A person suffering from amnesia can behave to all outward appearance in a perfectly normal way, so that — unless they know the circumstances — there is no reason for others to suspect he is anything but his real self in his USC. If in such a state the individual is capable of living with normal efficiency, distinguishing reality at least as well as an artist or a poet, can we say it is an ASC at all?

The short answer is that, however normally he behaves in his secondary state, it is none the less *not* his usual state, and something must have happened to trigger the switch. We shall deal more fully with this complication when we focus our attention on the states in which it arises.

How usual is the USC?
When we say of John that he's a down-to-earth realist, of Peter that he's a head-in-the-clouds dreamer, we mean that they respond differently to the world around them and the things that happen to them. Though both may be equally aware of their surroundings, their awareness may vary as much as an artist's view of a landscape differs from a property developer's; though both may be equally in control of their actions, their behaviour may vary as much as a journalist's differs from a nun's.

Ants, so far as we know, do not have such differences in temperament; horses and dogs, on the other hand, manifestly do. But the differences between John and Peter may go further than their personal make-up; their responses will be conditioned by the societies in which each was brought up and lives.

Suppose some personal experience occurs which threatens to upset their mental equilibrium.

John, born into a conformist society which prizes

allegiance to group values, will relate his situation to the belief-system of his community; if they include strong religious beliefs, he may for instance accept the notion that he has been possessed by the devil.

On the other hand, Peter, from a skeptical, permissive, radical background which respects the individual's right to make his own decisions be they right or wrong, might have difficulty in even conceiving satanic possession as a viable option; but because neither in his own mental resources nor in his cultural background can he find a nice, firm belief to which he can relate what's happening to him, he might be more disconcerted by his experience than John.

(Which is one reason why psychiatrists are thriving in our think-for-yourself age.)

We shall come across many Johns and many Peters in the course of our inquiry: we shall see that how a person responds to an ASC, and indeed often the fact that the ASC occurs at all, is the result of interaction between his personal temperament and his cultural conditioning. Moreover, this applies not only to deliberately-entered ASCs such as voodoo rituals, but even seemingly spontaneous ASCs such as the effects of sensory deprivation or diet deficiency.

So to the question, How usual is the USC? we can give only a relative answer. The USC of an Australian aborigine is something very different from that of a Parisian intellectual or of a fundamentalist Christian from the American midwest. Not one of the states we shall be looking at can be usefully considered, unless we also take into account the cultural milieu in which it occurs.

To some extent, as we have seen, the USC is measurable, and however unreliable the method, the fact that states are measurable at all is an indication that we are not talking about something which is entirely subjective.

As research continues, other, more precise and more subtle methods will surely be discovered. For example, it is evident that the USC is related to the level of sensory input — if we are bombarded with too much or too little, we will take refuge in an ASC. But how much is too much, how little is too little? No doubt these levels will vary from one individual to another, from one culture to another:

establishing norms for each type of person in each type of culture is a daunting task.

What is already clear is that the USC represents a delicate balance which can be upset more easily for some people, and in some cultures, than in others.

Are some people more ASC-prone than others?

Jules Romains, the French novelist who was also a prominent psychical researcher, wrote:

> Different individuals show unequal aptitudes for passing from the USC [his wording is 'ordinary regime of consciousness'] to other states. With some, a slight loosening is enough, as though the installation of the USC had always been more highly precarious, and as though other states, organised and ready, were only waiting for a signal in order to appear. With others, the first change of state requires prolonged efforts and the employment of a well chosen technique. In all cases there remains no difficulty, no appreciable resistance to switching, when it has been performed a number of times. (1924, p.33)

This seems borne out in practice: there do seem to be people who pass more easily than others into ASCs, whether it is 'artistic' people who go into rapturous reveries, or 'psychic' people who slip easily into trance or the hypnotic state.

A spirit medium will often say to a member of his audience or to a client, you too are a potential medium; it is an item of spiritist belief that there is a 'type' which is specially gifted to perform this function. Since an essential part of the work of a medium is an ability to pass easily into the ASC of the trance, it certainly seems true that so far as spiritists are concerned there are ASC-prone people.

We may reasonably assume that this psychological disposition correlates with some physiological characteristics, but though we have a few piecemeal indications — for example, that migraine-prone people are specially liable to have hallucinatory experiences — our knowledge is woefully incomplete.

American psychologist Josephine Hilgard finds that 'hypnotic responsiveness bears a complex relationship to personality development', and suggests that people's hypnotic susceptibility correlates with their ability to become involved in an imaginative way in reading, dramatic arts, religion, sensory experiences, imagery, imaginary companions, and physical and mental adventures.

Janet, in 1889, writes that 'in a general way, hysterics — in their waking or trance state, it makes no difference — are like little children, who don't have to be hypnotised to be persuaded of anything, and who believe whatever takes their fancy.' Almost a century later, Wilson and Barber, in a 1981 paper, confirm a correlation between high hypnotic susceptibility and being 'fantasy-prone'. Like children, such people live much of the time in a make-believe world, and continue to fantasise for as much as 50 per cent of their adult lives, continually playing games with themselves or with others: 'For instance, while riding on a bus just the day before the interview, one of our subjects introduced herself as an Eskimo to the person sitting next to her and then proceeded to tell the intrigued stranger all about her (imagined) life in Alaska.' We shall see in #3.1 that such role-playing is a key element in most ASCs: at the same time we shall also note the significance of this 'childlike' behaviour.

Of particular importance to our inquiry is Wilson and Barber's finding that 'the reason some individuals are excellent hypnotic subjects is that their addiction to fantasy leads them naturally to experience hypnotic phenomena in their own lives.' They suggest that 'perhaps this is the ''secret'' of hypnosis — it provides them with a social situation in which they are encouraged to do what they usually do only privately.'

Though the Wilson-Barber study is limited to hypnosis, their findings apply equally to other ASCs. Hysteria subjects display a tendency to restructure the world about them to conform to their subjective view of it just as do Wilson and Barber's subjects, 'whose everyday sexual fantasies can produce orgasms, whose fantasies of pregnancy can produce pseudocyesis [false pregnancy], or whose fantasies of eating spoiled food can produce illness.'

Even with the limited data we possess, there is no question that we do not all start equal when it comes to ASCs: some people, it seems, live continually on the threshold of ASCs and can be tipped from USC to ASC by circumstances which would not affect others. In #4.2 we shall see that approximately one person in three is considered to be 'weather-sensitive'; Reichenbach, one of the first researchers to recognise the psychological effect of geophysical forces, recognises also that some people are more sensitive to them than others (Rogers 1853, p.267); and Janet, though he considers hysteria too varied an ailment for there to be a simple hysteria-prone type, recognises the existence of a genetic disposition, and invariably mentions family history when describing a patient's background.

The signs by which a future shaman is recognised in primitive cultures indicate that a special kind of person is looked for. Among the Vogul of Siberia, 'the future shaman exhibits exceptional traits from adolescence; he very early becomes nervous and is sometimes even subject to epileptic seizures, which are interpreted as meetings with the gods.' Among the Tungus of the Transbaikal region 'he who wishes to become a shaman announces that the spirit of a dead shaman has appeared to him in a dream and ordered him to succeed him, but for this declaration to be regarded plausible, it must usually be accompanied by a considerable degree of mental derangement.' On the other hand, in the Sudan 'no shaman is, in everyday life, an abnormal individual, a neurotic, or a paranoiac; if he were, he would be classed as a lunatic, not respected as a priest.'

Evidently, different cultures expect different things from their shamans; but even if the African cultures place a greater emphasis on what the shaman *knows* rather than how he *behaves*, he must none the less be an exceptional person who 'stands apart from the world of the profane precisely because he has more direct relations with the sacred and manipulates its manifestations more effectively' (Eliade 1964, p.15,16,31)

Scientists are understandably hesitant to offer field explanations when so little information is available, but some theoretical models have been proposed, usually by people working within some belief-system such as theosophy or spiritualism. Robert Crookall, who devoted himself to exploring ostensible accounts of survival of death, proposes:

In some people the junction between the Soul and the

Physical Bodies is relatively 'loose'; they are less immersed in matter and tend to be 'mental' mediums with telepathic, clairvoyant and pre-cognitive faculties, i.e. they have flashes of 'super-normal' consciousness and glimpses of the 'next' world. Whereas those who possess a loose vehicle of vitality may, or may not, be of high moral type, people with loose Soul Bodies are often (though not always) spiritually inclined. (1961, p.56)

Unsatisfactory though this account of the matter is (though no more so than other such explanations), and unhappy though we may be with Crookall's terminology, it seems to me we must agree that some such differential exists. And Crookall deserves our respect for facing the possibility that the differential may have a physical basis — 'the looseness may be a purely bodily characteristic.' If what distinguishes mystic from materialist is in their genes, we may one day be able to chart the spectrum of human behaviour on a psycho/biological basis.

Abnormal or alternate?
Although it is today widely accepted that ASCs are not necessarily pathological, there is still a tendency to think of them as *abnormal*.

The machine on which I am writing this is, in its usual mode, a word processor; but I can override this to typewriter mode if I choose. Clearly, the typewriter mode is an alternate mode; when I switch the machine on, it is always in the WP mode, its usual state, and a specific act is needed to switch it to TP, an alternate state. But it would be ridiculous to think of the TP mode as 'abnormal'.

It is the same with SCs. Some departures from the USC — the effects of food poisoning or allergy, for example — may seem to be abnormal, but even these are the natural consequence of cause-and-effect processes, little understood though they may be — the equivalent of my switching to the TP mode by mistake. As for the majority, it is better to think of them as being like my typewriter mode, a facility available when we need it.

At the same time, there is the unfortunate fact that while some of us — spirit mediums, for example — seem to find it easier than most people to travel from USC to ASC and back again, there are others — for example, sufferers from amnesia or hysteria — who are easily switched from USC to ASC, but can't so easily reverse the process.

We shall have to consider the possibility that for these people, at least, the word 'abnormal' is appropriate. But even if this is so, we need not jump to the conclusion that it is the ability to switch into the ASC which is abnormal; rather, it may be the inability to switch back again.

3 Alternate states

If one person's USC can be so very different from another's; if attempts to measure SCs produce only elusive and ambiguous results; if what individuals themselves say about their states is unreliable; and if in many states, such as hysteria, amnesia and trance, they are unable to give any account at all — if the boundaries of the field are so uncertain and what lies within those boundaries so peppered with paradox, is there any point looking for ways to distinguish ASCs as a class from the USC, or one ASC from another?

So long as we are prepared to settle for less than hard-and-fast, clear-cut distinctions, the answer is Yes. We find that throughout the range of ASCs certain characteristics tend to recur, and at the same time that each is typified by a particular combination of characteristics which distinguish it both from the USC and from other ASCs. For example, though they have much in common and both are clearly not usual states, somnambulism is manifestly not the same as amnesia.

However, as we proceed, we will do well to heed Janet's warning: 'Given someone you can examine for only an instant, you just can't say what state he's in' (1889, p.125).

3.1 Characteristics which recur in ASCs

Diminished conscious awareness of reality

Drink and drugs, by and large, have a cumulative effect on us, in which our surroundings become less and less real. But it is not as simple as that: psychedelic drugs are often reported as giving visions, of which the individual is intensely aware, of what seems to him to be a *heightened* reality.

The matter is further complicated by the fact that we may be aware of reality on another level. When sleeping, for instance, we have no *conscious* awareness of reality, but our senses continue to register what is going on around us, and often this will be structured into our dreams — sounds from the street outside, the cold because the duvet has slipped off our shoulders, our need to pee. Similarly, surgical patients have recalled the conversation of the theatre staff to which they were apparently oblivious at the time.

How strongly a subject may sense an alternate reality was forcibly demonstrated by certain supposed witches. Calmet, writing in 1746, gives this account:

> A woman assures the Inquisitors that she can travel really and bodily wherever she wishes, even though she is shut up and watched, and though the place she travels to is far distant.
>
> The Inquisitors order her to go to a certain place, to speak to certain people, and to bring back news from them. She promises to obey. She is shut and locked in a room; as soon as she lies down, she is as if dead. They enter her room and shake her; she remains immobile and without any feeling, so much so that when they bring a candle close to her, they burn her foot without her feeling anything.
>
> A little while later she comes to herself again, and gives them the answers they requested, saying that the journey has been very troublesome. They ask her what is the matter with her foot? She replies that it has been very painful since her return, but she has no idea how she came by the injury.
>
> Then the Inquisitors tell her what happened, that she never left the place, and that the pain in the foot came from their candle. Faced with such evidence, she recognises her error, begs forgiveness, and promises never to do it again. (p.157)

Here, at the outset of our inquiry, we are faced with a difficulty we shall encounter throughout: just what kind of

ASC is this woman in? Clearly she is not simply dreaming, for few would fail to wake if burned with a candle. The rapidity with which she enters her state argues against drugs; she seems to go into her ASC as readily as a practised spirit medium dropping into her trance.

Another paradoxical aspect intrigued James Esdaile, a British doctor working in India in the 1840s, who performed many hundreds of surgical operations on hypnotised patients with no other anaesthetic. He tells us he frequently observed phenomena such as the following:

> I made a crucial incision into the patient's arm, without his shrinking in the least. He was then carried to the north door of the hospital; the blankets and sheet were suddenly pulled off, and he was exposed naked to the cold air; in about two minutes he shivered all over, his breathing became disturbed, and he clutched left and right for the bedclothes, but still sleeping; they were supplied to him, and he huddled himself up under them with the greatest satisfaction, still sleeping, however. (1852, p.174)

This illustrates how ASC subjects can have a partial anaesthesia, a narrowed focus of attention. In obedience to Esdaile's suggestion, his patient feels no pain from the surgery, yet retains his sensitivity to the infinitely milder sensations of heat and cold.

Diminished sense of personal control

A couple of gins, and we start to lose control of our physical and mental functions; the same is true when we are tired, or suffer a cold, or are harassed by too many demands on our attention.

But we know, too, that control is not synonymous with performance. A sleepwalker can move about in precarious situations which he could certainly not do when awake: a hypnotised subject will perform feats in obedience to the hypnotist's suggestions which would be beyond his normal capability.

'Robot behaviour' — behaviour which is seemingly intelligent but over which we don't seem to be exercising any conscious control — is a particularly interesting illustration of this separation of performance from control. Writer Aldous Huxley, who had a lifelong interest in human behaviour, developed the ability to enter a state of what he called 'Deep Reflection' in which he 'simply cast aside all anchors' of any type of awareness, though he could not describe how he did it:

> One day his wife came home and, after opening the front door which was locked as usual, found a special delivery letter on the hall table. She found her husband sitting in a state of profound thought. Later, she asked him about the letter, and found that he had no recollection of it. Yet he must have answered the doorbell, unlocked the door, taken the letter and placed it in the usual place, 'automatically'. (Erickson in Tart, 1969, p.48, paraphrase)

We shall consider the implications of such 'robot behaviour' in #5.

Enhanced awareness in a limited field

It is a common experience to have brilliant ideas come to us when we are half-asleep, and doing anything but focus our mind on the subject of the idea. Many ASCs involve some kind of enhanced awareness.

For example, a hyperaesthesia is demonstrated in many ASCs, sometimes so remarkably as to suggest clairvoyance. A dramatic form of hyperaesthesia is shown by certain religious subjects who, in ecstasy, are able to detect the blessed sacrament wherever it may be. Görres recounts several such prodigies: how Saint Casset, when some Franciscans tried to test him by putting the sacrament elsewhere than its usual place, knew at once where to find it; or how Joan Meatless of Norfolk was able to pick out the single consecrated host from a thousand unconsecrated ones. To the pious, such feats were seen as a sign of grace, even of miracle: but similar feats occur in a medical environment, suggesting that genuine powers, whether hyperaesthesia or actually psychic, may be involved. Tests carried out with hysterical patients indicate a remarkable ability to detect medical and other substances close to them:

> Théodore, a 23-year-old hysteria patient at an asylum in Grenoble, is able to detect several substances though introduced secretly into his presence in minute quantities. A packet of valerian roots (powerfully attractive to cats) placed

on his head under a thick woollen cap to prevent him smelling it, produces mental effects which are absolutely inconceivable. After a few moments, his expression becomes one of astonishment, he seems to be watching out for something: if a fly passes, he follows it with his eyes and even leaves his chair to chase it. We ask him what's the matter? Nothing, but I feel strange, I don't understand what's happening ... Suddenly he arches his back, gets down on all fours, and proceeds to run about the room like a cat, playing with a cork on the floor as a cat would do, licking his hand and using it to wipe his ears... in short, behaving as if he was a cat. The moment the valerian is taken away, or if his cap falls off, he gets to his feet, astonished to find himself on the floor, and with no memory for what has happened. (Cauzons, 1901–12, vol.4, p.241)

Was it the chemical qualities of valerian to which Théodore was reacting? If so, it is a different kind of hypersensitivity than that noted by Bramwell and other hypnotists, which displays an ability to distinguish *quantities*. One patient, when hypnotised, was able to detect differences in weight as small as six grains, which he was quite unable to do in the USC. Even if we decide that such detection is due to enhanced natural powers rather than a parapsychological ability, we still have to explain how and why it occurs to people when they are in ASCs.

For our present purposes, the point is precisely that: these abilities come hand in hand with certain ASCs. The WHO definition of hysteria notes 'restriction of the field of consciousness' as a characteristic symptom; but just as when we look through a telescope we see less, but see it more clearly, so it seems that a restriction in our field of consciousness may be balanced by enhanced awareness within that field.

Improved performance of certain tasks

Bramwell got one of his hypnosis subjects to control his pulse at his suggestion; others increased the range of their hearing and vision. Stigmata have been created to order: in contrast, wounds and injuries have been caused to heal faster. But what hypnotic subjects can be induced to do in response to suggestion is surpassed by the feats performed in spontaneous ASCs: we shall encounter many in the course of our inquiry.

A striking demonstration of enhanced powers, which we shall see recurring in many forms, is the ability for extemporised oratory — usually in a religious context.

This particular ability was most strikingly demonstrated by 'the Prophets of the Cevennes' who arose among the persecuted protestants in southern France at the close of the seventeenth century. Taking refuge from the catholic government in this isolated mountain district, the besieged communities sustained their morale only by an intense trust in their God, which they expressed in fervent religious gatherings.

Our sympathy for these innocent victims of religious intolerance should not prevent our noting that they were continually in or on the brink of alternate states. The maréchal de Villars, one of the commanders sent to subdue them, said, 'I have seen things which I would not have believed if I had not seen them with my own eyes: in one town, all the women and girls, without a single exception, seemed to be possessed by the devil, trembling and prophesying publicly in the streets.'

Whether or not the devil was responsible, the wide spread of the phenomenon is as astonishing as any single manifestation of it; for it shows us that the ability to 'prophesy' was not the gift of a few, but was attainable by many, though no doubt some demonstrated it more impressively than others.

In particular, all witnesses testify to the extreme youth of many of the 'prophets':

> At Aubessargues, at the house of Jacques Boussigue, one of his children, aged three, was seized by the spirit and fell to the ground. He was very agitated and pounded his chest, at the same time saying it was the sins of his mother which made him suffer. He added that we were in the Last Days, and must struggle bravely for the faith and repent our sins.
>
> A little girl of six or seven was seized by the spirit in our presence. She continually insisted that it wasn't her who was convulsed in this way, and that she hadn't any intention or wish to speak; it was something else, something stronger than her, even though she couldn't see it, which was doing all this inside her.

Yet another speaks of

> an infant of 13 or 14 months, swaddled in its cradle, not yet old
> enough to speak or walk. At least twenty of us heard him
> speak distinctly in French [i.e. not the patois spoken every-
> day], loud enough for us all to hear, exhorting us to repent so
> that we were all moved to tears. After the ecstasy, the child
> returned to its ordinary state. Its mother said there had been
> agitations of the body at the beginning of the ecstasy, though I
> saw nothing when I entered. (Calmeil, 1845, 2, pp.274–5)

The prophets might be overtaken by these ecstasies at any
time. The first observer quoted above saw his 16-year-old
brother, who had been posted in a tree as a sentinel to
watch out for the army, taken suddenly by one of these attacks, and fall from the tree, yet without hurting himself. Dr
Calmeil, of the Charenton Hospital, Paris, observes, 'I
know of only hysteria or epilepsy which occur in such a
way,' and notes that the Cevennes attacks present features
which resemble both the one and the other.

Whether in ecstasy or not, many of the Cevennois
reported other phenomena — visions of angels, mysterious
melodies coming seemingly from nowhere. But the
preaching was always the main item: some prophets were
inspired to speak as many as seven times on one day, and
some discourses would last three or four hours! Seventeen-
year-old Isabeau Vincent, one of the most celebrated of the
prophets, presented what Calmeil judges to be all the signs
of somnambulism; when in ecstasy, one could call her by
name, push and shake her, pinch or burn her, without waking her. Yet in that state of apparent sleep, she would sing
psalms in a clear and intelligible voice, improvise prayers,
recite long passages from the Gospels, comment on the
Scriptures, harangue the impious, deliver sermons full of
force.

Somnambulism, hysteria, epilepsy, ecstasy — evidently
the Cevennes phenomena have much in common with
many other ASCs; what makes them distinctive (though
not altogether unique) is the *public* character of the outbreak. Not only did the phenomena occur in public, but
they served a communal purpose, they were an affirmation
of solidarity in the face of persecution. This not only inspired the outbreak, but also dictated its character: in other

words, the individual performances were shaped by the shared circumstances. We shall be looking in #3.4 at the implications of such collective ASCs, which in many respects resemble individual states, yet differ from them in others.

A classic example of enhanced individual peformance is the ability to calculate, especially time. A hypnotised patient can be given a post-hypnotic suggestion to perform a certain act after, say, a million seconds; and this will be done precisely. We shall consider some of the implications in #7.

But we shall also have reason to think that the most important way in which performance is improved is in *creativity*. In ASCs, either our subconscious self is stimulated to become immensely creative, or the creativity it already possesses is stimulated to reveal itself.

The most obvious example is our dreams: which of us has not woken amazed by the ability of our dream 'producer' to devise wonderful and intricate fantasies? These everynight spectacles are a salutary reminder that we all of us possess within us this immensely creative force. So, whenever we come across some performance so astonishing that it seems it *must* have an otherworldly or supernatural explanation, our response should be to ask ourselves whether it is *really* beyond the capability of our dream producer? Consider, for example, the performance of Catherine Elise Müller, better known as 'Hélène Smith':

> Hélène was a Swiss psychic of the 1890s who, when she was about 30, began to claim a succession of parallel existences during which she lived successively as Marie Antoinette, as an Oriental Princess and as a traveller to the planet Mars. In each of these roles she displayed extraordinary inventiveness, and more, an access to obscure material which puzzled even her investigator, Théodore Flournoy.
>
> Hélène's greatest feat, though, was to back up her Martian claims by speaking and writing the Martian language. Although Flournoy was able to show it to be an artificial language based on French, the feat of creating from scratch a totally new language is a remarkable one. Nor did it stop there: Hélène *used* the language consistently, over a long period. Even the way in which she professed to learn it, gradually adding a phrase here, a word there, just like anyone

visiting a foreign country, was itself an impressive performance.

If the subconscious mind of someone who was outwardly a very ordinary person, working in a Geneva store, could perform this feat which so far surpasses what most of us could do in our conscious states, we must face the possibility that every subject, in every case we encounter in our inquiry, may have a subconscious self no less talented, endowed with powers no less creative.

From which it follows that whether we are considering hypnotic recall of past lives, abductions by otherworldly beings, possessions by spirits or near-death encounters with the dead, we must consider a creative performance by the subconscious mind as a possible explanation.

Increased suggestibility

As we lose conscious control from within ourselves, so we become more susceptible to suggestions from elsewhere. Janet's hysteria patients, at the height of their state, would respond to the most casual utterance made in their hearing:

> When Berthe happens to understand what is said to her, she displays a credulity which means that one must be on one's guard. Seeing how slowly she ate her lunch, someone said to her with a laugh, Have you put poison in your soup? and from then on she was haunted by the idea of poison, asking herself if she had poisoned herself or others. (1911, p.173)

Or the suggestion can be self-induced: Barthélemy quotes a dramatic instance:

> A young mother had her hands full of china which she was putting away in a cupboard, when she saw that her small child, playing near the stove, had touched some part of the mechanism and was in danger of having the chimney drop on his neck just like a guillotine.
>
>   In the shock of the moment, she said, 'her blood ran cold' — and in an instant, there formed on her own neck a raised red band in precisely the position where her child seemed about to be struck; the mark was still plainly visible some hours later when a doctor came to the house. (1893, p.82; with true scientific detachment, he doesn't tell us what, if anything, happened to the child!)

Janet notes that the suggestibility of his patients varies continually with the state of their health, making it clear that there is a *physical* correspondence. This is consistent with the symptoms of various states such as 'highway hypnosis' (#3.2), in which fatigue and sensory deprivation seem to make the individual more suggestible; on the other hand, in hypnosis itself, suggestibility seems to be an entirely psychological matter, the result of voluntary resignation by the subject to the hypnotist's will.

But what *is* 'suggestibility? As Breuer, Freud's collaborator, perceived, it is a state in which a suggestion proposed to the subject 'meets with no resistance...the field, so to speak, is clear for the first comer'. In other words, the subject *doesn't* or *can't* counter a suggestion put to him with any competing idea of his own. If a hypnotic subject is told by the hypnotist that the sky is green, he makes no objection, because he has *chosen* to abandon his customary reality-testing procedure. If someone is shocked by stress, drugs or anything else he can't cope with, he is *unable* to use his reality-testing procedure and so, similarly, lays himself open to suggestion from elsewhere.

So while we may see that suggestibility is a feature of ASCs, it is equally valid, and perhaps more helpful, to turn it the other way round and say: *An ASC is a state in which the individual chooses or is persuaded or compelled to abandon his customary reality-testing procedure, rendering him vulnerable to suggestions which he would at other times recognise as conflicting with reality, and making him liable to entertain ideas and pursue behaviours which are inconsistent with reality.*

Depersonalisation

The most real thing we know is ourselves. The most profound change we can conceive is a change in ourselves. Yet this is what every ASC does to a greater or lesser degree. There is a destructive aspect — ceasing to be our usual self — which has been given various labels, of which *depersonalisation* seems the most expressive. And there is generally a constructive aspect — in which we become something other than ourself: there are many terms for this, too, but I have chosen *role-playing* as the most all-embracing.

Whatever ASC he is in, the individual is liable to feel that he is no longer 'himself', whether he is a spirit medium who believes he is serving as a voluntary temporary channel for otherworldly beings, or a possession victim who believes his body has been taken over by some other entity. Each illustrates that depersonalisation is, as the word implies, a *negative* process. But we shall see that it can also be seen as a necessary preliminary to the *positive* process of assuming another identity in one of the various role-playing activities which characterise most ASCs.

There is a curious feature of many ASCs which seems to symbolise this process: the ease with which names are forgotten in ASCs. Gregory, in 1851, noted that the hypnotic subject

> often loses his sense of identity, so that he cannot tell his own name, or gives himself another, frequently that of the operator; while yet he will speak sensibly and accurately on all other points. He very often gives to his operator, and to other persons, wrong names, but always, so far as I have seen, the same name to the same person. (p.85)

One of the many puzzles of spirit communication has always been the reluctance of the 'spirits' to identify themselves correctly; visionaries frequently have the same difficulty — it wasn't until her 16th encounter with her otherworldly visitor that Bernadette Soubirous received an answer to her question, 'Mademoiselle, will you please be so kind as to tell me who you are, please?' — and then only the roundabout, not to say ambiguous, response: 'I am the Immaculate Conception.'

If the otherworldly entities are who they claim to be, there seems no reason why this should occur. But if they are simply actors in a drama, then their names are not so very important: how often do we watch a play on TV without really noticing the names of most of the characters?

Role-playing
In ceasing to be himself, the individual becomes, to a greater or lesser degree, another person:

> Janet: I suggest to Leónie [in the waking state] that she is wearing a fine dress of black velvet. This doesn't in any way alter

her medical symptoms...but she sits up straight in her arm-
chair, her face becomes serious with a composed smile, she
listens to me and replies with an affected gravity. In short, she
plays the part of a 'grande dame'. (1911, p.374).

As a rule, a hypnotised subject will respond readily to role-
playing suggestions. Some perform better than others:
Janet finds that Léonie's performance as a general is banal
and stereotyped, on the other hand she takes naturally to
being a princess dressed in black velvet, and plays the part
to perfection. No doubt private fantasy is at work here, such
as we all have — some of us feeling an urge to play the hero
we feel sure we could have been had circumstances been
otherwise, some trying to compensate for the rewards we
feel life has denied us, others choosing to play the role of
victim or even martyr, thereby justifying our present
situation.

A somewhat different kind of role-playing occurs when
the individual continues to behave in a rational way,
doesn't seem to have suffered any profound disintegration
of his personality, but none the less seems to become
'another person'. For example, there is a long tradition of
'inspired' preachers, such as the Prophets of the Cevennes
already noted in #3.1.

Reports of revivalist preachers, such as Wesley, suggest
that they are in some kind of ASC when at the height of
their performance; and there are actors who so lose
themselves in their role that even off-stage an Olivier remains Othello. Church ritual and the 'magic' of the theatre
will each in their way tend to enhance this. When a
preacher stands before his congregation as spokesman for
the divine, his performance parallels, however tamely, that
of the shaman in a primitive culture who believes himself to
personify — even to be possessed by — the deity of his people. Both, however sincerely they believe in their role, are
giving a performance, just as much as is the stage actor.

Something of the kind may be what is happening in spirit
trance states; and of course it is, almost by definition, what
is happening in multiple personality and possession cases.
The form it takes will depend on the context:

In a spiritualistic community we get optimistic messages,
whilst in an ignorant Catholic village the secondary personage

calls itself by the name of the demon, and proffers blasphemies and obscenities, instead of telling us how happy it is in the summer-land. (James, 1890, vol.1, p.228)

There are more extreme cases — most notably amnesia — in which the individual seems literally to become another person. And there are states to which it is hard to give any specific label, but in which role-playing seems to be the dominant feature (Sarah L was a former servant girl employed by Bramwell who subsequently came under his care as a patient):

In the normal state Sarah was quiet, respectful, and somewhat shy, and retained this character when I hypnotised her. Before coming under my care, she had been hypnotised and exhibited by a stage performer; and some time after, her mother told me that Sarah occasionally hypnotised herself, and that the condition then differed markedly from the one I induced. After some coaxing, the girl consented to hypnotise herself, and went through the following peformance: — First, she closed her eyes and appeared to pass into a lethargic state; then a few minutes later awoke with a changed expression: instead of having a shy and modest air, her eyes sparkled and she looked full of mischief. In place of addressing me as 'Sir' she put her hand on my arm and said in a familiar way, 'I say'. She then began to ask me impertinent questions about the persons she had seen at my house, and to criticise them in a particularly free and sarcastic fashion. The performance was so interesting and amusing that I got her to hypnotise herself on a good many occasions. The same phenomena always appeared; she invariably became familiar, inquisitive, and sarcastic.

After I had observed the condition for some time, I concluded that it was not likely to be beneficial to the subject, and suggested during ordinary hypnosis that she should lose the power of creating it. The suggestion was successful and the condition never reappeared. (1903, p.392)

One aspect of Sarah's behaviour may be more significant than it seems — her tendency to become more familiar when in her second state. She is not alone: similar behaviour is reported in other seemingly quite different ASCs. Kerner noted that Frederike Hauffe [#4.2], when in her 'magnetic' state, would address even strangers with the familiar 'du' (=thou), something which no well-behaved

German would think of doing; precisely the same was reported of the afflicted children in the Swedish 'preaching epidemic' [#3.3] and many of the Jansenist convulsionaries, when in ecstasy, would not speak except 'en tutoyant', i.e. addressing everyone as 'tu' not 'vous' [#7].

Bramwell's Sarah–2 shares another trait with Janet's Léonie–2: both would make fun of the doctor's visitors after they had left, and Léonie would imitate them in an amusing way. Neither would have behaved so in her normal state.

Why should going into an ASC so often have this effect? Why did the convulsionaries, as Montgeron observed them, revert to infantile behaviour:

> We see a childlike air suddenly take hold even of mature and serious people, affecting their facial expressions, their movements, their tone of voice, their body postures, their way of doing things; and at such times they will reason in a childish manner, both in the phrases they use and in the simple, innocent and timid way they express their thoughts. (Calmeil, 1845, vol.2, p.390)

Janet considered his hysterical patients to be 'like little children' in their fondness for make-believe; when he asked his patient Nicole how he should address her in her secondary state, she answered 'Nichette' — the name she had been known by as a little child. He observes that this is not a rare phenomenon: Deleuze had a patient who called herself 'Petite', Gibert one calling herself 'petite Lilie', and we shall see that Mary Wood [#3.3] does the same. Spirit mediums, too, frequently have as their 'spirit controls' lisping children, of whom Mrs Leonard's 'Feda' is just one example.

A further suggestion that ASC subjects revert to childishness in their secondary state comes from the 'death defying' feats they perform, and which we consider in #8.3.

This reverting to childish ways throws a new light on the nature of the depersonalisation and role-playing characteristic of ASCs. Remembering how children love to dress up and be anything other than themselves, should we perhaps see, as a major element in the process of entering the ASC, a divesting of adulthood, with all its problems and responsibilities, and a return to the imagined simplicity of childhood?

Personification

Not only do ASC-subjects cast themselves in roles in order to act out their ideas, but if others are involved in the ASC, they too become part of the performance. Cooper's hypnotic subject (#7), when asked to resolve an abstract problem, spontaneously does so by supposing the people involved to be actual people, whom she describes herself as visiting and talking with. When Madeleine [# 1] is enjoying her ecstasy she may be in turn Mary, Jesus, or herself as a kind of 'chorus': but what part can Janet himself play? Why, he can be Joseph, who naturally has a place beside Mary and Jesus; moreover, his dual role, as both Mary's husband and Madeleine's doctor, reinforces his position of authority and enables him to control her even when she's in the full flight of her ecstasy. Again, when Dr Voisin's patient [# 9] is induced to stab a pretended victim, he is subsequently 'haunted' by the reproachful spirit of the murdered lady.

American psychologist Hilgard provides a particularly ingenious instance: while regressing subjects to supposed earlier periods of their lives, he wondered how they would account for the presence of the hypnotist, who was assuredly not present at the time. He found that most subjects 'saw him as a stranger who had intruded into the regressed experience', and quotes one subject who, 'regressed to a birthday party in a park, saw me as the caretaker who was picking up paper on a pointed stick'.

Here we have further evidence of the creativity of the subconscious mind; the subconscious has *an urge to fabricate*, and it does it extremely well. Consequently, we must look twice at any scenario in which other characters appear, such as the claim of psychic Rosemary Brown that the spirits of dead musical composers, such as Liszt and Chopin, appear and dictate new compositions to her. Without questioning her sincerity, we must consider the possibility that they, like Hilgard's subject's park attendant, are actors created by the subconscious.

If that is so, then we are set on a long path; for the same

could apply to entities of every kind, whether it be the Virgin Mary who appears to Bernadette, the malevolent Devil who appears to others less fortunate, or the spirits of the dead who appear in near-death experiences. The question is a vast one, and deserves a book to itself (and indeed has one: Evans, 1984); here and now, we must recognise its very great importance for our study. Perhaps every being encountered by our ASC subjects is an actor, or we should better say, a *fellow*-actor, a supporting player in a drama whose protagonist is the subject himself.

One thing is clear: *suggestibility, depersonalisation, role-playing* and *personification* are the ingredients which, in combination, will more than anything else help us discover the nature and purpose of the ASC.

3.2   Spontaneous ASCs

Sleep and dreaming

Sleep, and dreaming which seems to be an inseparable part of sleep, are unlike other ASCs in that they appear to be essential to life. Though there are well-attested cases in which individuals have managed without sleep, either completely or very largely, it is probable that they made up for it by indulging in alternative ASCs.

Sleep itself is far from being a uniform state; in the course of a typical night, most of us pass through four or five cycles each involving a succession of states. There are many variations, no two sleeping patterns are identical, but there are overall similarities. Because behaviour is so different from one stage of sleep to another, it has been suggested that each should be thought of as a separate ASC; strictly speaking this is probably true, since some levels of sleep seem to be more necessary to us than others, and also since certain phenomena occur in one phase but not in others. Some phases are characterised by active dreaming (though there is evidence to suggest that dreaming of a sort is in fact continuous), and it is in these states that sleepwalking — a phenomenon which certainly merits classification as a special state — is likely to occur. There are also phases in which muscle tone relaxes so completely that if the sleeper is wakened he may find himself momentarily incapable of movement — a phenomenon relevant not only to sleep-related experiences such as 'bedroom invasions' but also other ASC-related experiences such as paralysis during encounters with extraterrestrials.

Though a lot has been learned about the phenomenology of sleep, much has still to be learned about *why* we sleep, why we have the various phases, what is the importance of each phase. We don't understand why some people need more, others less sleep: still less, why some people appear to sleep for immensely long periods — years on end, in some cases.

If sleep is still largely not understood despite much research, the same is equally true of dreaming. We do not know why we dream, we do not know why dreams vary so much, we do not know why it is necessary for us to dream.

Particularly intriguing, for our present purpose, is the fact that though dreaming is fundamentally a subconscious activity, there are clear indications that the dreaming mind is aware of normal sensory stimuli — temperature, sounds and so on. In one of the earliest studies of sleep (1834), Macnish noted:

> Dr Gregory relates that, having a hot water bottle at his feet, he dreamed he was making a journey to the top of Mount Etna, and that he found the heat of the ground almost insufferable. Another person having a blister applied to his head, imagined he was scalped by a party of Indians; while a friend of mine, happening to sleep in damp sheets, dreamed he was dragged through a stream. (p.54)

Moreover, it is clear that the 'producer' of our dreams acts to some extent in a purposeful manner, for instance, in responding to our current preoccupations or, in the case of psychiatric patients, coming up with dreams suitable for psychoanalysis.

A further paradox of dreaming is that, though for the most part it is a subconscious matter, some control can be exerted over it. I have learnt that if I am in an unpleasant predicament in my dreams, I can snap out of it — but only by waking. Others have far greater control, and enjoy 'lucid dreams' in which they seem to have a degree of conscious awareness. A French investigator, Hervey de Saint-Denis, published in 1867 a fascinating account of his own dreams, claiming that anyone could, like him, learn to exercise complete control over his dreams without waking.

Another indication of the complexities of dream activity is the evidence that some dreams show evidence of precognition — a fact I have proved to my own satisfaction, at least — and other manifestations of paranormal ability such as clairvoyance and telepathy. (Several other ASCs, as we shall see, also seem to favour psychic phenomena.) The classic Wilkins case is a particularly intriguing example:

> In 1754 the reverend Joseph Wilkins, living at Ottery in Devon, dreamed he was travelling to London, and decided to visit his family in Gloucestershire on the way. He seemed to arrive at his father's house; finding the front door closed, he went round to the back, and there entered. The family, however, being already in bed, he seemed to ascend the stairs and enter his father's bed-chamber. His father was asleep, but his mother seemed awake, so he walked round to her side of the bed and said, 'Mother, I am going on a long journey, and am come to bid you good-bye,' to which she answered, 'O dear son, thou art dead!'
>
> This, understand, was but a dream, to which he at the time attached no importance. He was, however, greatly surprised when, soon after, he received a letter from his father, addressed to himself, *if alive*, or, if not, to his surviving friends, since they believed him dead. For that on such a night (that on which their son had his dream), Mrs Wilkins had distinctly heard somebody try the fore-door, go round to the back, and enter. She had perfectly recognised the footstep of her son, who, entering the chamber, had spoken to her, and received her answer, as in his dream. Much alarmed, she had awakened her husband, and related what had occurred, assuring him that it was not a dream, for that she had not been asleep at all. (Rogers, 1853, p.283)

I cannot see how this can be categorised as anything but an OBE. If so, it provides us with another parallel between dreaming and other ASCs, for we shall see that people are liable to experience OBEs in many different states.

'Daytime sleep'
Many ASCs, because they weren't understood, were given

names relating to what they *seemed* to be: 'daytime sleep' is one such. In fact, this condition is sufficiently distinctive to merit classification as an ASC in its own right. A team of doctors (Guilleminault *et al.*) reported in 1975 that they had had nearly 200 patients afflicted by this condition: 'In addition to the complaint of hypersomnia, 95 per cent of this patient population presented what might best be described as "ASCs" that they do not identify as sleep. These states impair the patients' professional, social and familial lives and sometimes lead to severe accidents.'

One patient reported: I left Reno at 10 a.m. en route to Tahoe, a 100 km drive. I remember perfectly what happened up to Carson City (45 km away). After that, I had a complete blackout. I found myself at the reception desk of a hotel in Tahoe, knocking on the desk, and a receptionist asking me what he could do to help. I suddenly 'came back'. I could not remember why I was in that hotel, where I had parked my car, and what had happened in the past 90 minutes.

Another: I am a computer programmer. My last mistake was to run a completely inappropriate program for 3 hours which could have cost the company $25,000. During that time I had to do a certain number of tape rewindings, etc., which I did. It seems I even talked appropriately to one of my assistants.

A third: I was going to do the dishes...when I 'woke up' about 30 minutes later, the kitchen was a complete mess. I had put all the plates in the clothes dryer and turned it on. (Guilleminault *et al.*, 1975, p.378)

Investigation revealed that though the patients seem to sleep a lot during the day, they sleep *less* than normal at night, and their overall total is much like yours or mine; the authors speculate that 'this syndrome may be more related to an impairment of the "wakefulness" structures than to a dysfunction of the "sleep" structures'. They offer no suggestion as to how it originates, and none of their attempts to treat it gave more than marginal alleviation.

So we do not know whether it is of physical or psychological origin. What we *do* know is that it is embarrassing and potentially dangerous, and — judging by appearances — in no way beneficial. We cannot entirely rule out the possibility of a psychiatric explanation — that the act of putting the dishes in the clothes drier was perhaps symbolic of some domestic situation, that the running of an inappropriate computer program is significant of a repressed rebellion against the company or the fact of having to work at all. But it is easier to believe that in this case, at least, we are dealing with an ASC which is neither purposeful nor positive, but represents a physiological malfunction.

Threshold states

Hypnagogic (just waking) and hypnopompic (just falling asleep) states offer a special puzzle: though they are very like waking dream or reverie states, the phenomena they present are often of a kind not encountered in any other ASC. They are accompanied by visual experiences which, both in what is seen and in the way it is seen, are rarely found in other states. The most frequently described subject matter is *faces*, seemingly of strangers, which pass in succession before the mind's eye: here are some accounts collected by Mrs Leaning in her classic study (1925):

> The faces both come and go *gradually*, the eyes being generally the first to be observed, coming dimly as in a mist, till the whole face is clear and alive, then will fade, the eyes watching to the last...Sometimes the faces are flashed on and flashed out again...More lovely than any painting I have ever seen...More often than not beautiful or of strong character...None are ugly...Often look very ugly...Some grotesque, others beautiful...They appear gradually, an eye will appear, then part of a face...They evolve out of a circle of either blue or green, which unfolds itself in a lovely golden centre, and pass very rapidly.

Clearly, though many people in these threshold states see faces, they see different kinds of faces in different ways. But why should these strange processions of nameless faces be associated with this state? They do not seem to tie in with the other paramount feature of the passage from waking to sleeping, which is that the subject is at such times particularly open to hallucinations. This is when a high proportion of 'bedroom visitor' incidents take place, and UFO sightings are frequently reported by people who get up in the middle of the night to go to the bathroom and 'happen' to see a mysterious object as they pass the window.

Sleep paralysis

Akin to threshold states is 'sleep paralysis', which occurs when the individual believes himself to be awake, but is unable to move.

Often, though, instead of being simply a physical state, this is accompanied by experiences on quite another level, of which the 'bedroom invasion' is the best known. Typically, the individual is lying in bed, generally in the dark, and has the impression that some entity — almost always malevolent — has entered the room and is lying on top of him as though to stifle him; but the circumstances can be very informal:

George (24) is studying hard for an exam, and one evening decides to take a short rest on a sofa in the college library. The sofa gives him no choice but to lie on his back; he has a succession of brief dreams, each of which shocks him into waking suddenly. Then, seemingly awake but with his eyes closed, he hears footsteps approaching. The next thing he knows, a female voice is speaking to him: it's no one he recognises, but she speaks familiarly, saying 'You knew I would come' followed by a lot of talk about her face: she doesn't want him to look at her on account of her face. He keeps thinking, 'Who *is* this, who's playing this — who's talking?' and then he feels pressure on his arms, and he can't move. He opens his eyes — and there's no one there; he knows he's awake, because he can see the books above him, and thinks 'God, this is an incubus' — surprising himself with his own ability to be rational about it — and then he manages to free himself of the paralysis, and the moment he succeeds in moving, the experience is over.

Inevitably, psychoanalysts have had a great time with this phenomenon, linking it to incest, primal scene (watching parents making love) and masturbation guilt fantasies. Unfortunately for their ingenious theories, Hufford, from whose classic study I have taken George's case, has shown that sex is rarely an element. So, despite George's intuition, this is not quite the same thing as the succubus and incubus of traditional witch belief, or the nightmare of folklore.

There seems no reason to doubt that this particular experience is related to physiological factors which are liable to occur during sleep — body position, muscular relaxation, the slowing down of the metabolism, digestion, sensory distortion — all of which, as we know, influence our dreams. Bedroom invasions are not dreams as such, but clearly many of the same mechanics are involved.

There is one category of sleeper, narcolepts, who among other anomalies show unusual patterns of sleep, including the tendency to lapse straight from the waking state to the REM state, which is characterised by so complete a muscle relaxation that if a sleeper is awakened in this state, he is powerless to move and so may think himself paralysed. Possibly George is such a person; he takes what he intends to be a brief nap, but instantly plunges into REM sleep with complete muscle relaxation. Something wakes him — he is, don't forget, in a public library — and being unable to move, and in a hypnagogic state, he has his hallucinatory experience which seems so real to him.

Clearly, even if we see it as akin to sleep, this is a special kind of state with its own unique characteristics.

Waking trance

There are many states in which the individual is technically 'awake' but less than fully conscious of external events. Macnish, in 1834, uses the term *reverie* for a state in which the individual is unable (or perhaps unwilling) to focus attention on any one thing, but lets his attention drift; then he uses the term *abstraction* for a state which is outwardly similar, but in fact just the reverse, where the individual focuses his attention on one thing to the exclusion of others — the state of the stereotype 'absent-minded professor'.

'Waking trance' may be a reasonable term to include both these and other states whose distinctive symptom is a decline in the subject's overall awareness and attention, which may or may not mean that his attention is directed to a mental process or inner vision of some kind. This lack of attention can be quite extreme, to the extent that he may be oblivious to substantial stimuli in his vicinity.

Although I have included these under 'spontaneous ASCs', it is evident that someone who found abstraction useful might choose to enter it deliberately, so that it would qualify for the category of 'voluntary ASCs'. But most waking trance is involuntary, as is shown by its occurrence in hysteric patients: Janet compares his patient Berthe's concentration on her work with the scholar who concentrates:

> When she raises her head, she is confused as if emerging from a dream, and doesn't remember what she's just been doing. Her behaviour recalls that of men of genius who yield to their inspiration without being aware that they are doing the work. (1911, p.128)

Another similarity is with the 'sleepwalking' state we consider in #3.4, and La Tourette actually labels the following case one of somnambulism:

> A young shoemaker, age 22, is liable to be overtaken by attacks of somnambulism at any hour of the day, even in the middle of his work. When the paroxysm strikes him, he frowns, his eyes close, and all his senses go dead. You can now push him, pinch him, prick him, and he will feel nothing, not even if you call him by his name or discharge a pistol near his ears. Though his eyes are closed so fast that they cannot be opened, he carries on with whatever he was doing when the attack came, working or walking...One day, walking down the street in this state, he encountered some wood piled in the way, and jumped over it, proof that he could see. Another time, on a journey, he continued riding, passed through a wood, watered his horse at a trough, came to a market where he tied up his horse and made his way through the stalls and the crowd to the man he had business with, and spoke a few words to him before suddenly awaking in a fright, astonished to find himself there. (1887, p.176).

The similarity to somnambulism is so close that we may reasonably suppose it to be the same state, but with the obvious difference that it originates while the subject is awake rather than asleep.

'Highway hypnosis', 'kayak disease', etc.
Driving alone at night on a motorway or otherwise incident-free road is the most familiar of a number of situations in which something very like a waking trance may occur. It is notorious that this provides the setting for many of the most dramatic UFO-related incidents, and particularly of alleged abductions by extraterrestrials on to their spaceships. The classic abduction case, that of Barney and Betty Hill, involves just such circumstances: the couple were driving late

at night in a lightly populated area of New England, along a road which seemed totally deserted of traffic (Evans 1987).

There are two ways of accounting for this. If you believe these abduction events really happen, you can plausibly argue that of course the aliens choose isolated people in isolated situations so as not to draw attention to their doings. Since no independent evidence exists for any abduction event, we are left to make our own choice on the basis of probability whether witnesses are indeed abducted — or only imagine they are.

The question might be resolved if many Eskimo fishermen reported being abducted by extraterrestrials, for there is an evident parallel between 'highway hypnosis' and 'kayak disease', an ASC experienced by Greenland fishermen who have to spend several days alone in a kayak (a small oared boat) while hunting seals; the absence of sensory stimulation, the featureless land/seascape, the isolation of the individual intensified by the need to wrap himself up against exposure to the cold, combine to encourage deindividuation and openness to illusion, hallucination and suggestion of all kinds. The same factors, of course, should make them prime targets for the extraterrestrials, for what could be easier than beaming up a solitary Eskimo from his canoe under these conditions? If, however, it should turn out to be the case that few, if any, Greenlanders are abducted, we must suppose it more probable that abduction is a psycho-sociological phenomenon with no correlation in reality. Or, of course, that extraterrestrials are for some reason not interested in Eskimos.

This kind of state raises a very important issue: ostensibly, highway hypnosis is no more than 'robot behaviour'. The motorist's mind — that is, his conscious attention — is 'elsewhere'; the driving is being done by the brain which, as in other robot situations, is able to keep going remarkably well, responding to bends in the road and so on. Only if something demands particular attention does the brain alert the mind, like a subordinate at work calling in the boss.

In this it seems to differ from the robot behaviour of sufferers from functional disorders such as epileptic

automatism. These are liable not to be able to return to the
USC in time to deal with the situation; so either the robot
mechanism continues to operate even though it is out of its
depth, or the unfortunate individual comes to himself to
find himself in a totally incomprehensible situation, with no
notion how he got into it, much as in the 'daytime sleep'
states we noted earlier.

As for the alleged abductees, they offer yet another variation, for while the 'daytime sleepers' have no memory of
how they got to where they find themselves, in the case of
the abductees it seems that the robot behaviour is accompanied by a switch to a state of suggestibility in which they
may have dramatic hallucinations which they can subsequently recall — though sometimes only with the aid of
hypnosis.

Some of these hallucinatory experiences last an hour or
more. It is hard to believe that the subject keeps on driving
all this while, so we must suppose he parks his car —
presumably in the robot state — and goes into a trance-like
sleep or sleep-like trance or whatever, for as long as the experience occurs. Unfortunately, no one has ever come
across abduction subjects in the course of their experience, so we can only speculate on what happens to
them.

Waking dream

This is the state in which, if we direct our attention to it, we
find ourselves observing or actually involved in a dreamlike
story which is apparently being projected inside our mind.
It is like finding oneself in a cinema part-way through a film
about which one knows nothing. The action is highly detailed, clearly there is intense activity proceeding, certain facts
— those are terrorists, there is a kidnapped women in that
house — are apparent; but what the origin of the story is,
who wrote the script, why it is being enacted, we haven't
the least idea.

Such experiences have encouraged Myers and others to
speculate that we are dreaming all the time (see Evans,
1984), in which case the impression of walking unexpected-
ly into a cinema provides a very apt analogy. So far as our
present study is concerned, the waking dream provides fur-

ther evidence of our subconscious self's irrepressible creativity.

3.3 Externally triggered ASCs

States resulting from physical illness

Illness affects not only our body but also our behaviour. Often this involves nothing more than a diminishing of normal activity, ranging from mild lassitude to outright coma which, as it were, keeps us off the road while repairs are carried out.

Sometimes, though, specific symptoms such as hallucinations suggest that the patient has been switched to some kind of ASC. Because they do not appear to serve any biological purpose, these are generally supposed to be accidental malfunctions resulting from changes in body chemistry.

And so they may be. But though the *occasion* of such an experience may be no more than a physical accident, its *nature* is no less a product of the individual subconscious than any other ASC. Fever may put the patient into a delirious state in which he hallucinates, but it doesn't dictate *what* he will hallucinate.

ASCs originating in physical illness can lead to effects just as extraordinary as those originating in the mind:

In 1895 13-year-old Mary Wood suffered an attack of flu-related meningitis, during which she was afflicted with delirium bordering on mania; she called people snakes and did not recognise her friends. In the fifth week, during convalescence, her character changed, and she began to give those around her names other than their own; her father became 'Tom', her mother 'Mary Ann', etc. After a few more days, she developed a secondary personality of a rather rudimentary kind.

Fragmentation continued until eventually 16 different 'Marys' manifested, each of them quite distinct and unaware of anything that happened while another 'Mary' was in control. At the end of a year the normal condition only rarely appeared, and then only briefly — never for longer than ten minutes, sometimes only a few seconds.

Dr Wilson, who was treating her, listed the states:

a   Calls herself 'Thing'; vacant, knows nothing of her past life, cannot stand.

b   Calls herself 'Old Nick'; passionate and mischievous.

c   Cataleptic, deaf and mute; but writes anything she wants.

d   Has apparently lost much of the knowledge the primary self possesses, doesn't know what her legs and arms are, is childish in her talk, and when she writes her name, does so backwards, beginning at the tail of the last letter — not mirror-writing.

e   Terrified.

f   Calls herself 'Good thing'; docile, but usually without power in feet or hands.

g   Calls herself 'Pretty dear'; sweet and amiable, cannot write or spell.

h   Calls herself 'Mamie Wud'; recalls her childhood better than in her waking state, but remembers nothing of her illness.

i   Like d except that she knows nothing and thinks she has just been born.

k   Calls herself 'Old Persuader': wants to hit people with a stick if they won't do as she wants.

l   Calls herself 'Tom's darling'; a nice child.

m   Insists she has no name; violent and unkind.

n   Calls herself 'The dreadful wicked thing'; throws her slippers into the fire in a temper etc.

o   Calls herself 'Tommy's lamb'; blind and idiotic.

p   For two months, constantly repeats the word 'picters' and draws beautifully, which she cannot do in her normal self. Even if she can't see the paper she still draws perfectly. Her eyesight is abnormal and she is apparently insensible to sound.

q   Two years later she comes to something approaching her normal state, but she is still childish, and calls herself 'Critter Wood'.

Five years after her illness, she settles into stage g, and is reported as 'a fine, healthy, well-developed girl, who helps in the house and is anxious to learn typewriting in order to keep herself. Her character, however, differs slightly from her original one, and she is still somewhat childish at times'. (Bramwell, 1903, p.380)

There are other ASCs which so defy classification that we can't even be sure whether they originate in the body or the mind; but since they have an undoubted physiological aspect, whereas their psychological roots are uncertain, we may as well consider them here.

These are a group of states whose common ingredient is 'suspended animation', and which range from fainting through various kinds of spontaneous trance (as opposed to the voluntary trance of, say, the spirit medium) to the catalepsy which is so complete that it can lead to burial alive. Macnish (1834) describes the state:

> The whole body is cold, rigid and inflexible; the countenance without colour; the eyes fixed and motionless; while breathing and the pulsation of the heart are, to all appearance, at an end. The mental powers, also, are generally suspended, and participate in the general torpor which pervades the frame. In this extraordinary condition, the person may remain for several days, having all, or nearly all, the characteristics of death. (p.201)

He narrates the case of a lady who, after a long illness, was in just such a state, and was actually on the point of being nailed in her coffin when

> a kind of perspiration was observed on the surface of her body. It grew greater every moment; and at last a kind of convulsive motion was observed in the hands and feet... A few minutes after, she opened her eyes and uttered a most pitiable shriek... In the course of a few days she was considerably restored, and is probably alive at this day.

Adding to the interest is the victim's own account:

> She said it seemed to her, as if in a dream, that she was really dead; yet she was perfectly conscious of all that happened around her. She distinctly heard her friends speaking and lamenting her death, at the side of her coffin. She felt them pull on the dead-clothes, and lay her in it. This produced a mental anxiety, which is indescribable. She tried to cry, but her soul was without power, and could not act on her body. She had the contradictory feeling as if she were in her body, and yet not in it, at one and the same time. It was equally impossible for her to stretch out her arm, or open her eyes, or cry, although she continually endeavoured to do so. The anguish of her mind was, however, at its utmost height when the funeral hymns began to be sung, and when the lid of the coffin was about to be nailed on. The thought that she was to

be buried alive gave activity to her soul, and caused it to operate on her corporeal frame. (Macnish, 1834, p.205)

There are obvious parallels with the 'near-death experiences' we shall consider in #5: but what is most evident is that in one sense this is not an ASC at all, for the poor lady seems to have been conscious throughout. But was it her USC? The sensation of being 'in her body yet not in it, at one and the same time', suggests that some degree of dissociation was taking place.

If so, she shares with Mary Wood the fact that the origin of her state was a physical condition, but one which affected the mind and provoked a psychological malfunction.

In neither case do we know enough about the personal circumstances of the individual to know whether they may have contributed to the condition. If Mary Wood was experiencing family trouble, if the nearly-buried lady's illness was psychosomatic, this may have played a part in causing their physical state to have mental consequences.

A different kind of effect is produced by afflictions such as epilepsy: we shall have more to say on this subject in #4.

Spontaneous out-of-body experiences

Often associated with physical illness, though not exclusively, is the experience in which someone feels himself to be located outside his physical body, which he can often see at a distance from him.

An OBE is less an ASC in its own right than an experience which may or may not accompany an ASC. It may occur to a trance medium, to a hypnotic subject or to a patient under anaesthetics. Albert Hoffman, who discovered LSD and used it himself without knowing what its effects would be, was disconcerted to find himself seemingly out of his body; and American researcher Charles Tart found in a 1971 test that 23 per cent of experienced marijuana users reported having OBEs.

While psychologists by and large regard the OBE as a special form of hallucination, many accounts support the face-value scenario — that some part of the self, including the senses, is indeed detached in some way from the body and is able to move about more or less independently:

In 1957, at the age of 16, I was in hospital, when I found myself standing beside one of the beds, looking down at the occupant. The most exquisite feeling of pity filled me. I was looking down at myself. The pity and sorrow was for the clumsy, ailing creature lying in that bed. Yet it was not ME, for I was standing there looking down. THIS was me, not that body on the bed. It was with great though impersonal regret that I moved away from that bed, towards the door of the ward. At the door I turned to look again and was compelled, with a force greater than any that I had possessed, to return. There was a nurse at the bedside, holding the hand of that body to which I felt neither association nor responsibility. 'You are not ready, you must go back' repeated itself over and over. I did not want to go back, and replied NO...NO...I was still saying NO when I looked up into the worried face of the young nurse, which filled with relief as she realised that I was all right. (Bord, 1973, p.38)

Thousands have reported such experiences, and the fact that they are so lifelike, and that information is obtained in a way which seems paranormal, has encouraged many to take them at face value as some kind of 'supernatural' experience. However, there are reasons why we should hesitate before jumping to this conclusion.

First, OBEs may be induced by drugs — ketamine, for instance. True, we are finding that physiological and psychological processes are so inextricably interwoven in many ASCs that it is impossible to trace them to their origin; nevertheless, the way we interpret a case like the one just narrated must be affected by our knowledge that it could have been the effect of some chemical administered to her system.

Second, while the information reported by people when 'out of the body' is often correct, this isn't always so; sometimes it is demonstrably incorrect. We find the same thing in spirit trance and hypnosis; this suggests that the OBE, like them, is an ASC in which access to seemingly paranormally-acquired information is combined with a tendency to mix true and false information in a somewhat indiscriminate manner.

To consider the OBE as a psychological process, rather than an indication that the soul, astral self or whatever has truly separated from the body, may seem to be belittling a rather remarkable experience. But in fact the phenomenon is none the less a remarkable one, for it remains a fact that somehow true information is often acquired in what seems to be a paranormal manner. However we explain the OBE, we have somehow to account for this seemingly psychic performance.

We shall be discussing the NDE, with its particular implications, in greater detail in #6. For the moment, let us note that OBEs, while they are particularly associated with near-death, or at any rate serious illness situations, also happen at other times when no such crisis seems to be occurring: in one major study, it was found that only one OBE subject in ten is in a near-death situation. The same study notes other circumstances, among them the following (some of which overlap):

- about 78 per cent of subjects were physically relaxed/ mentally calm;

- 15 per cent were unusually fatigued;

- 8 per cent were using a drug, 6 per cent were under a general anaesthetic;

- 6 per cent were in severe pain;

- 9 per cent were in an active situation (in an accident, having a sexual orgasm, driving a vehicle);

- only 22 per cent were under emotional stress.

There was no correlation with holding a specifically religious belief-system.

As for the character of the experience, a massive 93 per cent emphasised that it was *more real than a dream*. Not only does the subject feel himself to be conscious while having the experience, but he is likely to feel himself *especially* so: and the overwhelming majority find the experience rewarding, non-frightening, reassuring, enlightening and generally life-enhancing (Twemlow *et al.*, 1982).

On the face of it, the OBE seems a clear-cut case of the depersonalisation we find in so many ASCs. But it is a different kind of depersonalisation: not a vague and negative feeling, but a consciously felt and physically real separation in space. Moreover, not only is there an apparent physical separation, but there is an emotional separation. Author Rosalind Heywood had a revealing experience:

> I was lying in bed thinking about an agreeable but selfish action I ardently wanted to take. Suddenly I appeared to split into two, one of me very idealistic and impersonal, who stood at the foot of the bed, the other entirely egocentric, who remained lying in bed. These two 'mes' had a heated discussion and I remember vividly that the standing 'me' looked upon the selfish one with cold contempt, and that the selfish one in bed angrily called her a pious prig.

Some time later she was talking to another lady who had had an OBE, and

> in view of my own experience I asked, very casually, 'What did you both think of each other?' She replied, using the actual words I had used in my own case, 'The one standing looked on the one in the bed with cold contempt.' (PF, 1961)

The spontaneous OBE may turn out to be something altogether different from the OBE-like experience that may occur in the dream state, as in the Wilkins case [#3.2], or from the voluntary OBEs we shall consider in #3.5. But all these experiences have sufficient in common for us to presume that though the OBE has its own unique characteristics, it is related to many other ASC experiences.

States triggered by physiological or environmental factors
In #4 we shall see that ASCs may be triggered by a host of physical factors, ranging from diet — too much, too little, or the wrong kind — to the state of the weather.

It does not seem that there is a specific kind of ASC which is induced only by these triggers, nor does it seem that a particular trigger induces a particular effect. Rather, they seem to put the person into a state where he can more easily be switched into a waking trance, an OBE, a hallucinatory state or whatever. But there may be times when such an event — a thunderstorm, for example — may be the last straw in a cumulative build up of ASC-inducing factors.

Crowd-induced states
Most of us behave differently when we are with others than

when we are alone. A member of a crowd is more suggestible, less ready to make decisions which go against the majority, or to think for himself. This poses the question: is
group behaviour a number of single processes happening
to the individual members of the crowd, or a collective process that happens only to crowds as such?

In a sense, this is a meaningless question, for how could it
be tested? However, it is meaningful to ask: Is crowd
behaviour different in kind from individual behaviour?
Philippe de Félice, writing of the Prophets of the Cevennes
(#3.1), asks (1947, p.240):

> Should we see, along with some alienists, the effect of a sort of
> contagious hypnosis, complicated by epilepsy-like fits, or
> even the consequence of a specific malady of the nervous
> system? Without disregarding the part played by individual
> morbid conditions, what is manifest in these cases is a state of
> *generalised hypnosis*. Both the preachers and their audiences
> succumb to the suggestions continually made to them by their
> leaders, whose influence paralyses their conscious self and
> delivers them to the impulses of a common subconscious, in
> which the individual subconsciouses meet and mingle. In
> short, what we have here is something like a huge collective
> intoxication, whose mechanism is as mysterious as any other
> intoxication, but which results in sweeping the group as a
> whole from waking state to that of a dream...in their case, a
> dream of triumph of the faithful over their satanic foes.

That something of the sort takes place is evident enough,
and really, it doesn't too much matter how we label it. The
key to the process is that it takes place at the subconscious
level; and any state in which the subconscious takes
precedence over the conscious is by definition an ASC.

The phenomena of collective behaviour have been much
debated but insufficiently researched; it seems safe to
assert, though, that people in crowds abandon their usual
reality-testing and decision-making procedures. Notable
examples can be found in the histories of Russian religious
sects such as the Khlysti, of whom it was observed by a
government inspector that 'hundreds of them live as
though they had but a single soul, obeying orders mechan-
ically and with a joyful intoxication' (Félice, 1947, p.214).

The Norsemen who invaded France in the tenth century had a fearsome reputation which helps to explain why the idea of the 'barbarians' became so emotional a concept at that time:

> From time to time a frenzy overtakes them...They froth at the mouth, they distinguish nothing, they lash out at random with their swords, striking friends and enemies, trees, stones, living things and lifeless. They swallow burning coals, they hurl themselves into the fire...and when the fit is over, they are for a long time drained of all force. (Salverte, 1856, p.309)

Should we dignify such a loss of critical sense as an ASC? It seems to be no more than an abandonment of normal rhyme and reason. But we must not be premature, for we shall come across other states which seem likewise to be entirely negative, in which the individual loses his adult intelligence, his knowledge, his memory, all that he has acquired as a maturing individual, yet where behind these seemingly negative symptoms there is a positive motivation: though the individual ceases to be himself, he may become something other.

In short, we shall see that though we rightly describe 'crowd-induced ASCs' as externally triggered, the experience which results is shaped by interaction between the individual and the group.

ASCs specific to a particular culture

Pibloktoq is a disorder which appears to affect only Eskimos — nearly always female — living in Greenland and the polar areas. In Peary's account of his 1909 Arctic expedition he says that eight out of the twenty women on his ship suffered an attack:

> Inahloo, a married woman, was taken with one of these fits in the middle of the night. In a state of perfect nudity she walked the deck of the ship; then seeking still greater freedom, jumped the rail onto the frozen snow and ice... She was finally discovered at a distance of half a mile, pawing and shouting.

The attack usually lasts 60 to 90 minutes. No two people behave in quite the same way, but the first sign is likely to be a soft singing accompanied by rhythmic hand-clapping;

the victim will generally tear off her clothes; then she may crawl around barking like a dog, or lie on her back placing ice on her breasts; or jump into the water and wade among the ice, singing and yelling. Inahloo tried to walk on the ceiling like a bird, uttering bird cries.

A person suffering *pibloktoq* is clearly impervious to feeling, if she can stand water at a temperature of −40 degrees. She seems oblivious of her surroundings, but will resist attempts to restrain her, sometimes fiercely. The attack usually culminates in writhing on the ground and orgasm-like convulsions, terminating in sobbing and deep sleep, after which she is perfectly normal. Victims have no recollection of their experience, and it is regarded by others as something that can happen to anyone and nothing to be concerned about. It is accepted that bystanders' involvement will be limited to seeing that the victim comes to no physical harm during the attack.

Pibloktoq is more likely to occur towards the end of the polar night, when the prolonged dark is starting to weigh even on those accustomed to it. The fact that it rarely, if ever, occurs among Europeans living in the area suggests a cultural basis; however, we should also take into account factors such as diet. Eskimos tend to suffer from calcium deficiency, known as a cause of mental disorder.

Another localised variety of outbreak is *ikóta*, which occurs among the Samoyeds of northern Russia:

> Except very rarely, it afflicts only married women, but somewhat remarkably frequently afflicts them on their wedding day. There seems to be no specific trigger — it may be the spectacle of another woman in the throes of convulsions, the mere sight of a person or a given thing, the sound of a certain word, the inhaling of the smoke of a cigarette. Generally the fit is preceded by a feeling of giddiness, constriction in the throat, oppression in the upper part of the chest or in the diaphragm, torpor in all the limbs. Some subjects declare they have the sensation of a rat running all over the body and inflicting innumerable and very painful bites. Then comes a shrill cry, a fall, general convulsions, violent contortions; the eyes roll in all directions, the teeth are ground, the hands tear the hair and rend the clothing. In other cases the subject flings herself upon the bystanders as if to attack them, upsets

everything she can lay hands on, breaks the furniture and utters devilish cries. Sometimes during the fit she cannot speak a word; in other cases she utters the most atrocious abuse, making use of obscene expressions. Sometimes she falls into an ecstasy or begins to predict the future, speaking in the name of the demon who has taken possession of her.

After the fit, which is of variable duration, there is a return to the normal state; nothing survives except at most a slight heaviness of the head, and no memory remains. Usually the possessed continues to suffer from the same fits until an advanced age. (Oesterreich, 1930, p.204)

The similarity of *ikóta* to *pibloktoq* and to other outbreaks noted thoughout this study shows that we should see it as a local variation on a universal phenomenon, given its specific form by conforming to a known behaviour. We may suppose that, like *pibloktoq*, the social situation of Samoyed women plays a crucial part. While it is worthy of note that *ikóta* victims believe themselves to be possessed, this is probably no more than local custom.

The 'preaching epidemic' which enlivened the peasant communities of southern Sweden in 1842 is typical of the short-lived outbreaks which have been reported here and there thoughout history. Unlike *pibloktoq*, or the Malayan *látah* we shall note in #6.2, it is not a recurrent phenomenon which affects an ethnic group on a permanent if intermittent basis, but seems to have been a one-off event, though of course inspired 'preaching' occurs in many other circumstances.

To the Swedish peasants, the preaching was seen as a divine miracle, though the church authorities looked upon it with less favour. The Bishop of Skara, whose district was among those most affected, made a personal study of the phenomenon, and concluded

that it is a disease originally physical, but affecting the mind in a peculiar way. Bodily sickness is an ingredient, as is proved from the fact that although everyone affected by it mentions a spiritual excitement as its original cause, close examination proves that an internal bodily disorder, attended by pain, preceded or accompanied this excitement. Besides, there are persons who, against their own will, are affected by the quaking fits, which are one of its most striking early outward symptoms, without any previous religious excitement; and these, when subjected to medical treatment, soon recover.

The Bishop finds the symptoms of the Preaching Epidemic to correspond with some of the effects of animal magnetism [the name then given to hypnosis] as practised at that time. In both cases there is an increase of activity of the nervous and muscular system; and further, frequent heaviness in the head, heat at the pit of the stomach, prickling sensation in the extremities, convulsions and quakings; and finally, the falling, frequently with a deep groan, into a profound fainting fit or trance. In this trance, the patient is in so perfect a state of insensibility to outward impressions, that the loudest noise or sound will not awaken him, nor will he feel a needle thrust deeply into his body. Mostly, however, he will hear questions addressed to him, and reply to them. The power of speech in this state is of great eloquence, lively declamation, and the command of much purer language than was usual, or apparently possible, in the natural state. The invariable assertions of all the patients, when in this state, are that they are exceedingly well, and that they have never been so happy before; they declare that the words they speak are given to them by someone else, who speaks by them.

There is in some families a greater liability to this strange influence than in others; it is greater also in children and females than in grown-up people and men. The patients invariably show a strong desire to be together, and seem to feel a sort of attraction or spiritual affinity to each other. In places of worship, they will all sit together; and when one of them is questioned individually, he will always give his answer on behalf of them all, saying 'we' when the inquirer naturally expects 'I'. Another circumstance is peculiar: although these children differ from one another in their natural state, yet while under the influence of the disease, their countenances become so similar as greatly to resemble each other.

The Bishop says he has seen several persons fall at once into the trance, without any preparatory symptom. In the province of Elfsborg, the patients preach with their eyes open, and standing; while in his own province of Skaraborg he has seen them preaching while lying down, with closed eyes, and as far as he can discover, in a state of perfect insensibility to outward impressions.

He gives a detailed description of one girl, aged between 8 and 12: There came on, in the first place, a violent trembling or quaking of the limbs, and she fell backwards with much

violence, but no apparent injury ensued. The patient was now
in the trance, or state of total unconsciousness; and this
trance, which lasted several hours, divided itself into two
stages, acts or scenes, totally different in character. In the first
place, she rose up violently, and all her actions were of a rapid
and violent character. She went through — for what purpose,
it seems impossible to say — the operating of loading, presenting, and firing a gun, and performed most realistically a combat in which she presented the actions of both parties...

The child next passed into the second stage of the trance,
which was characterised by a beautiful calmness and
quietness, and with her arms meekly folded she began to
preach. Her manner in speaking was that of purest oratory;
her tones were earnest and solemn, and the language of a
spiritual character which, when awake, it would have been
impossible for her to use. The Bishop noted down her little
discourse, and an analysis shows it to be an edifying practical
address, perfectly suited to an unsophisticated audience. During its delivery the child had something saint-like in her appearance. Her utterance was soft and clear, not a word was
retracted or repeated; and her voice, which in her waking state
was hoarse, had now a wonderful brilliancy and clearness of
tone. (Ennemoser, 1854, vol.2, pp.503–ff.)

I have quoted this account at some length because the
Bishop's observations are rich in significant detail. We shall
consider in #6 the motivations which may be at work in
these collective outbreaks, but we should note now some
interesting features of the Swedish epidemic:

* The apparent origin in some kind of physical state. This
  may have been a mistake on the Bishop's part, but there
  seems little doubt that physical *symptoms* were present.
  We should at least consider whether climate, diet, etc.
  played any part.

* The extraordinary *communal* character of the outbreak
  which drew those affected together and caused them to
  physically resemble one another: I know of no other case
  in which the last feature has been noted. The fact that the
  ailment, if ailment it was, caused each victim to behave in
  much the same way is something we have seen in other
  collective ASCs and will see in many more; but the
  Bishop leaves us with the impression that something
  more than the customary contagion effect was operating.

* As with every collective ASC occurring within a religious context, the Preaching Epidemic raises in a striking manner the question of whether such outbreaks are beneficial or not. The Bishop's conclusion, after conducting his first-hand investigation, is that, while the extraordinary character of the phenomenon has indeed produced a great religious movement and wrought much good, sending multitudes to church who never went there and reclaiming many from the error of their ways, none the less it *is* a disease, those affected are in an unnatural state, and the practice should be discouraged.

In the event, the clergy and the doctors between them had extinguished the epidemic by the end of 1843.

3.4 Mentally triggered ASCs

All ASCs operate *through* the mind: some seem to originate *from* it, and these are especially interesting because we can often see evidence of *purpose.*

Such experiences suggest that in certain situations a person will — probably at the initiative of his subconscious self — deliberately switch from his USC to an ASC, because that is the most effective way of coping with his situation. Usually this is done simply as a temporary expedient, and the individual reverts to his usual state when the situation no longer requires it.

Sometimes, however, he gets 'fixed' in the behaviour pattern and cannot snap out of it; he may become chronically unadapted to life in the real world, he may develop neurosis or some other form of mental trouble. It is this which has led to the traditional view, still widely prevalent, that all ASCs are signs of mental illness. Rightly, however, *they should be seen not as mental illnesses in themselves but as processes which may degenerate into mental illness.* It is not the ASC itself, but the fact that it has become chronic, which is the mental illness.

A leading contributor towards this more intelligent way of looking at the matter is Thomas Szasz, an American psychiatrist who argues that many conditions currently diagnosed as mental illness are nothing of the sort. He is not denying that mental illness exists, of course: clearly there are many 'true' mental illnesses which are malfunctions of the organism. Many others, however, are not the accidental malfunctions they seem to be, but ASCs deliberately entered into, albeit the decision may be made by the subconscious rather than the conscious self.

Hysteria

Hysteria is defined by the World Health Organisation as:

> Mental disorders in which motives, of which the patient seems unaware, produce either a restriction of the field of consciousness or disturbances of motor or sensory function which may seem to have psychological or symbolic value.

Two types are distinguished:

> It may be characterised by conversion phenomena or dissociative phenomena. In the *conversion* form the chief or only symptoms consist of psychogenic disturbance of function in some part of the body, e.g., paralysis, tremor, blindness, deafness, seizures. In the *dissociative* variety, the most prominent feature is a narrowing of the field of consciousness which seems to serve an unconscious purpose and is commonly accompanied or followed by a selective amnesia. There may be dramatic but essentially superficial changes of personality sometimes taking the form of a fugue [wandering state].

It is important we realise that 'hysteria' is merely a label designating various kinds of behaviour which may or may not qualify as specific states in their own right. Indeed, hysteria is probably best conceived of as a *process* which leads to a variety of behaviours, many of which qualify as ASCs.

It was from their hysteria patients that Charcot, Janet, Freud and Breuer, and others gained many of their greatest insights into the working of the human mind. The protean character of hysteria, taking a different form with each individual patient, presented them with a bewildering repertoire of symptoms: Freud and Breuer list 'anaesthesias as well as neuralgias of the most varied kind, often of many years' duration, contractures and paralyses, hysterical attacks and epileptoid convulsions, symptoms of the nature of tics, chronic vomiting and anorexia carried to the point of refusal of food, the most varied disturbances of vision, constantly recurring visual hallucinations' — and other doctors could add many more.

It was evident to these doctors that the fact that each patient is afflicted by his own individual brand of hysteria means that it is not, like measles, an ailment which is more or less the same for each patient, but a made-to-measure affair. Consequently, to establish its cause means examining the individual patient.

Clearly, too, the choice of symptoms and modifications to the basic pattern are not made arbitrarily: cause and purpose are involved. Freud noted:

> A girl watching in harrowing anxiety at the bedside of a sick person wants to pray but can find no words; finally she succeeds in repeating an English prayer which she learnt in childhood. Later hysteria develops in which she can speak, write and understand only English, while for a year and a half her mother-tongue remains unintelligible to her. (Freud and Breuer, 1892, p.26)

In other cases the link may be symbolic only, and sometimes utterly elusive.

Underlying the outward behaviour, the doctors perceived, is a private motivation. Freud saw it as the festering memory of an incident which the individual cannot forget, but to which he did not properly respond at the time (for instance, 'crying himself out' after the loss of a loved one) and which was not absorbed into the common stock of his memories where he could see it in proper perspective. Why was the memory not processed in the usual way? Perhaps because it involved some kind of psychological conflict — for instance, the loss of a loved one which the subject cannot bring himself to accept, or feelings of guilt, shame, etc. which he dare not face. Or it could be that he was in an abnormal mental state at the time and so unable to respond normally.

Instead, the memory is stored away intact like an unwanted wedding present shoved in the attic without being used, till everyone has forgotten it is there. Freud and Breuer found that, when recalled under hypnosis, 'recollections dating back 15 to 25 years were of astonishing integrity and intensity; on reproduction their effect had the full force of new experiences.'

Once it was seen that this kind of process underlies hysterical states, the road was open for treatment, not as hitherto by treating the hysteria itself, but by going beyond it to discover its origins. The result was psychoanalysis and the other schools of psychotherapy.

As the WHO definition notes, one interesting form taken by hysteria is *partial* blindness, deafness, etc., the degree of partial-ness relating to whatever caused the hysteria. Clearly, in such cases, since there is no organic damage but only a functional defect, the affected area has been *selected*. But the moment we use that word, we raise the question: selected by *whom* or by *what*? Since it cannot be the conscious mind, which is totally bewildered by the phenomenon, the presumption must be that it is the subconscious mind.

Confirming this view is the observation that the symptoms often do not make sense anatomically, but conform with the patient's *idea* of how they should be; someone with hysterical paralysis of the hand has, simply, a hand he cannot use, whereas anatomically paralysis of the hand should involve muscles and nerves in the forearm, etc.

This 'pseudo-paralysis' is displayed vividly by UFO witnesses who claim to encounter extraterrestrials who stun them with a ray gun. When French farmer Maurice Masse met some aliens with their landed saucer in his lavender field one morning in 1965, they pointed a kind of weapon at him which prevented him from moving. But his lungs continued to breathe; his legs continued to support him; his eyes continued to watch the aliens. His pseudo-paralysis is a strong indication that he was in an ASC at the time, in which case it is a fair guess that his experience was hallucinatory.

It is significant that patients react quite differently to subjective and objective symptoms. Pierre Janet tells of a patient of his brother Jules:

> Annette had put her hand through a window, cut it, and developed a partial anaesthesia in the palm of her hand. While examining her, Janet discovered to his astonishment that she was *completely* anaesthetic on the *other* side of her body; this, however, was hysterical in origin — she was somehow subconsciously responsible for it — and so presumably it was ac-

companied by some kind of instruction from her subconscious that it wouldn't bother her at all, whereas the relatively tiny loss of feeling in her other hand, being of external origin, she found extremely bothersome! (1911, p.19: name added)

Note the parallel here with Esdaile's Indian patient (#3.1), who readily went along with the suggestion from the hypnotist via his subconscious that he would feel no pain from the surgery, but was bothered by the far less severe draught of cold air. Both hysteria and hypnosis, evidently, involve a process of *selection*.

Selectivity of a different sort is demonstrated by one of Pierre Janet's patients who had anaesthesia of the hand, but recognised by touch certain personal possessions such as her ear-rings or her hair-clips. Only what was familiar was recognised. Here we note another parallel, this time with robot behaviour: someone who suffers an attack while performing an action can often continue to function — but only so long as he is not required to do anything but what is habitual and familiar.

It is arguable whether hysteria should be thought of as an ASC in its own right; but it is a condition whose characteristics are paralleled in many ASCs and as such it is clearly relevant to our study.

Somnambulism

'Sleepwalking' is a patent example of how ASCs confuse us. For though it originates in sleep, it is quite clear that the individual has shifted into a quite different mode; in fact, more than anything else, somnambulism resembles the robot behaviour of a victim of epileptic seizure. Nineteenth-century French doctors used the word 'somnambule' to describe anybody who carried out natural functions while in a state akin to sleep; for them, hypnosis was 'artificial somnambulism', and closely connected with it. When Dr Dufour of Lausanne inquired into the background of hypnotic subjects, 'all the young people I questioned had just the one thing in common — they were somnambules who, as children, used to get up in the night, leave their beds, wander around the house, go to a desk and write, etc.' (La Tourette, 1887, p.172).

But the sleepwalker is capable of performing not only the

actions of waking life, but also feats beyond his waking ability. Notorious are instances when sleepwalkers go out on to roofs or other dangerous places: the dramatic climax of Bellini's opera *La Sonnambula* involves just this sort of act. Indeed, the tendency to do dangerous things is so common that it may be a clue to understanding the phenomenon: is the subject's dangerous behaviour symbolic of some urge to transcend the limitations of his daily life? We shall consider this point in #8, when we compare it with other examples of risk-taking in ASCs.

Other features of sleepwalking offer clues to understanding ASCs as a whole; some are vividly demonstrated in one of the earliest cases to be seriously studied and used as a basis for experiment. It is narrated by Diderot in his 1760s *Encyclopédie*, to whom it was reported by the Archbishop of Bordeaux:

He told me that when he was at the seminary, he had known a young cleric who was a sleepwalker. Curious to know the nature of this malady, he went every evening into his room, as soon as he was asleep; he saw, among other things, that this cleric would get up, take paper, compose and write sermons; when he had finished a page, re-read it from top to bottom (if you can call it reading, when his eyes were not used): if there was something he didn't like, he would cross it out and write a correction above it, perfectly placed. I have seen the beginning of one of these sermons which he wrote in his sleep, it seemed to me very well done, and correctly written; but there was a surprising correction; having at one place written 'ce divin enfant', he decided when re-reading to substitute 'adorable' for 'divin'; this he did, but then found that he would have to change 'ce' to 'cet' before a vowel, so added a 't' in exactly the right place.

To test whether the sleepwalker was making any use of his eyes, the observer placed a card under his chin, so as to come between the paper and his field of vision; but he continued to write without noticing it. To test how he knew what was before him, the sheet of paper on which he was writing was removed; but he always noticed, because the size was different. Only when a sheet of paper of precisely the same size was substituted did he mistake it for the original; he would then proceed to mark his corrections on it in a place corresponding to the place on his original sheet.

What was even more remarkable was to see music written

with the same exactitude — first the five lines, then all the notes, which were all written first as white notes, and only afterwards he went over the score filling in the black notes.

Somnambulism, Diderot comments, must be accepted as a fact, but when it comes to explaining it, it is a rock on which many hypotheses have been wrecked. He notes as specially difficult to explain the fact that the attention of the writer was limited only to those things he was actually using — pen, paper and ink; but these he perceived very exactly. He was totally unaware, on the other hand, that there was another person in his room; yet in other incidents, in which other people were specifically involved, he would talk to them quite naturally though still asleep.

This narrowed focus of attention is characteristic of ASCs as a whole.

Diderot found particularly baffling the fact that the priest could 'see' with his eyes closed. If he had to correct an upper line while the ink on the lower lines was still wet, he would carefully avoid putting his hand where it might smudge, but if it was perfectly dry, he did not take this precaution. On the other hand, the fact that he would accept a substitute sheet of blank paper, provided it was exactly similar, for the one on which he had written, shows that it was not the thing itself, but a mental image of the thing, that he perceived.

Diderot notes another significant feature of somnambulism, that a sleepwalker, when questioned, can recall not only the events of his waking life, but also what he did during other fits of sleepwalking, though when awake he will be totally unaware of his sleepwalking activities. This 'inter-state data-sharing' is a recurrent feature of ASCs which we consider in #7.3.

Amnesia

I make no apology for illustrating amnesia by the best-known case on record, because it helps us see how ASCs have been inadequately examined, with important questions not being asked. Though this case has been frequently retold, it has been almost always with an eye to the *mechanics* of the event, the psychological process involved. For the purpose of our inquiry, however, that is something we can take in our stride, for amnesia occurs so often in ASCs as to be almost a standard ingredient. On the other hand, as is becoming more and more apparent with each category of ASC we look at, these experiences are meaningless unless we inquire *why* they occur.

On 17 January 1887 Ansel Bourne, a 61-year-old carpenter of Rhode Island, draws $551 from the bank to purchase a piece of land, and boards a Pawtucket horse-car. He fails to return home that day, and nothing is heard of him for two months. He is published in the papers as missing, and the police seek his whereabouts in vain. On the morning of 14 March, at Norristown, Pennsylvania, a man named Brown, who six weeks previously rented a small shop and set up in trade in stationery, fruit and confectionery without attracting any particular attention, calls in the people of the house to ask them where he is? He tells them his name is Ansel Bourne, he is a stranger in Norristown, he knows nothing of shop-keeping, and the last thing he remembers — it seems only yesterday — is drawing the money from the bank in Providence. He cannot believe that two months have elapsed. The people of the house at first think him insane, but on telegraphing to Providence, they receive confirmation of this story; a nephew arrives, settles his affairs, and takes him home.

Often omitted from accounts of Bourne's experience, or if mentioned, never emphasised, is the information that thirty years previously he had been converted from atheism to Christianity under dramatic circumstances — like Saul on the road to Damascus, he was deprived of sight, hearing and speech, and had to be carried home in a cart. In the climate of the day, when all America seemed seething with religious fervour, this had been hailed as a miracle, and a leaflet was published vaunting it as such, though so far as his doctor was concerned 'Mr Bourne's case is clearly attributable to a disturbed and disordered condition of the functions of the brain'. Even before his conversion he had been subject to headaches and blackouts.

Following his conversion, he was told by a celestial vision to give up work as a carpenter and become an itinerant preacher (a curious parallel to the career of Jesus); for more than twenty years he kept up the good work, but after remarrying in 1881 he gave up his preaching vocation and returned to carpentry.

In short, we are not talking about just any old man in the street, but one whose past life is surely relevant to his present experience. I don't think we need be in any doubt that Bourne's amnesia was a dissociation ASC, induced by mental conflict related to his spiritual life. Referring to the case in his classic *Principles of psychology*, William James writes: 'The case (whether it contains an epileptic element or not) should apparently be classed as one of spontaneous hypnotic trance... The peculiarity of it is that nothing else like it ever occurred in the man's life, and that no eccentricity of character came out.' This we have seen to be very far from the case: we must suppose either that James was not in possession of the full data or that he failed to see the relevance of Bourne's early career. Both suppositions seem improbable.

We, too, would like to know more. Michael Kenny's fine study puts Bourne's late fugue in perspective, but the mystery of why he should board a bus as Ansel Bourne and step off as A. J. Brown, why he should make his way to Philadelphia and set up shop there — these have not been resolved. Was it merely chance, or does it relate to some experience from his earlier life?

We shall understand better *why* amnesia subjects behave in this way when in #6 we focus our attention more particularly on the question of what motivates ASCs.

Amnesia demonstrates once again how hard it is to draw a clear line between one kind of ASC and another. The career of Ansel Bourne has affinities with hysteria, with somnambulsim, with role-playing, with vision-seeing, with multiple personality; what is distinctive is the almost total replacement of the primary self by an almost fully developed secondary self, which has the ability to function capably to all appearances as a human personality in its own right.

However, I use the word 'almost' advisedly, for it is evident that Bourne carried over many skills from one life to another — his new self must have known what money was, how to get off a bus, and so on. It is a pity we do not know more about how Bourne behaved when playing the role of Mr Brown.

Some indication of how people behave in amnesia is given us by another case:

> Emile is a 33-year-old Paris lawyer, who in 1888 quarrels with his stepfather: this suffices to put him into a hysterical state which leads to amnesia. Three weeks later he recovers himself 150 km away. He is able to learn a few of the things he has done during his amnesia: these include visiting a village priest who thinks his behaviour is 'odd'; staying with his uncle, a bishop, where he behaves very badly; and committing a petty theft for which he is fined in his absence. (Myers, 1903, vol. 1, p.137, citing Dr Proust)

It seems likely that psychiatric investigation could have elicited some motivation behind this: why did the quarrel trigger off the event? Why did he visit the priest? What made him behave so badly at his uncle's house? Why did he commit theft? Is it significant that he, who is of all things a lawyer in normal life, should behave so badly in his secondary state?

Aside from these questions, though, the account confirms that someone in the amnesic state can perform quite capably: though the priest found him 'odd', his behaviour wasn't so very odd, or the priest would have called the police or a doctor; clearly his uncle had recognised him and accommodated him — unfortunately we do not have his side of the matter with regard to the misconduct. It all points to a switch involving a secondary personality, of a type we shall be looking at in a moment.

Spontaneous dissociation of the personality

The cases of Mary Wood and Ansel Bourne are just two among those we have looked at in which the individual not only loses some aspects of his personality, but seems to acquire others in exchange. Had they been investigated in the right way, they might well have revealed the kind of fragmentation which manifests in the specific form known as 'multiple personalitity disorder'.

Multiple personality can reasonably be regarded as the 'key' alternate state. It displays, in their most extreme form, the twin processes — the negative process of *depersonalisa-*

tion, the positive process of *role-playing* — which occur, though usually less dramatically, in most, perhaps all ASCs. Every ASC, almost by definition, reveals another facet of the personality: in multiple personality states this process is carried to its logical extreme, and the dissociated facets set up in business on their own, as more or less independent personalities.

They can never be wholly independent, of course. They have no choice but to inhabit the same body as the primary personality, look through the same eyes, and share its resources of intelligence, memory, etc. However, they make very different use of what they possess in common: secondary personalities will make both body and mind do things which the primary personality would never do, revealing latent powers and abilities. For instance:

> In 1888 a patient named Marceline, treated by Jules Janet, developed a series of hysterical troubles, including so marked a distaste for food that she would vomit at the sight of a spoonful of soup. Death from exhaustion and lack of nourishment seemed imminent. However, Janet put her under hypnosis and evoked a secondary personality who, in addition to many other personality differences, was able to eat and digest well.
>
> Janet found that as soon as he returned Marceline to her primary state, her troubles returned also; consequently he decided the only way to save her life was to switch her permanently to the secondary personality. This proved entirely beneficial: Marceline-2 was contented and nourished, and passed a nurse's examination which Marceline-1 had failed. (1911, p.369)

Typically, a multiple-personality case comprises a three-way dissociation, generally something like this:

* Self-1, timid and introvert, which left to itself would never achieve anything much.

* Self-2, reckless and extrovert, which left to itself might achieve all manner of things but only by taking unacceptable risks (for example, it is often found that Self-2 will smoke, drink and engage in risky sexual liaisons while Self-1 does none of these things).

* Self-3, prudent and wise, which keeps a kind of balance between the others.

Put like that, it may seem that Self-3 is the ideal, and that the doctor's efforts should be directed at eliminating Self-1 and Self-2 in favour of Self-3. But in practice this does not seem to be desirable. Self-3 tends to be serene but somewhat remote; the more 'involved' Self-1 and Self-2 provide necessary qualities for the practical purposes of daily life and for social interaction. The ideal, it seems, is a synthesis of all three.

This recurrent pattern emerges so frequently that it raises the question, whether *all* our personalities may not essentially be a trinity of complementary selves, each contributing essential ingredients to the mix? In the healthy state, the three are more or less evenly balanced; in the disorder state, something has upset the balance, the selves are in conflict, and treatment is called for.

Thinking along some such lines, some researchers have sought to match the three personalities with the concepts of psychoanalysis — ego, libido and so on. Neat though such a matching would be, however, it seems that the fragmentation process is too complex to be compartmentalised into the tidy categories of the theorist. For example, there is the perplexing unevenness in the way the personalities are aware of one another and share their memories. It seems generally to be the case that Self-1 is unaware of the others, that Self-2 is aware of Self-1 but not of Self-3, and that only Self-3 is aware of all. Thus in the famous 'Three Faces of Eve' case, Sizemore's primary personality, 'Eve White', doesn't suspect the existence of 'Eve Black', but 'Eve Black' knows that 'Eve White' exists; when the third personality, 'Jane' appears, she 'showed awareness of what both Eves did and thought, but had little or no direct access to their stores of knowledge and their memories prior to her emergence upon the scene' (Thigpen and Cleckley, 1957, p.145). So there is a complexity to the inter-personality relationships which defies any formal scheme.

In several multiple-personality cases, many more than three personalities emerge — 'Sybil' had 16, Billy Milligan produced 24. However, there are grounds for speculating whether these should all be regarded as personalities in their own right. No doubt each has its own characteristics, like the characters in a Tolstoi novel: but they do not have the 'archetypal' qualities of the leading characters of Sizemore's Three Faces.

My own suggestion is that we should look at them in the light of the 'role-playing' process discussed in #3.1, as variations on a theme, each adopted because it offers some nuance which seems appropriate to the specific occasion. In the Mary Wood case cited in #3.3, for instance, we find her playing at one time the part of 'Good Thing', at another that of 'Dreadful Wicked Thing'.

It is because multiple-personality cases so clearly reveal the complexity of our subconscious activity that they are, of all ASCs, the one most likely to help us reach an understanding of them. What we see openly enacted on the stage, as it were, of an MP case may be what is happening, behind the scenes, in other categories of ASC. Here is a revealing detail from the amazingly involved 'Sally Beauchamp' case which Morton Prince treated in the early years of the twentieth century:

> Prince found that Sally's malicious Self-2 would cruelly present fantasy images to the unfortunate Self-1, which she would mistake for reality, often with frightening results. One morning, for example, he receives a terrified phone call from Sally-1 who is convinced that her feet have been cut off at the ankles and are still inside her boots, bleeding stumps, on the far side of the room! He hurries round, sends Sally-1 to hypnotic sleep and calls up Sally-2, who cheerfully admits putting the idea into Sally-1's simple mind.

Here is another, less macabre example:

> Janet's patient Meb puzzles him; he can't understand why, in a sleepwalking state, she prepares little objects to surprise her waking self, which finds them and believes them to be 'apports' miraculously brought from Heaven by Saint Philomela. So he puts her under hypnosis and asks her to re-enact the placing of the apports. She obediently does so, and Janet sees that as she performs the actions, 'her face wears a serene smile, she utters good advice or phrases of the catechism: in a word, she has undergone a change of personality and has transformed herself into Saint Philomela. (Janet, 1911, p.505)

The implications of the process operating in these instances are all-important for our inquiry. If in multiple-personality cases one part of our mind can impose a suggestion on another part of our mind, we may reasonably suppose that the mind is equally capable of doing so in its unfragmented state. If so, we may suppose that the subconscious self can impose suggestions on the conscious self, particularly when it is in the suggestible state we have seen to be characteristic of ASCs. We may therefore conjecture that *any anomalous behaviour pattern, as manifested in hysteria, amnesia, somnambulism, etc., may be the result of a suggestion imposed by the subconscious mind.*

In the World Health Organisation index of mental disorders, 'multiple personality' is just one of a list of subdivisions under the overall heading of 'hysteria'. Though for labelling purposes this may be convenient, it hardly does justice to one of the most remarkable — and one of the most revealing — manifestations of human behaviour.

That a multiple-personality *state* frequently leads to a multiple-personality *disorder* is certainly a fact, just as a disabling hysteria may result from other states. But there is more to the multiple-personality state than that. Like so many other ASCs, it is basically a natural psycho-biological process whose initial raison d'être is positive and purposeful.

We shall have much more to say about the multiple-personality state as we proceed with our inquiry; for the moment, we would do well to see it, not as a unique and alarming ailment, but as no more and no less than the ASC carried to one of its logical extremes.

Possession

A young girl, a gifted spirit medium, goes into a violent nervous crisis when confronted with a blessed rosary while she is in trance. 'Clearly this is because demons have a horror for the rosary,' say those who believe she is possessed by the devil. Yes, perhaps, Janet replies, but we may be allowed to entertain an alternative explanation...(1889, p.404)

Possession cases bring us slap up against the internal/ external problem. Those who accept them at face value suppose that the victim's mind is 'invaded' by some external agency who takes it over and controls his behaviour. The 'invaders' are supposed to be either non-human entities, typically 'the devil'; or human, typically the spirit of a dead person, generally someone known to the individual.

Possession by a non-human spirit

The possibility that a human may be possessed by a malevolent spirit has been a popular belief throughout history. The Roman satirist Lucian tells us that both possession and exorcism were well established practices in the second century:

> Everyone knows the famous Syrian of Palestine who, when people fall down at the sight of the moon, rolling their eyes and foaming at the mouth, calls on them to stand up and sends them back home whole and free from their infirmity; for which he charges a large sum each time. When he is with a sick person he asks him how the devil entered into him; the patient remains silent, but the devil replies, in Greek or in a barbarian tongue, saying what he is, where he comes from, and how he entered the man's body. This is the moment to conjure him to come out; if he resists, the Syrian threatens him and finally drives him out. (cited in Oesterreich, 1930, p.6)

It is not difficult to see how the idea might come about. When a person starts behaving differently from usual, and is not able to exert that control over his own behaviour which we regard as normal, it is an easy jump to the idea that some other force is controlling him. Since this is unnatural, the subject or those around him assume it is being done with evil intent; consequently the invader must be an evil spirit. Since virtually every religious belief-system presumes the existence of such malevolent beings, there is no difficulty in naming the culprit.

That such ideas should seem reasonable to the primitive mind is understandable; that they should be taken up by the intelligent and subtle minds of theologians, leading ultimately to the witchcraft mania of the Middle Ages, is a revealing instance of the persistence of primitive thought-processes even in the most ostensibly sophisticated of us.

In his monumental *Discovery of the unconscious* (1970), Ellenberger writes as though belief in possession, like belief in witchcraft and the Devil himself, went out with the Enlightenment of the eighteenth and nineteenth centuries.

I wish it was so, but I am sorry to say I have a shelf of books which prove him over-optimistic. Belief in demonic possession is still alarmingly prevalent in our own day, particularly among fundamentalist Christians, who are as convinced that Satan is alive and well and taking up his lodging in the puzzled minds of Swiss or American teenagers as were their predecessors in sixteenth century Geneva or seventeenth century Salem.

Two levels of demonic possession must be distinguished: first, the individual has an outbreak, epileptic, hysteric or whatever, which is diagnosed as possession by priests, witch-doctors, etc., who cannot explain it any other way; second, the individual himself makes the identification, and genuinely believes this is what is happening to him.

In both cases, of course, the belief-system in which the individual has been brought up provides the scenario; but whereas in the first category we see little more than an automatic following of a patterned behaviour, as I think probably occurs in the *ikóta* of the Samoyeds [#3.3], in the second we see a specific act of role-playing: the subject is externalising his personal situation in terms of an entity who represents a malevolent power on to whom he can shift responsibility for his actions.

Belgian writer Jacques Bourgaux, himself an actor, shows how role-playing is used both by the victim of hysterical attack and by the exorcist who is seeking to 'cure' him:

> The exorcist's first task is to transform the convulsions into possession. By getting the devil to reveal his name, he in effect persuades the subject to abandon his threatening anonymity and enter into a scenario which has the blessing of tradition. Once a label has been found, the victim is constrained to conform to it — which he is not always ready to do: the exorcist often has a hard time forcing the victim into playing the specific role. (1973, p.17)

French occultist Eliphas Lévi observed: 'He who affirms the devil, creates the devil'; and that is just what the exorcist does. He not only imposes his authority on his suggestible patient, but imposes a role on him taken from his own belief-system, which may or may not be shared by the patient. In such cases it is the exorcist, not the patient, who brings the possessing demon into existence. Exorcism is nothing less than mind-control.

Possession by a human spirit

Will such an explanation enable us to explain the subtler form of possession in which the individual shows signs of being invaded by a *human* personality, usually that of someone now dead?

There is an obvious parallel between such cases and spirit trance, which we shall look at in #3.5: the difference is that in spirit trance the medium voluntarily chooses to allow his or her mind to be taken over temporarily by a deceased communicator, whereas in possession cases the individual *seemingly* has no choice in the matter.

While the majority of doctors who treat multiple-personality cases reckon that role-playing is involved, some feel that not all secondary personalities can be explained in this way. Ralph Allison, an American psychiatrist, believes:

> An alter personality serves a definite and practical purpose — it is a means of coping with an emotion or situation that the patient cannot handle. It might express anger, pain, sexuality, joy, love, or fear, but there is always a logical reason for the alter personality's 'existence'...Thus, the discovery of an entity who doesn't serve any recognisable purpose presents a diagnostic problem. Interestingly enough, such entities often refer to themselves as spirits. Over the years I've encountered too many such cases to dismiss the possibility of spirit possession completely. (1980, pp.184 ff.)

One instance was 24-year-old Elise, who

> 'had 16 alter personalities and a hierarchy of five Inner Self Helpers [Allison's term for personalities who represent the conscience or superego]. Each served a specific purpose in her life and each was created to handle a trauma that Elise herself couldn't face. Eventually, I was to discover more than double this number, since Elise coped with all the problems in her life by creating alter personalities...She would often create a personality simply to handle a relatively minor decision or problem.'

Allison discovered that one of Elise's personalities was a somewhat unscrupulous young man, Dennis, who had invaded her because he was sexually attracted to Shannon, another of her personalities. When Elise, as Shannon, made love with a man, Dennis would share the experience by possessing her lover, which Shannon understandably resented.

Baffled, Allison consulted Elise's Inner Self Helpers, who insisted that Dennis was *not* an alter personality like themselves, but an invading spirit, who unlike them was able to come and go in and out of Elise at will. Dennis himself claimed to be the spirit of a Louisiana stockbroker who had been murdered in the 1940s.

His invasion of Elise was facilitated by her participation in 'black magic' practices with teenage companions; 'he had entered her mind while she was trying to open herself to Satanic possession.' Working from this knowledge, Allison was able to work on his patient and eventually bring about 'Dennis's' expulsion.

We can understand how Allison might be baffled by this bizarre case; however, there are other cases which justify us considering alternatives to the invading-spirit hypothesis. For example, that most hard-headed of psychical researchers, Frank Podmore, quotes this revealing case from his personal experience:

Ann Brown, a young woman of about thirty, experienced a sudden and demonstrative attachment for a man, Charles Dunn, living in the same neighbourhood. The affair attracted unpleasant notoriety, and the young man, who had apparently acted a rather passive part throughout, abruptly discontinued the acquaintance. Ann continued, however, to cherish the belief that the man had been influenced by the malice of her enemies, and that he was still profoundly attached to her.

A few weeks after the breach she felt one evening a curious feeling in the throat, as of choking — the prelude probably, under ordinary circumstances, to an attack of hysteria. This feeling was succeeded by involuntary movement of the hands and a fit of long-continued and apparently causeless sobbing. Then, in presence of a member of her family, she became, in her own belief, possessed by the spirit of Charles, personating his words and gestures and speaking in his character. After this date she continually held conversation, as she believed, with Charles's spirit; 'he' sometimes speaking aloud through her mouth, sometimes conversing with her in the inner voice. Occasionally 'he' wrote messages through her hand, and I have the testimony of a member of her family that the writing so produced resembled that of Charles. Occasionally also Ann had visions, in which she claimed to see Charles and what he was doing at the moment. At other times she professed to hear him speaking or to understand by some inner sympathy his feelings and thoughts. (Podmore, 1910, p.279)

While we can't rule out the possibility that Charles had projected his spirit into Ann, most of us will find it easier to suppose that it was all a fantasy devised by Ann's subconscious self. And if that is true in Ann's case, we should consider whether it may also be so in Elise's. Is it not possible that Elise's subconscious self is presenting a particularly elaborate instance of role-playing, staging a private fantasy in the way which has become customary to her, that is, by creating a set of personalities to embody her conflicting impulses?

If so, we must ask why has her subconscious self chosen this way of doing things? Only detailed analysis would tell us, but one possibility is that she is using the Dennis/Shannon affair as a way of externalising some hang-up of her own about sexual relations. The intention may have been, by shifting the problem outside herself, to evade personal responsibility for a situation she did not feel able to cope with. The information that she had previously played around with the occult is very revealing, telling us that this is part of her cultural background: whether or not she subscribes fully to occult beliefs, she would find in them an appropriate format for her fantasy.

We can see the same sort of process occuring in many other ASCs which involve dissociation; for example, in the classic case of 'The Watseka Wonder', as it was named in a contemporary pamphlet (Stevens, 1887):

In 1877 a 14-year-old girl of Watseka, Illinois, Lurancy Vennum, becomes strangely ill, with what seems to be a combination of physical symptoms similar to those displayed by hysterics, visionary trances and ecstatic visits to Heaven. It is generally supposed by family and friends that she is insane and should go to an asylum.

This is opposed by others, including a family acquaintance, Asa Roff, who introduces Dr Stevens, who like Mr Roff is inclined to take a spiritist/occult view of the girl's ailment.

Stevens finds Lurancy 'near the stove, in a common chair, her elbows on her knees, her hands under her chin, feet curled up on the chair, eyes staring, looking every way like an "old hag". She savagely warns Dr Stevens not to come nearer. She appears sullen and crabbed, calling her father "Old Black Dick" and her mother "Old Granny".'

Eventually she seems to acknowledge that Stevens is well-disposed, and reveals to him a succession of beings that she claims to 'really' be — a 63-year-old lady named Katrina from Germany, a young man named Willie Canning, and so on.

. Stevens suggests to her that she find a better spirit than these to control her. She says there are several spirits around who are willing; one of those she names is Mary Roff, the daughter of Asa Roff who is present at the time—Mary died 13 years previously, at the age of 19, of an ailment very like Lurancy's, but which deteriorated until she was a 'raving maniac', dying in an asylum in a fit.

Asa Roff approves Lurancy's suggestion, and shortly after Lurancy becomes 'mild, docile, polite and timid'. But she no longer recognises her own parents; instead, she pleads to 'go home'. The Roffs agree to take Lurancy as though she is Mary; asked how long she will stay, she says, 'The angels will let me stay till some time in May.'

'Mary' remains in possession of Lurancy's body for the predicted three months: 'She has been nothing but Mary since she has been here, and knows nothing but what Mary knew.' Mr Roff reports. She recognises Mary's friends and relatives, and every object in the Roff home.

To make matters more complicated still, she displays many paranormal powers including clairvoyance and precognition, and has frequent trances in which she will visit Heaven. On several occasions she refuses meals at the Roff's, saying, 'O, nothing, I thank you, ma. I'll go to heaven for my tea.'

On 19 May Mary leaves control, and Lurancy repossesses her own body. However, it seems that 'Mary' continues to watch over her; after Lurancy marries, 'Mary' puts her into a trance when her first child is born and 'the work of deliverance went on painlessly'.

Richard Hodgson, who looked into the case on behalf of the American SPR, inclined to a face-value interpretation — that Mary's spirit was indeed involved; however, he recognised an alternative, in terms of 'secondary personality with supernormal powers'. The same choice is open to us today; the evidence that Mary's spirit was indeed engaged is very compelling, but we have to recognise that, as with demon possession, we have the alternative of supposing that what was happening was an extreme instance of role-playing.

Several factors favour this alternative view. Lurancy's behaviour, for example, seems very similar to that of Mary Wood [#3.3], whose disorder was manifestly of pathogenic origin. It is significant that Roff was an ardent spiritualist — one of Lurancy's relatives said when it was proposed to send her to the Roff home, 'I would sooner follow a girl of mine to the grave than have her go to Roff's and be made a Spiritualist' — and it is evident that suggestion could have played a major part, filling Lurancy/Mary's head with thoughts of heavenly visits and more besides — the original account is full of echoes of spiritualist belief.

How was Lurancy so familiar with Mary's life and circumstances? The two girls lived in the same small town, their families were at least distantly acquainted, Mary's insanity had been much talked about in the town, and Lurancy didn't go to the Roff home until after Asa Roff had been a constant visitor to her home for several weeks; he must often have spoken about his family affairs during that time. All this, even without bringing in psychic powers, which we should be prepared to consider in addition.

Impressive as the evidence for spirit-possession is, then, it seems we do have a viable alternative: role-playing of a particularly dramatic kind. My private suspicion is that behind the whole business was some kind of identity crisis simmering within the adolescent Lurancy, perhaps exacerbated by a domestic situation which, reading between the lines of the published account (which naturally had to tread discreetly in the matter), does suggest a less than totally harmonious family background. Why she should choose this particular way of resolving her problem is something we shall consider in #6.

Visionary encounters

Whether or not Bernadette Soubirous met the Virgin Mary at Lourdes in 1858, believers and skeptics agree that she was in an ASC of some kind. Whether or not the 'miracle of the candle' was indeed miraculous, it is characteristic of the anaesthesia which occurs in one after another of our ASCs:

> On 7 April 1858, Bernadette has her 17th meeting with Mary at
> the Grotto, in the presence of the usual large crowd. She car-
> ries a large candle; during the vision, the candle droops
> towards the ground in such a way that its flame burns up bet-
> ween her fingers and licks the palm of her hand. Those nearby
> cry out (in local patois) 'Moun Diou! qu'es brulla!' (My God,
> she's burning herself!) — but Dr Dozous, standing nearby,
> says 'Leave it be' so that the flame plays on her hand for
> several minutes. Finally her ecstasy ends, and the candle falls.
> Dozous seizes her hand, wipes it with his sleeve, examines it,
> and shouts 'Nou ya pas arré!' ('There's nothing there!'); the
> words are carried to the back of the crowd whose enthusiasm
> is on the verge of delirium. Dozous then re-lights the candle
> and hold the flame against Bernadette's hand, who quickly
> snatches it away saying 'You're burning me!' (Trochu, 1953,
> p.249)

Since a similar anaesthesia is displayed by suspected witches, by hysterics and by persons in many other ASCs, it
seems reasonable to suppose that Bernadette's anaesthesia
was not so much a miracle as a characteristic ASC symptom. Trochu, from whose authoritative biography I take
this account, uses the word 'extase' to describe Bernadette's state, and so does Laurentin, whose massive
documentation includes 56 pages of testimony solely on the
subject of Bernadette's ecstasy — making it quantitatively,
at least, the most fully documented ASC in this book.

While in general the testimony is consistent, Laurentin
recognises some contradictions — for example, the degree
to which she is aware of those around her while she is having her visionary experiences. She herself says she was not,
but on one occasion at least, when the candle she held went
out, she held it out for someone to re-light. Laurentin accounts for this — I think reasonably — by suggesting she
was sometimes more and sometimes less aware of her surroundings at different phases of her ecstasy. Alternatively it
could have been robot behaviour of a kind we shall look at
in #5.

However, both Trochu and Laurentin are unhappy, to
put it mildly, with the report made by the Lourdes doctors
(*catholic* doctors, note) at the request of the Préfet Massy,

who had hoped that the public excitement caused by the early visions would die down, and asked for a medical examination of Bernadette with a view to establishing her mental state. On 31 March 1858, at which time Bernadette had had 16 of her 18 encounters, the doctors reported as follows:

Is this child suffering from mental illness? Does she merit treatment? These are, we suppose, the questions we have been asked to resolve.

The young Bernadette is of a delicate constitution, with a lymphatic and nervous temperament; she is 13 years old [actually, she was just 14], though seeming no more than 11; her appearance is agreeable, her eyes are lively...She says her health is very good, she has never suffered from headaches or nervous crises, she has a healthy appetite and sleeps well. However, young Bernadette isn't as healthy as she thinks she is; she has severe asthma, and she has breathing troubles.

[Then follows the story of the encounters as told by Bernadette herself.]

Such are the facts which seem to merit our attention, and which have been hailed as miraculous. Well, has little Bernadette imposed on the credulity of the public, or is an impairment of the intelligence sufficient to explain the incidents she narrates?

To resolve this question, it would have been helpful to know her family background, her daily existence, in short all the influences which might have acted on her. However our examination of the young girl seems to us sufficient to reach a satisfactory solution.

There is nothing to suggest that Bernadette has tried to impose on the public: the child is impressionable by nature, she could have been the victim of a hallucination; no doubt her attention was caught by a reflection of light in the Grotto; her imagination, under the influence of a mental predispostion, gives it a form which always impresses children, that of those statues of the Virgin that one sees on altars. She tells her vision to her friends: they drag her back to the Grotto, the story gets round the town; a crowd gathers, larger every day; it is hailed as a marvel, as an Apparition of the Virgin; isn't it to be expected that the girl's state of mind would be affected and her exaltation be carried to a greater height? What was at first a simple hallucination takes greater hold on her, absorbs her more and more, isolates her from the external world at the time of the encounter, so that she goes into a true ecstatic state, an impairment of the intelligence in which the subject is dominated by the idea which preoccupies her.

The conclusion of the undersigned, then, is that Bernadette Soubirous has displayed an ecstatic state which has recurred several times; that it is a mental affect, whose effects account for the visionary phenomena. Is there any need for treatment? We do not think so. The malady we attribute to Bernadette doesn't, as things are at present, involve any risk to her health. On the contrary, when Bernadette is no longer pressured by the crowd, when people stop asking her for her prayers, when she has resumed her normal life, we expect that she will cease to dream about the Grotto and the marvellous things she recounts. (Laurentin and Billet, 1958, vol, 1, p.297)

Needless to say, Trochu and Laurentin, firmly believing that Bernadette truly met the Virgin, are scornful of this report, and it is true that in the light of further developments it is inadequate. But considering the many ambiguous features of the matter, including Bernadette's own doubts that 'Aquéro' [= 'that one'] was actually the Virgin, it seems to me the doctors did a fair and balanced job of evaluating her experience.

Against their estimate must be set that of Dr Dozous, already cited, who was converted from skepticism to belief by first-hand observations such as that quoted. He is at pains to distinguish her ecstasy from 'l'extase maladive':

This state, altogether different from a morbid ecstasy, deprived her neither of the use of her senses nor of voluntary movement; it didn't leave her exhausted, nor with bruised limbs, nor accelerated heartbeat or any nervous disorder. She remembered every detail of the event and reported it perfectly. (Laurentin, 1962, p.89)

More recently, a group of Yugoslav teenagers have claimed experiences very similar to Bernadette's: but whereas the eighteen Lourdes visions were spread over five months, after which they ceased, those at Medjugorje have occurred almost daily since the first on 24 June 1981, and are still continuing in 1988, making the visionaries by far the most favoured mortals in history, quantitatively speaking.

The visions are hard to evaluate because of the immense controversy they have generated. A commission of theologians and psychiatrists, set up by the local bishop, delivered their conclusions on 2 May 1986 after three years of examining the evidence: two of the fifteen commissioners accepted the visions as real, two abstained, and eleven rejected them. However, the visionaries themselves continue to assert the reality of their experiences (though two have ceased to see them), their champions continue to give them fervent support, and the pilgrims continue to flock to Medjugorje.

Sensitive to skeptical opinion, those who champion the visions have conducted a fair number of scientific tests, and Joyeux and Laurentin conclude that:

> these young persons are normal, healthy in body and mind. Meticulous studies in and outside the clinic enable us to affirm scientifically that their ecstasy is neither epilepsy, nor sleep, nor dream, as is demonstrated by the electro-encephalograph. Nor is it hallucination in the pathological sense of the term: nor hysteria, neurosis or pathological ecstasy, for the visionaries display none of the symptoms of these ailments. Nor is it catalepsy, for during ecstasy the muscles function normally. (Joyeux and Laurentin, 1985, pp.96–7)

An even more dramatic test was conducted by Father Lipinski of Boston, who sought to measure the intensity of 'spiritual energy' during the ecstasies: his instruments recorded that the intensity in the chapel of the apparitions on 15 March 1985 was 100,000 millirads, compared with 20 to 70 millirads at an ice hockey match. However, it is not clear what this proves.

The visionaries are, understandably, reluctant to be tested — some have refused altogether. In evaluating these findings, we must bear in mind that they were conducted by persons sympathetic to the visionaries and anxious not to betray their confidence. The nearest thing to objective scientific testing occurred, first, on 2 June 1984 when the Abbé Bulat stuck a pin in the shoulder of Vicka, one of the visionaries, while she was supposed to be in ecstasy: she reacted, showing that she was not — as was claimed by Laurentin and Joyeux — totally detached from external reality. Then, on 14 January 1985, Jean-Louis Martin, a French visitor, suddenly darted his fingers towards Vicka's eyes; her flinching was recorded on video by Canadian researcher Louis Bélanger. Disconcerted, Vicka explained that her flinching was not from Martin's fingers but because just at that moment she had seen the infant Jesus who seemed to be slipping from Mary's grasp and her movement was an instinctive one to save it from falling.

Despite the coincidence that this should occur at precisely the instant of Martin's experiment, we cannot prove it was not so: or possibly this explanation was a rationalisation improvised by Vicka's subconscious mind, just as it does in dreams to account for external sounds. Or, of course, she may have been lying.

There are many grounds for questioning the authenticity of the Medjugorje phenomena, but even if they are not authentic they confront us with the very remarkable phenomenon of pseudo-ecstasies being maintained by a group of people over many years. Theologically, there is all the difference in the world between a true and a false vision of the Virgin; from our psychological viewpoint, on the other hand, the difference may be more apparent than real. Visionaries or pseudo-visionaries, the Medjugorje teenagers are undoubtedly in an ASC of some kind, even if it is not the profound spiritual ecstasy their supporters would like us to believe.

The Belgian stigmatic Louise Lateau (1868) would, every week from Thursday to Saturday morning, enter a state during which she would eat and drink nothing — if she was forced to take anything, she would vomit it; she had no bowel movements; she could not see or hear; she had total anaesthesia, whether to tickling or to ammonia held under her nose, to pinpricks or to electric shock.

During this period of ecstasy she had visions which began with finding herself in a great light; then figures would appear, and perform the scenes of Jesus' passion, in chronological order and great detail:

> She saw the naked cross, then Our Lord carrying his cross; she saw him stripped, describing each article of clothing, she saw him attached to the cross, described his wounds, the crown of thorns; she saw his body placed in the tomb. Then she saw the Holy Virgin in a great light. (Bourneville, 1879, p.23)

Can we say that *all* visionary encounters occur during an ASC? Teresa de Avila had her visions in the course of meditation; Catherine Labouré was awakened from sleep by a little child who led her to the chapel where she met the Virgin Mary. Saint Paul says of his own experiences, 'whether in the body, I cannot tell; or whether out of the body, I cannot tell; God knoweth.'

Here, by contrast, is a vision which occurred not to pious teenagers but to an American railroad engineer, though it shares a religious character — as do most visions. It should be noted that Mr Skilton's experience, which occurred in 1890, is only one of several anomalous incidents that he reported to the SPR:

I was engaged with two other men one day about 2 p.m. in taking out some evergreen trees from a boxcar; they were large and heavy. There had been a great deal of other freight put in the car after mine, so it was necessary to take out some of it before I could get at mine. I opened the car door, and a barrel of eggs fell out on the ground, and just at that instant I saw a medium-sized person standing at my right hand clothed in white with a bright countenance, beaming with intelligence. I knew what he wanted in an instant, although he put his hand on my shoulders and said, 'Come with me.' We moved upward with the speed of lightning, as it were; I could see the hills, trees, buildings and roads as we went up side by side till they vanished out of our sight. As we passed on, this glorious being told me he was going to show me that bright heavenly world. We soon came to a world of light and beauty, many thousands times larger than this earth, with at least four times as much light. The beauties of this place were beyond any human being to describe. I was seated by the tree of life on a square bunch of what appeared to be a green velvet moss; there I saw many thousand spirits clothed in white, singing the heavenly songs...I wanted to see my dear mother, two sisters, and a child of mine that had died some time before. The request was granted at once; they seemed very much pleased to see me, but I was not allowed to converse with them...

My attendant told me we must go back; I wished to stay, but he told me my time had not come yet, but would in due time, and that I should wait with patience. At this we started back...I saw everything as it looked from a great height, till we came to the car that I had opened the door of, and I found myself there in body, and he vanished. I spoke then (just as I

opened my watch and found it had been just 26 minutes that I
had been engaged with that mysterious one), and said I
thought I had left this world for good. One of the men said,
'There is something the matter with you ever since you opened the car door; we have not be able to get a word out of you,'
and that I had done all the work of taking out everything and
putting it back into the car, and one item was eight barrels of
flour I had taken off the ground alone and put them back in the
car, a metre high, with the ease of a giant. I told them where I
had been and what I had seen, but they had seen no one.

This I count the brightest day of my life, and what I saw is
worth a lifetime of hardship and toil. (*PSPR* 11.5.60)

3.5   Voluntary ASCs

Some ASCs are considered to be valuable in themselves,
providing therapy, relaxation and so on. Others are
thought to confer benefits, such as enabling contact with
spirits of the dead. Either of these may be sought voluntarily, and often there are established procedures to help the individual do so most effectively.

Usually these involve long and dedicated self-disciplines,
but some individuals seem to be able to dispense with that.
A certain Captain Townsend

> possessed the remarkable faculty of throwing himself into a
> trance at pleasure. The heart ceased, apparently, to throb at
> his bidding, respiration seemed at an end, his whole frame
> assumed the icy chill and rigidity of death; while his face
> became colorless and shrunk, and his eye fixed, glazed, and
> ghastly: even his mind ceased to manifest itself; for during the
> trance it was as utterly devoid of consciousness as his body of
> animation. In this state he would remain for hours, when
> these singular phenomena wore away, and he returned to his
> usual condition. (Macnish, 1834, p.204)

Had Captain Townsend lived in another era, I dare say he
would have been pressured into putting his gift to work, as
a spirit medium, healer or whatever. Living when he did,
he seems to have regarded it simply as an anomalous talent.

Many people report a practice of entering a state like Dr
Halliday's 'active introversion' in which he was instructed
by a Jungian analyst:

> Active introversion is the procedure of relaxing on a chair or

couch, closing the eyes and watching the inner imagery which develops. Some people are quicker at achieving this than others. I never succeeded in achieving it in bright sunlight or when I was tired or depressed. The best condition seemed to be one of relaxation, ease and slight elation or expectancy. [After a series of visual impressions] a great variety of shapes, forms and figures are encountered. At first these can usually be related to childhood experiences, but later as one becomes more proficient the scenery includes archaic buildings, temples, strange animals, ancient priests, medicine men, etc. Throughout, constant changes occur and a story may unfold in which one may be either observer or participant. Yet one must be passive and not actively force or alter what emerges. Things must be allowed to happen on their own. (PF, 1961)

This sounds very like the 'waking dream' we looked at in #3.2; the difference being that in this case the experience is specifically sought. Whether that makes any difference to the content of the experience is an unresolved question; Halliday's references to 'archaic buildings' and 'medicine men' suggest cultural influences are at work, but whether they are meaningful to the individual is another matter.

The other difference is the 'foreplay', which is reminiscent of some descriptions of hypnagogic experiences; this combination of technique and content seems to justify regarding 'active introversion' as a specific process.

Intoxication

By far the most common of voluntary ASCs is the taking of alcoholic drinks or other inebriating substances, for the 'high' they provide. Though it is most commonly used as either a private means of escape from reality or a lubricant easing social intercourse, in many cultures it provides the basis for religious practices.

Because the effect of alcohol on the body is almost wholly negative, reducing ability and effective functioning, the ASCs it induces are almost entirely of a releasing sort, removing inhibitions and bestowing an illusion of euphoria. Some momentary insights may be gained, but it is rare for any real benefits to be obtained except the short-term release from reality in itself, which could be beneficial, for instance, after a sudden shock or a bereavement.

That intoxication is a true ASC is indicated by the fact that it displays many features found in other ASCs — anaesthesia, suggestibility and so on. The amnesia-and-recall which occurs in the following case are just what we find in hypnosis and other ASCs:

> An Irish porter to a warehouse, in one of his drunken fits, left a parcel at the wrong house, and when sober could not recollect what he had done with it; but the next time he got drunk, he recollected where he had left it, and went and recovered it. (Macnish, 1834, p.78)

Psychedelic states

In 1953, a number of American soldiers were given LSD unawares by their medical officers to find out the effects. Today, after thirty years of drug research, we can be aghast at such irresponsibility; we can only guess what the effect must have been on the subjects, who would have no idea what was happening to them and must have thought they were going out of their minds — which, in a very real sense, they were.

Even now, when the effects of drugs are more widely known, there must be many people who are taken by surprise by the experiences they induce, with an ever-present risk of psychological if not physiological damage if the experience is not properly controlled.

Nevertheless, many find the risks worth taking; and provided proper caution is observed, the risks are not so very great. The danger is that whereas alcohol-drinking has relatively marginal effects on perception, so that the individual is liable to pass out or at any rate become incapable of any but the most automatic of actions before his sense of reality is seriously impaired, psychedelic drugs enable a person to be aware of what is happening, and often be fairly active, at the same time as his perception of reality is distorted.

This can be very exciting; and if sometimes it is alarming, it can also be a supremely life-enhancing experience, conferring a deeper insight into cosmic processes, broader perceptions and so on. In 1961, in the euphoric early days, Canadian psychologist Duncan Blewett declared, 'The discovery of the psychedelic drugs marks the greatest advance yet made in the field of psychology,' and though he recognised that in the present state of our ignorance 'some subjects take the drug and become ill, some become psychotic, while others have transcendental reactions', he assumed that in the course of time we would learn to eliminate the unfortunate effects and obtain the full benefit of their positive effects (PF, 1961).

Clearly there is a substantial element of subjectivity involved in a person's experience under drugs. In Blewett's view, this is a matter of approach: those who attempt to resist the effects of the drug are liable to make themselves ill, those who seek to rationalise the essentially irrational experience are liable to become paranoid; only those who attempt neither escape nor explanation will obtain the transcendental benefits that psychedelic drugs have to offer.

Much of the argument about psychedelics is directed at just how transcendental the resulting states are, compared with the mystical states we will be looking at in a moment. Many commentators, particularly those who are committed to religious beliefs, are reluctant to see the states as comparable; champions of drug culture refuse to recognise any difference. Personally, I take the view, again, that it is a question of the individual; if a saintly person takes LSD, he may well have an experience as valuable as the mystical experiences he obtains via meditation, whereas a person who takes the drug out of scientific curiosity or simply for kicks would be less likely to have his spiritual horizons raised.

One who has no doubts on the matter is Timothy Leary:

> Three years ago, on a sunny afternoon in the garden of a Cuernavaca villa, I ate seven of the so-called 'sacred mushrooms' which had been given to me by a scientist from the University of Mexico. During the next five hours, I was whirled through an experience which was without question the deepest religious experience of my life... I have repeated this biochemical and (to me) sacramental ritual over fifty times, and, almost every time, I have been awed by religious revelations as shattering as the first experience. (Leary, 1973, p.36)

Encouraged by his own experience, Leary championed further understanding of hallucinogenic drugs as spiritual aids, and believes that the psychedelic experience has been proved experimentally to be similar to the mystical experience reported by religious figures. A notable 1962 experiment conducted by Walter N. Pahnke of Harvard involved a group of 20 divinity students who attended a three-hour Good Friday devotional service. Some had taken a dose of psilocybin (the chemical synthesis of the active ingredient of the 'sacred mushroom' of Leary's experience), others a placebo; neither the subjects nor the experimenters knew who had taken which. Pahnke concluded:

'Those subjects who received psilocybin experienced phenomena that were apparently indistinguishable from, if not identical with, certain categories defined by the typology of mystical consciousness' (in Tart, 1969, pp.413 ff.).

ASCs may occur not only when drugs are taken, but also in the course of withdrawal, especially if this is abrupt — recalling the French proverb, 'Visitors always give pleasure, if not when they arrive, then when they leave.' This reminds us that the experience is, at bottom, a modification of the chemical balance of the body, which is no less upset when substances are subtracted than when they are added.

Meditation and spiritual disciplines
In principle, the church disclaims any intention of directly encouraging its members — even the most saintly — to have mystical and spiritual experiences: they are seen as a gift of God, and come unsought to those whom God wishes to reward.

However, there are many practices which, whether or not they are performed with the specific intention of bringing about such experiences, do have that effect. Many aspects of the spiritual life, especially in past times, are potentially conducive to ASCs: the isolation, the absence of stimulus, defective diet exacerbated by fasting, sexual abstinence, sleep interrupted by prayer sessions which are in themselves repetitive — these in themselves would put someone halfway to having an ASC. Deliberately performed spiritual exercises would complete the process.

Such factors have been combined in many cultures into systems for spiritual development: yoga and zen are two among thousands of systems, and each of these exists in almost as many varieties as it has exponents. Many of those who take part in such practices contribute towards the probability of obtaining ASCs by a life-style which includes an abstemious diet, minimal stimuli and so forth.

Just how greatly they vary is shown by the fact that though all aim in their various ways at enhancing consciousness and spiritual awareness, some will do so by seeking to achieve maximum control over the body, including heartbeat, oxygen consumption, etc., while others will advocate withdrawal from such concerns, encouraging indifference to the body and all material things. The fact that such widely divergent means can lead to comparable ends is an indication that, ultimately, it is the subjective workings of the mind, not the objective means employed, which shape the experience.

Almost the only thing on which their proponents are agreed is that there are no short cuts — a lifetime is not enough to master the techniques; hence, of course, their distrust of the 'instant ecstasy' methods favored by Leary, Blewett and others. The most respected of Christian mystics, Teresa de Avila, set out elaborate manuals charting the different levels to be attained, and other systems have their own ways of laying out the process. Here, for instance, is a glimpse of the alternatives on offer:

> One way of classifying meditation techniques is the threefold division into what has been called in the East the Inner Way, the Middle Way, and the Outer Way. In the Inner Way, one concentrates on the spontaneously arising contents of one's own mind, upon the images and feelings that arise. In the Middle Way one strives for stillness of the mind; one withdraws from both internal and external perceptions. It has been called the Way of Emptiness. In the Outer Way one concentrates on and meditates on an externally given perception; one relinquishes spontaneity and disciplines the mind to stay with this perception until it blends with oneself. One contemplates one thing, following the statement of William Blake: 'If the gates of perception were cleansed, all things would appear as they are, infinite.' (LeShan, 1974, p.116)

Do all these ways lead to the same destination? It is hard to know, because each practitioner uses his own terminology to describe what is done and what is achieved. Language is inadequate to express either the subjective feelings of being in the state or the otherworldly rewards the disciple hopes to attain.

For the same reason, it is impossible to say whether the practice of these disciplines, or the results achieved, are giving each practitioner the same kind of satisfaction. What is certain is that all of them seem, in their own various ways, to give satisfaction to some. This does rather suggest that *neither* the end prescribed *nor* the means adopted matter all that much: rather, what matters is that one should make the effort, submit to the discipline, formulate a goal. This in turn supports the view that all ASCs are no more than facets of an ultimate 'super-self' which transcends not only the everyday self of our USC but also the other selves which are revealed in our ASCs.

Shamanic trance

Throughout the world, in primitive societies from the Americas to the Pacific, from Africa to Siberia, a would-be shaman is initiated in rituals in which he seems to be dismembered, his bones broken, his eyes removed, etc., whereupon either his organs will be replaced, or magic substances will be implanted, so that thereafter he will not be as his fellow-men. Instead, thanks to his operation, he is now qualified to perform the role of intermediary between his people and their gods; this he will do by performing some kind of ritual practice, involving dance, intoxication or whatever, which will get him into a trance-like ASC of some sort, in which he will be able to make the magic journey to meet the deity.

Access to the shamanic state is by various methods, often in combination. Nearly always there is a sacred food or drink, which is often seen as the incarnation of the god himself, much as the Christian sacrament is seen as being the flesh of God. These substances, unlike the Christian one, are generally hallucinogenic, and of themselves, or in combination with ritual dance, switch the shaman into the requisite state.

Spiritual practices, wherever they are performed, consitute a harnessing of the ASC to pre-determined ends. In shamanism, as in so many other contexts, we see that the outcome of the practices will be shaped by personal expectation, which will itself be based on the cultural beliefs the shaman shares with the community.

Spirit trance

In spirit trance the individual, in effect, switches off his USC in order that the mind may be used as a 'channel' by otherworldly entities. Most often, this is done within a spiritist context: the entities are supposed to be spirits of the dead who communicate with living humans, and are sometimes able to perform physical feats with the aid of the medium's powers, and even temporarily extract a psychic substance from him or her with which they can create short-lived three-dimensional representations of things — usually themselves — called 'materialisations'.

That these things happen is firmly believed not only by spiritualists, for whom communication with spirits of the dead is an article of religious faith, but by many who, after experiencing the remarkable phenomena associated with the practice of spiritism, are convinced that the ostensible communication should be taken at face value. Of these, the most thoughtful and authoritative was surely F.W.H. Myers, co-founder of the Society for Psychical Research, who is quoted frequently in these pages. At the end of his life he wrote, regarding spirit trance:

> The claim is that the automatist [= the medium], in the first place, falls into a trance, during which his spirit partially 'quits his body': enters at any rate into a state in which the spiritual world is more or less open to its perception; and in which also it so far ceases to occupy the organism as to leave room for an invading spirit to use it in somewhat the same fashion as its owner is accustomed to use it. (Myers, 1903, vol.2, p.190)

Holding this belief, it is not surprising that Myers uses the word 'possession' to describe the phenomenon whereby a dead person is able to speak via the medium with the living. The fact that few other researchers have used this term in this connection is perhaps a sign of their continued doubt whether what *seems* to be happening is what is *really* happening.

There is no doubt that under these circumstances a very marked change of personality takes place, and that the personality who 'uses' the medium is often able to give a convincing performance as another person. If this is, as skeptics suggest, a subconscious simulation on the part of the medium, it is one which involves quite remarkable talents far beyond his everyday abilities.

What supports the skeptics' view is that, for every amazingly persuasive performance, there are a score of lamentably *un*persuasive ones, in which there is little to encourage belief and often much to discourage it. Such discrepancy is hard to account for if we hold the view that otherworldly forces are truly at work, but not so hard if we hold that dramatic impersonation is taking place. For we all know that some actors are better than others.

What *is* a spirit trance? No medium would accept what French author Jean Lignières (1928) has to say about it:

> It's no good playing with words: the fact is that most mediums are neuropaths or hysterics. For their mediumistic powers to reach their maximum intensity, they have to enter a sort of crisis which they politely term 'trance'. Every medium is in a state of permanent imbalance. (p.72)

None the less, Lignières gives us a salutary reminder that trance *is* an alternate state, and the person in the trance is, by definition, in a condition of disequilibrium. American researcher Karlis Osis writes:

> It is very difficult to judge in what 'state' of mind the successful mediums give results. Deep trance seems to be de-emphasised, and a somewhat modified state of consciousness or disassociation appears to prevail in most instances where the results are good. (PF, 1961)

He suggests that drugs might serve a useful purpose in enabling us 'to induce this dreamlike state of consciousness physiologically, by pharmacological means'.

In 1915 Mrs Sidgwick, a former President of the SPR, published a detailed study of American medium Leonora Piper, the 'one white crow' who convinced William James that not all mediumship can be explained away. She offers an explanation in terms of auto-hypnosis combined with subconscious role-playing:

> To sum up very briefly my own conclusion about Mrs Piper's trance, I think it is probably a state of self-induced hypnosis in which her hypnotic self personates different characters either consciously and deliberately, or unconsciously and believing herself to be the person she represents, and sometimes probably in a state of consciousness intermediate between the two. (*PSPR* 28: p.330)

It is important to remember that not every medium is committed to the spirit interpretation of what he does. One notable doubter was Eileen Garrett, whose perceptive self-examination has probably contributed more than any clinical analysis to our understanding of what psychic powers *are*. Her account of what happens to her when she goes into trance not only helps us to see how spirit trance may relate to other ASCs, but offers insight into the fundamental process of *every* ASC:

> When I go into a trance situation and withdraw, I breathe very deeply into the solar plexus. The last thing I am aware of is a terrific cloud of yellow light. Within my trance state there are two personalities, both of them, fortunately, constructive. I have no control over them. I invite them once I enter the state of auto-hypnosis. What they are I cannot tell you. I think that somewhere in my infancy I may have laid the groundwork for them, why I do not know.
>
> During that period of my life when I gave much time to analysis and being investigated, I worked with people of strong spiritualistic beliefs. They may have left these names in my subconscious, and subconsciously I may have liked their sounds, and clung to them. These personalities are still there. I have tried to dispose of them by various forms of hypnosis and analysis, but in vain. They remain their own length of time, permit themselves to be analysed by all and sundry, and bring forth valuable material that sometimes gives great comfort, and is also used therapeutically. (PF,1961)

It seems that this combination of depersonalisation and role-playing with the process of auto-hypnosis is similar to what Mrs Sidgwick supposes Mrs Piper to employ. We shall see that these two ladies, Eileen Garrett describing the experience from within, Mrs Sidgwick analysing it from without, bring us close to the essential nature of the ASC.

Hypnosis

The more we learn about hypnosis, the more difficult it becomes to define its limit and pinpoint its essence. To say, as did many early researchers, 'hypnosis is an artificial hysteria', is certainly an over-simplification; what does seem true is that, because hypnosis, like hysteria, can take an infinite variety of forms, it too is best thought of as a process rather than a single state.

For the same reason, it is often difficult to know what a particular researcher intends when he uses the term. Should the term be used at all for spontaneous states such as 'highway hypnosis' or the subjective process of 'auto-hypnosis'? Since it is possible (in my opinion, probable) that each of these involves a very different process from that of voluntary person-to-person hypnosis, such use is liable to cause confusion.

Over the 200 years during which it has been studied, the concept of hypnosis has evolved from a purely physical process, involving an electrical fluid transferred to the subject via 'animal magnetism', to a purely mental process in which the hypnotist performs no more crucial a role than that of an authority-figure who directs the subject into a state of enhanced suggestibility, and then guides him with suggestions.

A century ago elaborate instructions were given as to how the subject could be induced to enter the state; today it is little more than a verbal agreement between subject and hypnotist. Often subjects remain almost fully aware of what is happening around them; I remember a hypnotised subject interrupting a session in order to change over a cassette in a tape recorder, apparently without quitting the hypnotic state. Often, today's subjects find it hard to believe they have been under hypnosis at all — very different from the dramatic scenes demonstrated a century ago in the 'golden age' of hypnosis, when a Dr Dufay could report such a case as this:

> When medical attendant at the theatre at Blois, I had to attend a young actress, who was subject to frequent exhibitions of hysterical passion. I witnessed attacks seven or eight times during the two months the company remained at Blois, but

after my third visit it was sufficient to command Mlle Béatrice to sleep, or even to fix my eyes on hers, to produce a perfect calm.

Having noticed that intelligence is much more highly developed in the hypnotic state, I had sometimes hypnotised this very indifferent little actress by merely telling her, just as she was about to make her appearance on stage, that she was going to sleep, which always procured her a great success with the public. [Unfortunately, Dufay doesn't tell us what instructions he gave her, but presumably they were to the effect that she would not be inhibited by lack of confidence. It seems, however, that this was not a post-hypnotic suggestion, but that she actually played her part in the hypnotic state, which is interesting in view of our interest in the role-playing abilities of ASC subjects.]

One evening I arrived late at the theatre. The manager was waiting anxiously for me: his 'grande coquette' had missed the train, and he was relying on my assistance to substitute Mlle Béatrice without ruining the performance.

'Does she so much as know her part?'

'She has seen it played several times, but she has not rehearsed it.'

'Have you expressed any hope that I might come to her assistance?'

'I took care not to do that: any doubt as to her talents would have been sufficient to produce one of her attacks.'

'Very well, do not let her know I am here. I will take advantage of this opportunity to make a very interesting experiment.'

I did not show myself on the stage, but took my place in an unoccupied box. Then, drawing myself together, I willed intently that Mlle Béatrice might fall asleep.

At this same time, I later learned, the young artiste stopped suddenly in the middle of her toilette, and sank on to the sofa in her room, begging the dresser to let her rest a little. After a few minutes of drowsiness she got up, finished dressing herself, and went down to the stage.

When the curtain rose I was not very confident of success, not then knowing what had taken place in the dressing-room; but I was not long in satisfying myself, merely by seeing the action and attitude of my subject. She had retained in her memory this part which she had not learnt, but had only seen played, and acquitted herself marvellously.

I was obliged to awaken Mlle Béatrice so that she could take part in the supper which was given by the delighted manager.

It was only on seeing her companions surrounding her, congratulating her, that she understood what had taken place, and thanked me with a glance. (*PSPR* 6, p.409)

Four years after this report was published, George du Maurier wrote *Trilby*, the story of a singer who is able to perform well only when hypnotised by her manager. Was Dufay's experience the inspiration for the novel?

Trilby's hypnotist, the sinister Svengali, has become a synonym for control of hypnotic subjects by their hypnotists. Du Maurier's book, with its tragic finale, must have confirmed traditional fears about hypnosis — that once a subject has placed himself under a hypnotist's control, he will for ever be subject to that person's will. It does seem as if this is true of only a very few hyper-suggestible subjects; evidently, if we can believe Dufay's account, Mlle Béatrice was one such.

Doubts and fears continued to accompany the study of hypnosis: La Tourette's excellent 1887 study is largely concerned with the misuse of hypnosis for criminal purposes, especially rape. But the achievements of the nineteenth-century doctors were real enough. Esdaile carried out 261 operations on his hypnotised Indian patients without any of the side-effects of drug-assisted surgery. Janet won from his hypnotised patients not only insights into their condition but also suggestions as to appropriate treatment.

Not only is hypnosis complex in itself, but it raises the question, should we think of it, not as a single state, but as a succession of states? There is no doubt that there are different levels; and these can be as distinct as, say, the personalities in a multiple-personality ASC. This was demonstrated by Gurney of the SPR who, after carrying out repeated experiments using different hypnotists and different subjects, wrote:

After being brought into a light stage of trance — what we may call Stage A — the subject is told something, with a direction to remember it. He is then carried into a deeper stage of trance — state B — and is asked what it was he had just been told. He proves quite unable to recall it, and even that anything has been told him. He is now told something fresh, with a direction to remember it, after which he is recalled to state A; and now he cannot recall what he heard in State B but repeats what had been told him in the prior state A. (*PSPR* 4, p.515)

Gurney seems to have reached, as it were, two separate 'personalities'; in principle, today's sophisticated brain-probing techniques should be able to establish whether these separate 'selves' correlate with separate systems in the brain.

Today the tendency is to rate subjects along a fairly complex scale, of which the best known are probably the Stanford Hypnotic Susceptibility Scales developed at Stanford University from 1957 by Hilgard, Weitzenhoffer *et al*, which identify a series of physical responses as indicators of depth of trance. As for the characteristics of the state, these are identified as follows:

1. Reluctance to plan or initiate actions.

2. Narrower focus of attention.

3. Improved access to memory

4. Reduced reality-testing.

5. Increased suggestibility.

6. Tendency to role behaviour.

7. Subsequent amnesia for what happens in hypnotic state.

(adapted from Hilgard, 1965)

How does hypnosis fit into the pattern of ASCs? It seems best to see it as a process whereby, thanks to co-operation by the subject, the hypnotist can get the subject voluntarily to enter states which are equivalent to those he spontaneously enters in hysteria, somnambulism, etc. If we use the term 'hypnotic state' at all, we mean one of several levels of suggestibility which the subject has entered voluntarily, and which are not in themselves different from those states which occur to the subject spontaneously.

In this sense, there is truth both in the allegation of some modern researchers that there is no such thing as hypnosis, and in the assertion of their nineteenth-century predecessors that hypnosis is induced hysteria. But there are parallels with other ASCs too. Hilgard rightly sees the significance of the following case:

> A subject was regressed under hypnosis to a childhood visit to a department store, during which she had become separated from her family. The hypnotist, in the role of a sympathetic stranger, comforted her and assured her that her mother would come soon. She saw her mother come to meet her, and was happy again.

The reason for telling this little story, Hilgard writes, was her account of it after she was aroused from hypnosis:

> 'I felt so sorry for that little girl, because I knew all the time her mother was going to find her, but *she didn't* know it.'

As Hilgard observes, 'here we have almost a multiple-personality type of dissociation between the regressed ego (that of the child) and the observing ego (that of the watching adult), both belonging to the hypnotised subject' (1965, p.171).

Artificial dissociation of the personality

Perhaps the single most important advance in our understanding of ASCs was the discovery that, via hypnosis, dissociation of the personality could be artificially induced.

Janet observed that a patient, each time he was hypnotised, would revert to an alternative behaviour which was always the same, and which gradually became habitual for that state. This Self-2 acquired memories and experiences independent of Self-1, and eventually developed as rich an existence as the primary self.

The pattern is typified by 'Léonie', a hysteria patient whom Janet treated and studied over a period of years. The primary personality *Léonie* was sick and hysterical; under hypnosis, however, there emerged the extravert *Léontine*, cheerful to the point of tiresomeness; and eventually a third and more balanced personality, *Léonore*, revealed herself, more positive than Léonie, less obtrusive than Léontine, and who acted as a moderating influence.

This poor peasant is in her normal state a serious and somewhat melancholy woman, calm and slow, very gentle and extremely timid. No one would suspect the existence of the personage she contains within her. Hardly is she entranced than she is metamorphosed: her face is no longer the same; her eyes indeed remain closed, but the acuteness of her other senses compensates for the absence of sight. She becomes gay, noisy, and restless to an insupportable degree; she continues to be good-natured, but she has acquired a singular tendency to irony and bitter jests. (Janet, 1889, p.129)

Aside from the fact that this dissociation was brought out by Janet in the course of hospital treatment, there is no intrinsic difference between the artificial and the spontaneous forms. In practice, of course, there was a world of difference, simply because Janet was around to keep a watchful eye on Léonie and keep the secondary selves under control.

The completeness of the dissociation was just as marked as with the spontaneous cases: one day Léonie, out walking, meets a gentleman who has visited her in hospital when she was under hypnosis. He greets her politely, and is astonished that she fails to recognise him — but of course he has never met Léonie, only Léontine... Again, as with spontaneous cases, Léontine (Self-2) knows about Léonie (Self-1) but not the other way about.

Artificial multiple-personality cases raise, even more acutely, the question How 'real' are the personalities thus evoked? They also lend additional force to the claim frequently made, that the doctor himself is often responsible for creating the secondary personalities, by suggestion. However, I am not sure that this is a useful line to pursue, since it is evident that once a subject starts fragmenting his personality, he is apt to do so at will, whether at other people's suggestion or in response to some impulse of his own.

What is going on? This is precisely the question one of Janet's more intelligent patients, while in the hypnotic state, put to him:

'I'm not asleep, it's absurd to say so. It's just that I'm changed, there's something funny about me... what have you done to me?'

To which Janet replies:

> We now have a pretty good idea what we have done to them. We have taken advantage of their psychological instability to change the state of their senses, by paralysing — or more usually by exciting — one relative to the others. So a patient who is deaf in the waking state hears when he is under hypnosis. And sometimes things happen otherwise, and either gradually or abruptly, the subject refuses to recognise his identity, derides his former personality and claims to be someone quite new. (1889, p.130)

To what extent are the 'states' of hypnotic subjects, or Gurney's levels of suggestibility, equivalent to secondary personalities? Hypnotising someone often seems to *create* a new personality — but maybe it is simply *revealing* it?

What we *can* say, though, is that the personalities adopted during *role-playing* are distinct from secondary personalities. If Janet suggests to hypnotised Léonie that she is a princess, she cheerfully hallucinates being a princess for a while, enacting the part in an appropriate manner. Then she will revert to one or other of her secondary selves. If it is Léontine (Self-2), she will comment that she's just had a funny dream of being a princess; however, if it is Léonore (Self-3), who knows so much more than the others, she will say, 'Isn't she stupid, this poor Léonie? She believed she was a princess, when it was only you making her think so!' (1889, p.164)

Here, then, we have a clear distinction between role-playing on the one hand, and dissociation of the personality on the other.

In fact, the differences are more striking than that. Role-playing is never more than a performance — often done remarkably well, but also sometimes not done very well at all. Janet found his patient Lucie to be a superb mime, giving for example a wonderful performance (she was totally irreligious) of an archbishop hearing confession. Léonie, on the other hand, though excellent in the part of a princess, gave only a mediocre performance as a general, made up of obvious clichés and stereotypes.

By contrast, subjects in secondary states are often as

much individuals as in their primary state: their behaviour is not simply a question of mannerisms, it involves a radical and total change in outlook and values. Janet remarks:

> M. Beaunis tells us he has never come across a hypnotised subject who tells lies. If so, he's been very lucky. There are hypnotic subjects who lie like Lucie, others who are honesty itself like Léonie, just as in everyday life there are good people and bad. (1889, p.128)

Since the 1960's we have received a great many reports from people who claim to have been abducted by extra-terrestrials on board their UFOs. In one of the first and best-known of these cases, one of the witnesses became ill, and it was suggested that suppressed memories of the alleged incident might be responsible — a classic psychological situation. Consequently, the classic psychological treatment was tried — to recall the incident under hypnosis — with dramatic results. Both Barney and Betty Hill independently recalled in vivid detail a UFO abduction.

There are good grounds, none the less, for doubting whether the incident occurred as related, just as Freud discovered there were good grounds for doubting whether all his patients had suffered from sexual molestation in childhood. Subsequent experiments by Alvin Lawson and others have confirmed the ability of hypnotic subjects to elaborate remarkably detailed but entirely fictitious abduction stories (Evans, 1987).

The conclusion to be drawn from all this is that in the ASC there are *two kinds of depersonalisation* which may take place: there is *role-playing*, which though often remarkably clever is apt to be no more than a superficial performance; and there is *dissociation*, which creates or reveals the existence of beings who are to all intents and purposes distinct individuals.

Furthermore, we must consider the possibility that the role-playing behaviours are not always initiated by the primary personality, but the secondary personalities may be responsible. The Self-2, in the classic multiple-personality trinity, is the child-like, suggestible, impressionable personality. It seems reasonable to hypothesise that it is this personality which shows such a fondness for role-playing and story-telling, such a lack of concern to distinguish between the real and the imaginary.

Induced out-of-body experiences
Like other effects of ASCs, OBEs may be deliberately sought. From time to time, experiments are made in 'psychic projection', 'astral travelling' etc., and the evidence is impressive that some are successful. We have a good many well-attested accounts such as the following:

> Having been reading of the great power which the human will is capable of exercising, I determined with the whole force of my being that I would be present in the spirit in the front bedroom of a house in which slept two ladies of my acquaintance, aged respectively 25 and 11 years: I was living at a distance of about 5 km. I had not mentioned my intention of trying this experiment, for it was only on retiring to rest this Sunday night that I made up my mind to do so. The time at which I determined I would be there was 1 a.m., and I also had a strong intention of making my presence perceptible.
>
> On the following Thursday I went to see the ladies, and in the course of conversation (without any allusion to the subject on my part) the elder one told me that, on the previous Sunday night, she had been much terrified by perceiving me standing by her bedside, and that she screamed when the apparition advanced towards her, and awoke her little sister, who saw me also. (Beard in Gurney, *et al*, 1886, vol. 1, p.104 Case 14)

Additional details increase the credibility of the story, and it is significant that though Beard had never visited the room, not only did his apparition find the right room, but positioned itself appropriately in respect of the furniture.

We are not obliged to take this account at face value; there are alternative explanations, though none of them is wholly convincing. What is of interest for our inquiry is that Beard himself recognises that he may have been in some sort of special state:

> Besides exercising my power of volition very strongly, I put forth an effort which I cannot find words to describe. I was conscious of a mysterious influence of some sort permeating my body, and had a distinct impression that I was exercising some force with which I had been hitherto unacquainted. (*Ibid.*)

When we considered the spontaneous OBE, it seemed right to say that it does not constitute a specific ASC in itself, but is an effect which accompanies some ASCs. Can we say the same of the voluntarily-sought OBE? It seems to me there is a parallel here with the mystical phenomena of ecstasy and visionary encounter: those who seek them cannot command them, but can put themselves in a state where the probability of their occurrence is increased. It would be absurd to suppose that the effort of will plays no part; but it may simply be to *guide* the course of events, just as a patient undergoing Jungian analysis will wish to help his analyst by dreaming Jungian dreams, just as Catherine Labouré, desiring above all things to meet the Virgin Mary, had her wish granted.

3.6 What ASCs are: a provisional model

We are not yet far enough along in our inquiry to attempt any final formulation of what ASCs are; but we can construct at least a provisional model from the elements which our rapid survey has shown to occur in virtually every ASC:

1. *Depersonalisation*: whether spontaneously, as the result of appropriate circumstances, or by a more or less voluntary process of hypnosis/auto-hypnosis, the individual is released from his usual state of consciousness. In so doing he is liable to shed his habitual personality to a greater or lesser degree; this entails, among other things, abandoning the reality-testing procedures he employs in his usual state.

2. *Suggestion*: because his mind is no longer screening the input it receives, he becomes very open to suggestion, whether from outside or from his own subconscious mind.

3. *Role-playing*: suggestion is most likely to lead to his assuming some form of alternative self, either a secondary personality, a possessing or channelling entity, a character in a hallucinated encounter with other entities, etc.

These we have found to be the essential building blocks of

most 'active' ASCs. The exceptions are those 'passive' states, such as waking dreams and hypnagogic visions, in which the subject, while free of his primary self, remains inactive, without assuming another self or playing any role beside that of observer.

We have seen that these basic elements come in all manner of shapes and sizes, dictated by personal needs and cultural patterns. Each ASC has its own array of characteristics, which serve to distinguish one from another: for example, Bernadette's visionary ecstasy differs from the trance of a spirit medium in that she remembers every detail of her experience, whereas a medium generally has no idea what occurs during the seance. Evidently, the two states are *not* the same, despite similarities in other respects.

Any model we construct at this early stage must be tentative only; but at least the *depersonalisation — suggestion — role-playing* model which has emerged from our survey is something we can carry with us as we proceed to see how the ASC is shaped, both by the circumstances which determine *how* it comes about, and by the reasons *why* it comes about.

4 The trigger

Many factors, physiological, psychological, environmental or cultural, can cause a person to switch from his usual to an alternate state.

Some are simple cause-and-effect processes, which would affect anyone at any time to a greater or lesser degree — I take a drink too many, I start to lose my sense of reality. Others are once-only events, such as the sudden loss of a loved one by someone who is already in a vulnerable state due to his upbringing or his health history. Without that previous conditioning, the trigger might not have the same impact: more often than not, it is a *combination* of factors which brings about the effect, the trigger factor being simply the last straw.

It is important, though, that we be clear what we mean by 'trigger'. We mean (1) a circumstance which will cause (2) a physiological process to occur which will in turn bring about (3) a change of state. For example, when we say that voodoo drumming puts a person into a state in which he believes himself possessed by a deity, we may mean that the drumming stimulates electric discharges in the brain which cause seizure-like effects which activate those parts of the brain into a hallucinatory state whose specific form will be determined by what he has been culturally conditioned to expect to happen in such circumstances — in this case, that he will be possessed.

Each of the three elements — cause, means, effect — is almost infinitely variable, so two people will not necessarily respond to the same triggers nor respond to them in the same way. Any of us can get drunk, any of us may attend a voodoo ceremony, but we will not all enter ASCs. One person's trigger is not necessarily another's.

4.1   Physiological triggers

Madeleine's 'nights of love and madness with the good Lord' became much less frequent after I had treated her for an irritation of the external genital parts caused by her deformed thighs being too close together. (Janet, 1926, p.86)

We are physical beings. Whatever the metaphysicians may say, that we possess mind and spirit is less certain than that we possess bodies. So first, we should look for simple physical causes for switching from USC to ASC. Here is a case of amnesia:

In 1896 a 50-year-old businessman of Virginia, while away on a business trip, suddenly vanishes. He has reserved a cabin on a steamship in a northern city, and leaves his belongings on board while he goes into the town; but he never returns to the ship. It is presumed that some accident has occurred, but no trace of him is found and eventually he is supposed dead.

Six months later, he suddenly turns up at the distant home of a relative. He is in a deplorable physical state, dazed, able to recognise only a few of his friends. A day or two later an abscess breaks in his auditory canal, discharging a large quantity of matter: immediately there is a striking improvement both physically and mentally, and he is soon back to normal. He has no recollection of what has happened during the 6-month interval, except that he has had a few flashes in which he part-remembered his real self.

Clearly the abscess is closely associated with his amnesia: but it is also noteworthy that an uncle has also had an amnesic experience, suggesting the possibility of some hereditary disposition which combined with the immediate cause, the abscess, to bring on the amnesia.(Myers, 1903, vol.1, p.319)

Even this is not the whole story, but before we could attempt anything like a full explanation we would need to know more about the circumstances of his 'alternate' life. It

seems that, like Ansel Bourne (#3.4), he must have func-
tioned more or less normally, otherwise he would not have
survived without medical or police intervention. But was it
a true 'other life', conscious and controlled; or did he
simply drift, as might a tramp or some other social drop-
out, living from moment to moment oblivious of past or
future?

A physical cause seems equally plain in the case of Mary
Wood (#3.3), whose role-playing began on her sickbed. But
that still doesn't tell us why her illness turned so dramatically into a case of dissociation; it is only our guess that
family troubles were ultimately responsible.

Here is an ASC of yet another kind induced by a physical
cause — a dental patient's experience under anaesthetic
(nitrous oxide). The dentist told him he would count up to
twelve, but by that time the patient would be under and not
hear him count 12; when he heard a musical-box he would
know he had 'come to':

> At 'two' the gas was turned on. At 'six' I was conscious, but
> aware that I could no longer stop the operation. I heard
> 'seven' and 'eight', and then the conversation between the
> dentist and the anaesthesist became so absorbing that I forgot
> to listen to the counting. They were discussing the question of
> my sensibility, and saying that they were only pretending to
> give me gas. The last remark was addressed to me, 'You see, it
> is entirely a question of faith.' As I heard this, I also heard the
> musical-box, and one part of me knew that the teeth were out
> and the remark of the dentist imaginary, while the other part
> knew that the remark was *real*, and that nothing but conversa-
> tion had occurred since I sat down. Another part of me, which
> I can only call *I*, waited to see which was the correct version.
> (*JSPR* 7, p.116)

On another such occasion,

> The dentist was urging me to sit up, but I made no effort, as I
> felt I was not quite sure that I was *complete* enough to move. I
> was not certain that the person who heard the order to move
> was able to convey the order to the person who had to move. It
> was only when I actually sat up that I was sure that 'I was I'.
> (*ibid.*)

It is interesting that the effect of the gas was to bring about a fragmentation into two 'persons', with a third adjudicating between them, matching the pattern we find in multiple-personality states.

Body chemistry

The seventh-century English hermit Guthlac of Croyland left sufficiently detailed accounts of his personal life for twentieth-century researchers Kroll and Bachrach (1982) to compare his diet with the United States Recommended Dietary Allowance. They deduced that he probably suffered from protein and vitamin B deficiency, whose likely consequences would be night blindness, scurvy and hallucinatory states.

When we read that Guthlac was continually troubled with horrifying visions of demons, we are not only not surprised, but can confidently say that if he had enjoyed a better diet, he would not (other things being equal) have had the visions.

But that is not the same as saying that his defective diet *caused* him to be visited by demons. It could lead him to hallucinate, but it could not make him hallucinate demons rather than pink elephants. The demons came from his cultural programming: they are what a pious seventh-century hermit would *expect* to be visited by, given that he was going to be visited by anything.

Guthlac's diet, then, was a *contributory* cause of his experience, and perhaps a *necessary* one; but surely not the *sole* cause.

The same applies to dance. Sargant, a behavioural scientist, was intrigued by dancing he witnessed in northern Kenya:

While the Samburu were overbreathing and harshly expelling their breath, they were rhythmically dropping back hard onto their heels. The whole movement required much muscular effort and obviously would soon start to cause bodily and nervous exhaustion. I showed a film of this to a research biochemist who felt that, if it had been possible to take arterial blood samples, a high degree of blood alkalosis would have been found leading to brain alkalosis. We know that brain alkalosis tends to produce suggestible behaviour and trance. Undoubtedly the heavy stamping and rhythmic dancing would create more lactic acid in the bloodstream, which might counteract some of the alkalosis. However, the total effect on the biochemistry would still seem to be an increasing tendency to brain alkalosis, which is what is required if a state of trance is to be fairly rapidly induced. (1973, p.117)

Here again, studies of chemical activity show *how* the dancers would proceed to the trance state, but don't tell us what they would experience when they reach it.

Allergy seems evidently a response related to body chemistry, but there are indications that bioelectric factors are also involved. Though it is currently the subject of intense research, we are still very much at the fact-finding stage, and so far the facts found do not add up to a very coherent picture. If someone reacts to the presence of a cat in the room even though it is hidden behind a sofa, this would seem to be a straightforward physiological response — the cat emits some chemical to which the person is hypersensitive. Alternatively, the irritant could equally well be one of electromagnetism. However, we cannot rule out a third possibility, that it is not physiological at all, but psychological or even parapsychological: some kind of extra-sensory awareness — a 'sixth sense' — which tells the person there is a cat in the room.

Not only our behaviour, but our body itself is changing from one moment to the next; at different times of day we react differently to stimuli. Each meal we eat loads our body with a batch of new chemical substances which it must deal with, absorbing what it finds useful and excreting the rest. Many of these substances act in a particular way on the body. Alcohol and drugs are obvious examples, but the same is true to some extent of everything we eat, drink or even touch. For example, German researcher Schmeing in 1937 claimed to have found that second sight is inhibited by adding calcium to the body, from which he inferred that second sight is caused — or enabled — by a calcium deficiency in the blood. American writer Scott Rogo notes that ketamine, frequently used as an anaesthetic, produces NDE-like and OBE-inducing effects. American pharmacologist Cedric Wilson in 1958 reported experiments showing that 'ergotrophic drugs, such as dexamphetamine and caffeine, depress ESP ability, whereas drugs of the trophotrophic series, such as the tranquillisers, appear to cause heightened ESP ability' (PF, 1961).

Wilson's use of the word 'cause' seems rather premature: 'enable' or at most 'encourage' would seem as far as we have a right to go. In changing the chemical balance of the body, drugs may have releasing or inhibiting effects, but opening or closing a door is a meaningless exercise unless there is somebody there.

A further complication comes with the finding that it is not only a matter of which drugs you inject into the system, but also how much or how little. The American parapsychologist Rhine, in 1948, found that when the narcotic sodium amytal was administered to subjects, small doses improved performance, but large doses reduced it. If caffeine was administered to counteract the narcotic, scoring improved again.

Moreover, many of these chemical processes can be put to good or bad use. When insulin is given to a patient, the amount of sugar in his blood is reduced, which leads to mental confusion, excitement and ultimately to coma; this can be used as an effective treatment for schizophrenia, but can equally be exploited for mind-control purposes.

Apart from the chemicals we introduce into it, our body is maintaining its own chemical balance: for instance, supplying adrenalin to the system when a boost is needed, or serotonin as an antidote to emotional stress. But under the appropriate circumstances, this too could lead to ASC effects.

For instance, it has been suggested (Lindley *et al.*, 1981) that in cases of critical illness, the patient's hypothalamus might seek to offset near-death stress by releasing endorphins, and/or enkephalins into the brain; these might have the requisite euphoric effect, making the patient happier and more relaxed — but they could also lead to hallucinations. These effects could actually be inhibited by drugs, and this would explain why patients under heavy sedation or feeling the after-effects of anaesthetics are less likely to report NDEs. We may, indeed, be doing patients a *disser*-vice by keeping them under heavy sedation, and would do better to let their bodies deal with the situation in their own way.

Such a finding is a salutary reminder how far we are from possessing anything approaching a coherent picture of the way in which our body is acted upon by these chemical factors. Our information is no less piecemeal when it is a matter of the body's electricity.

Body electricity

Just as we are chemical machines, so we are electrical machines: electricity is involved throughout our system. Consequently, we are liable to be affected by interactions with atmospheric electricity. Links have been shown in the timing of deaths and births, the discomfort of the sick and injured, and statistics for accidents at work or on the roads. Magnetic storms correlate with suicide statistics; schizophrenia with variations in Earth's magnetic fields; blood clotting with solar activity, whose effects are predominantly electrical.

However, it is evident that some of us are more 'electric' than others, and more at certain times than others. There is certainly more than chance in the fact that the people most likely to display electrical effects are teenage children, mostly girls around the time of the menarche.

In the 1830s and 1840s there was a sudden flurry of interest in 'electric girls', which unfortunately died down almost at once, and though subsequently there have been intermittent references to the phenomenon, there has been no methodical investigation.

Rochas (1896) lists about a dozen cases, of which the best known is that of Angélique Cottin:

> In January 1846, a 13-year-old village girl named Angélique Cottin, small, robust, but extremely apathetic physically and mentally, suddenly began to present strange phenomena; objects touched by her or even by her clothing would be violently pushed away; sometimes she had only to approach people for them to feel the movement and for objects to be displaced.
>
> These phenomena lasted for about a month, with occasional intervals. Not only family and neighbours observed the phenomena, but also qualified persons, and when she was brought to the Paris Académie des Sciences for investigation, even though by then her powers were much on the decline, Dr

Tanchou, who twice examined her, vouches for the reality and strength of the phenomenon: for example 'a chair held down by strong men, on which I was sitting in such a way as to occupy only half, was violently tugged away from under me the moment she sat on the other half'. (p.432)

There can be little doubt that Angélique's age is a crucial factor. Rochas comments:

It is noteworthy that these anomalous talents almost always manifest to young girls at a time when their organism is preparing for the onset of menstruation. We know that many women, when their period occurs, break their needles while working. The age of menopause seems sometimes to be accompanied by electrical manifestations, though of a different sort. (1896, p.448)

Dr Tanchou notes that Angélique's greatest feat, the movement of a heavy dining table simply by the contact of her clothing, was at the level of her pelvis, and Rogers (1853, p.272) comments that 'the point of nervous derangement appears to have been about the uterus: it was from this point that the most powerful discharges of force took place, which instantly overturned chairs, tables, and everything related to her, even when at quite a distance.'

If Angélique's was a one-off instance, we would have to attribute the outbreak to her as an individual; but her feats have been duplicated by a sufficient number of others for us to acknowledge a recurring phenomenon. But though the facts are well enough established, their significance eludes us. What is certain, however, is that the phenomena are linked both with the subject's physical state and her state of mind. Not only is Angélique described as unusually apathetic, but Dr Tanchou gives several indications which correlate with other ASCs, noting, for example, that 'it's when she isn't thinking of anything, or when she is distracted, that the phenomenon is the most sudden and the most intense'.

It is surely significant that this is exactly the same class of persons who are most given to seeing visions — long before Bernadette, it was nearly always young girls who claimed encounters with the Virgin — and who are most prone to harassment by 'poltergeist' phenomena, which for a long time were blamed on 'naughty little girls'.

The complexity of the matter is well illustrated by the following case:

> A young woman, sister of a professor of theology at Strasbourg, on a sudden fright, was seized with a nervous malady, which continued for a long period, and finally terminated in her death. Among the remarkable symptoms in her case were the following:
>
> First, those of *somnanbulism*, with more or less lucidity. Second, her body became so highly charged with electricity that it was necessary to conduct it away by a regular process of conduction.
>
> Third, her body would impart powerful shocks to those who came in contact, and even when they did not touch her. Fourth, she controlled its action so as to give her brother a 'smart shock' when he was several rooms off. When the professor received the shock, he started up and rushed into her chamber, where she was in bed; and as soon as she saw him she said, laughing, 'Ah, you felt it, did you?'
>
> She was subject, also, to spasms and paroxysms of rigor and trembling. (Rogers, 1853, p.107)

Even the sparse information we are given about this case raises intriguing questions. Why should 'a sudden fright' produce such strange effects? And how was the girl able to control them — for it seems she knew very well what she was doing when she gave her brother a shock in a distant room? If we could understand the basis of the mind-body interaction in these 'electric girl' cases, we would be a long way towards understanding the physiological basis of ASCs.

Greater progress has been made in the area of research into electrical processes in the brain. Neurosurgeons have demonstrated that electric stimulation of the temporal lobes of the brain can produce a wide range of effects, many of which are strikingly similar to the sensations reported by people in ASCs. These include emotional effects such as anxiety or fear, perceptual effects such as hallucinations and OBEs, or 'mystical' effects such as a sense of oneness with the cosmos or of the meaningfulness of existence.

If such effects can be produced artificially by the surgeon's probe, they can also occur spontaneously: and here we come closer than anywhere else in this study to the fundamental physical mechanism involved in the process of switching into an ASC.

Brief electric microseizures occurring within the temporal lobe — he calls them *temporal lobe transients* (TLTs) — are seen by Canadian psychologist Michael Persinger (1983) as a likely trigger in many events which the subject sees as meaningful in a personal religious sense. The overall effects would be the same for everyone: the specific form of the experience would depend on the individual's personal experience and cultural background.

In support of his hypothesis Persinger points out, for example, that the onset of puberty is accompanied by 'temporal lobe peculiarities', which correlates with the very high proportion of cases cited in our inquiry which involve teenage children. He claims that TLTs may be precipitated by a whole list of factors, which matches pretty well the list of triggers we examine in this chapter.

What Persinger offers us, then, is a physiological basis for the psychological experience. His TLTs could be the means whereby material from our latent store of experience and memory is retrieved, giving our ASCs their specific form. As such, it may be a valuable contribution to our understanding of what is occurring in these states.

But even if it is established that TLTs, or something of the sort, are the physical trigger for ASCs, we have still to establish what it is that, as it were, makes the finger pull the trigger? In fact, we see that we have so many possible choices that it is rarely possible to say which is operating in a particular instance. Even if we can point to a specific event — being stuck in a lift, witnessing a death — we are not going to find it easy to identify the predisposing factors within the individual which will interact with that event to set off the TLT and trigger the ASC.

Apart from anything else, the physiological make-up of even a healthy individual is continually changing. We are different people when we wake in the morning than when we go to bed at night — some of us are 'morning people' who wake alert and ready for anything, but can't work at night; others are just the reverse. These dispositions are caused by fluctuations in our body chemistry and electricity.

Then there are longer cycles; it is, for instance, probably true to say that most women are particularly susceptible to ASC triggers at the time of their monthly period — some before, some during, some after. Attempts have been made to formalise the various cyclic influences which affect us, so that we can benefit from knowing when our body-cycles coincide to give us 'best' and 'worst' days, but though the evidence for biorhythms is intriguing, it has yet to be proved scientifically. It remains a matter of subjective experience; and here other factors come into play, which may be as much psychological as physiological. There are many instances of persons who have regular recurrences of some affliction. For example, many stigmatics receive a renewal of their marks on Fridays — and clearly this is an effect of suggestion, done in commemoration of Jesus' crucifixion. But what lies behind the Cambridge athlete who suffered a predictable swelling of his knee every nine days? (Luce, 1971)

Sensory deprivation

Shut someone up in a dark room with minimum contact with the outside world, and he is liable to suffer hallucinations, emotional disturbances and intellectual impairment. When some American volunteers submitted to such a test in 1959, they experienced:

> hallucinations of playing baseball, skin diving, being on a troop ship, feeling chips of paint or specks of dirt falling from the ceiling, water dripping, delusions of the refreshment being poisoned, feeling shocks from the electrocardiograph leads, smelling the electrode jelly melting. (Davis *et al.*, 1960, p.889)

In another experimental situation, in 1950 the US Air Force sent subjects up in high-altitude balloon flights, equipped with radios with which they were supposed to send back physical data. More than one individual, instead of reporting data, described his own feelings: thus one man, alone in a balloon at 18,000 metres, reported back 'I have left the world. There is only the ship to identify myself with. Her vibrations are my own. I feel them as intensely as those of my own body. Here is a kind of unreality mixed with reality that I cannot explain to myself.' Another, flying at 30,000 metres, felt 'as if I was literally in another world and had lost all sense of time and distance judged by ordinary standards' and seemed to be 'above the trials and tribulations of earthly existence' (Taylor, 1979, p.6). If such effects occur when the subject knows roughly what is going to happen to him, and has the reassurance of contact with people who will terminate his condition whenever he wants, it is not surprising that much stronger effects result when he is taken by surprise, as in the case of trapped miners who experience dramatic hallucinatory experiences (#4.3).

If too little stimulus can lead to ASCs, so can too much; we shall see examples of the effects of sensory overload when we look at what stress does to people.

Fatigue, exhaustion

One of our best mediums in Paris is a man who has been suffering for some time from a serious chronic disease. He says that his best moments of clairvoyance come before lunch when he has been especially tired, irritated, harassed by a tedious customer and nervous. (Dr Alain Assailly in PF, 1961)

Similarly, Father Reginald-Omez, a French graphologist, reports:

When I am generally at rest I am not as successful as if I have to do it under stress — at a time when I am impatient to finish something and get away. I am then in a state of annoyance that creates a nervous condition, an increase in speed of pulse, and this assists my abilities. And it is often when in the first place I have been tempted to say no — when pressure has been brought to bear on me to make the analysis — that I am able to do ever so much better than under other circumstances. (PF, 1961)

Studies of front-line soldiers in the Second World War revealed the effects of combat fatigue, which eventually destroy the efficiency of even the most highly trained soldier:

The men lost their ability to distinguish the various noises of combat. They became unable to tell friendly from enemy artillery. . . They became easily startled and confused, lost their confidence and became tense. They were irritable,

frequently 'blew their tops', over-responded to all stimuli . . .
This state of general hyper-reactivity was followed insidiously
by 'emotional exhaustion'. The men became dull and listless,
mentally and physically retarded, preoccupied and had
increasing difficulty in remembering details. This was accompanied by indifference and apathy. (Swank, cited by Sargant,
1957, p.23)

In certain physical conditions, such as polar exploration or
moutain climbing, the intensity of the physical effort —
perhaps combined with sensory factors — induces a hallucinatory state, and apparitions are quite often reported.

We know that after 48 hours without sleep, the body
starts to release a substance chemically related to LSD,
noted for its hallucinogenic properties. After 90 hours, even
comfortably situated volunteers start to hallucinate. Fatigue
would accelerate this process, especially if combined with
stress and sensory deprivation.

Pain, injury

When pain becomes too intense, most of us will just 'pass
out' — lose consciousness altogether. But for some people,
pain can induce an ASC. Some torture victims are said to
retreat into a state where pain ceases to be felt in the normal
way; some martyrs and witches are reported as going to
their deaths in a state of ecstasy.

There are many accounts of religious fanatics who are
unhappy unless they are suffering. Thus the seventeenth
century French visionary Marguerite-Marie Alacoque tells
us:

> The more my body was afflicted, the more happy was my soul
> and the more free to join my suffering Jesus . . . I made myself
> a bed of broken pottery, on which I laid down with an extreme
> pleasure, despite my body which protested, but in vain, for I
> would not listen to it.

Clearly, in such cases there is no question of anaesthesia,
for it is the pain itself which Marguerite-Marie sought ever
since Jesus himself had shown her a cross covered with
flowers and told her:

> 'This is the bed of my chaste brides, on which I will make you
> consummate the delights of my love; the flowers will fall little

by little and all that will be left will be the thorns, and you will need all the strength of my love to support their pain.'

We must suppose, then, that she felt the pain, but welcomed it in some kind of ecstatic state; we know that such states were common for she describes them too.

We have seen that anaesthesia can be induced by a hypnotist, as Esdaile did with his surgery patients; but the indifference to pain of the martyr goes beyond both induced anaesthesia or the spontaneous anaesthesia displayed by hysterics such as Jules Janet's Annette (#3.5), who while fully conscious and living a seemingly normal life was quite unaware that she was totally anaesthetic on one side of her body. In cases like Marguerite-Marie's, pain is not simply over-ridden but transcended, just as fatigue is transcended by the voodoo dancer.

4.2   Environmental triggers

Habitat

It may be easier to enter ASCs in some places than in others. In his study of his remarkable patient Frederike Hauffe (1801–29), the German doctor Justinus Kerner (1845) noted a disposition to 'nervous derangements' among the mountain folk of her part of Germany — 'a thing scarcely to have been expected among so robust a people':

> Thus it is observed, in a place called Neuhütte, situated, like Prevorst [Frederike's home], upon the mountains, that a sort of St Vitus's dance becomes epidemic, chiefly amongst young people, so that all the children of the place are seized with it at the same time. Like persons in a magnetic state, they are aware of the precise moment that a fit will seize them; and if they are in the fields when the paroxysm is approaching, they hasten home, and immediately fall into a convulsion, in which condition they will move, for an hour or more, with the most surprising regularity, keeping measure like an accomplished dancer; after which they frequently awake as out of a magnetic sleep, without any recollection of what has happened. It is also certain, that these mountaineers are peculiarly sensible to magnetic influences, amongst the evidences of which are their susceptibility to sympathetic remedies,

and their power of discovering springs by means of the divining rod. (p.31)

Frederike herself displayed perhaps the most extraordinary range of anomalous behaviours ever recorded of a single individual — they included OBEs, visions and apparitions, precognitive dreams, hyperaesthesia, poltergeist phenomena, and all manner of spasms, catalepsies and trances. Clearly, no one is going to blame all this on her habitat; equally, it seems certain that geophysical factors played a contributory part, for Kerner observes:

> The higher she was in space, the more abnormal and magnetic was her condition; this was observable even in the different floors of a house. In a valley, she felt oppressed and weighed down, and was attacked by convulsions. (p.72)

That these symptoms had a physiological basis is suggested by some traits she displayed, notably a sensitivity to electro-magnetic forces, and to certain minerals. It is true that, as one reads the biography of this much-afflicted lady, she seems to have been sensitive to just about *everything*: nevertheless, she may well have been a sister under the skin to the electric girl of Strasbourg (#4.1).

Weather

It seems to have been local weather conditions which dashed the hopes of the 'Smyrna Girls':

> The two Greek girls came to France from Izmir in 1839, hoping to make their fortune by exhibiting their remarkable powers of moving furniture and other objects by deploying some sort of body electricity. Several persons, 'including various men of science' examined them and acknowledged their feats; unfortunately, 'the temperature having become cooler, and the atmosphere having loaded itself with humidity, all perceptible electric virtue seemed to desert them'. (Rogers, 1853, p.100)

As Eric Dingwall observes with his customary common sense, 'One has only got to live oneself to know the effect of climate and weather and other things on human life and human personality.' It is a matter of everyday experience that many of us react unfavourably to thunderstorms, and there is a good solid scientific reason for it; during such a storm the air is supercharged with positive ions, which belie their name by having a marked negative effect on a substantial proportion of humankind. The effect of 1000–2000 positive ions in a single cubic centimetre of air is, on the one person in three who is 'weather-sensitive', to make him irritable and anxious, and if he is hypersensitive, to induce heart oppression and migraine (Sulman, 1980).

Though the findings are piecemeal and sometimes ambiguous, it has been shown that changes in the weather correlate with statistics for suicide and for aggressive crime; neurotics, psychopaths, alcoholics and drug addicts are all liable to be particularly affected. Dutch researcher Solco Tromp (1972) investigated several such effects, and concluded that 'there is hardly an organ of the human body which escapes the effects of changes in the meteorological environment, and these effects are reflected either directly or indirectly in the mental process of man.' Meteorological conditions affect, in particular, the pituitary and hypothalamus, which in turn affect the emotional centres in the rhinencephalon: so 'it is not surprising that the mental processes in man are influenced by even subtle changes in the physical environment.'

Studies by Israeli scientist Felix Gad Sulman show that 'weather-sensitive patients encompass about 30 per cent of any population, no matter of what ethnic origin.' He concentrated particularly on the effects of the hot, dry winds which throughout the Mediterranean region are traditionally associated with unpleasant effects on health and behaviour.

His study of nearly 1000 weather-sensitive Israeli subjects showed that they were affected by the *sharav* — the local version of the wind — in three ways:

1 43 per cent displayed an *irritation syndrome* due to serotonin hyperproduction. Among the symptoms relevant to our inquiry are sleeplessness, irritability, tension, anorexia, migraine, abnormal sensitivity to light, etc.

2 44 per cent displayed an *exhaustion syndrome* due to adrenal deficiency. Symptoms included fatigue, apa-

thy, 'blackout', depression, psychic impediment to performing tasks, etc.

3 13 per cent displayed an *intermittent hyperthyroid syndrome* due to latent hyperthyreosis. Symptoms included insomnia, irritability, tension, palpitations, fatigue, depression, confusion, anxiety, etc.

After a month-long *sharav* ordeal, a weather-sensitive could emerge as a 'complete wreck'; in contrast, rainy winter days produced effects comparable to the elation many feel near a waterfall, and on a snowy winter's day, not one patient complained. So even the excitement we all feel at seeing the year's first fall of snow has a biological basis!

What causes these effects? Clearly, the hot dry wind is the villain, bearing an excessive proportion of positively charged ions, generated by friction of sand particles. The problem, therefore, is not so much atmospheric as electrical, and presumably will eventually be found to involve interaction between external electrical conditions and our own physiology, which varies from one individual to another.

It is noteworthy that Izmir, like Israel, is in the eastern Mediterranean area, so the Smyrna Girls may have been hoping to turn to good account precisely those effects which cause so much distress to Sulman's subjects — a nice illustration of the saying that it's an ill wind that blows nobody good! At the same time, their disappointment at Marseille is a nice demonstration of the way weather and environment can modify behaviour.

Artificial environments
'Electrosensitive people may react with the serotonin syndrome to passing electric street cars, telephones, radio receivers, television apparatuses, radar, infrared heaters, ultraviolet generators and even to the extension wires crossing their living rooms' (Sulman, 1980).

The things people do to the environment may be small compared with what nature can do, but they too can affect behaviour, causing headaches, fatigues, etc. For a large minority of people proximity to high-tension wires can cause stress; for an unfortunate few, the effects can be crippling.

Working environments, which more and more tend to be controlled by air-conditioning systems, can be detrimental if the designer fails to take into account every relevant factor. The increased use of electrical appliances, each of which creates its own electrofield, contributes to the hazards. To take just one factor, it is only recently that office planners have begun to take account of the effects of an imbalance in negative/positive ionisation, which has the same effects as the *sharav* winds mentioned earlier. Put over-simply, positive ions encourage the over-release of serotonin, a hormone that is apt to produce allergies; negative ions inhibit serotonin release and promote its breakdown.

In short, an unfavourable working environment is liable to put an electro-sensitive person into a condition where he will be more vulnerable to involuntary ASC triggers: he would in consequence be more readily affected by a quarrel with a colleague, by having to perform a monotonous, unstimulating task, or by any of the stress factors we are about to consider — particularly in regard to the phenomenon of multiple psychogenic illness.

4.3 Psychological triggers

Stress

> Perhaps the MPI [mass psychogenic illness] symptoms represent a 'last resort' means for low-status persons (female, young, poor, etc.) in high-stress situations, to express their distress. (J. McGrath in Colligan *et al.*, 1982, p.73)

The symposium on MPI from which I quote achieves a consensus rare in such debates, in that each of its authors accepts that *stress* in the work environment is a primary cause of remarkable outbreaks of pseudo-illness in offices, factories and similar contexts which at first sight seem to have a down-to-earth material cause. For example, in one classic case, first one or two and then an increasing number of the workforce complained of being bitten by a bug; in another, staff believed themselves poisoned by chemical fumes. In both cases, and in dozens more, investigation revealed that no such cause existed; yet the illness itself was real enough.

The fact that this phenomenon was previously labelled 'mass hysteria' is an indication that it has affinity with other ASCs. It hardly qualifies as an ASC in its own right, since its symptoms are predominantly physiological — the victims are physically ill, even if the cause is within their own minds. At the same time, we discern traits which are also seen in other states: first and foremost, of course, the abandonment of normal reality-testing process, so that the ostensible cause — a 'June Bug', a gas leak — is accepted without question, so long as it is sufficiently plausible (after all, there *are* nasty insects about, gas *does* leak . . .).

As the quotation from McGrath's paper indicates, those affected are nearly always low-ranking members of the workforce, and often the immediate trigger is an increase in stress — additional work, a decline in working conditions, etc. The victims are people who are not in a position to make any effective protest or resolve the situation themselves, hence their developing the MPI may be a 'last resort' strategy just as multiple personality or amnesia may be a last resort for the individual in family circumstances. It is significant that in both cases, the behaviour is essentially one of *role-playing* — the MPI victims are 'playing' at being ill, just as the amnesiac is 'playing' at being someone other than himself.

Overwork makes people less aware of what they are doing. Sometimes it makes them work *better* up to a point, because they act intuitively; but it can result in wrong because of over-hasty decisions. When it is combined with psychological stress factors, such as anxiety about passing an exam, it can notoriously lead to suicide, whose occurrence among university students is evidently an indication that individuals have been driven by stress to abandon their hold on reality.

Personal crisis

It is not surprising that the recently widowed frequently

hallucinate the comforting return of the lost spouse, as did this woman:

> One day she returned home tired: 'We always used to meet in a doorway that led into the kitchen and I saw him as plain as I see you, I walked through him in fact.' He appeared to be dressed in his normal manner, was life-sized and was seen in natural colour. As she walked through him she felt 'shall I say protected, I felt that he was there . . . I felt comforted'.

She was, however, able to apply her normal reality-testing procedure:

> As to its origin she said, '. . . I put it down to being very tired, you see, sort of wishful thinking.' She had in fact been thinking of him all the way home. She saw him on other occasions when she had been thinking particularly of him. She knew all the time that it was not reality: 'Well, I knew it couldn't be.' (Sedman, 1966, p.52)

Had circumstances been otherwise, however, she might well have believed the apparition was real, as other widows have done throughout history. We may suppose, as she did, that tiredness was responsible: it put her into a mild ASC where she was just sufficiently suggestible for her subconscious mind to present the image, but not so deep a state that her conscious mind could not bring her back to reality.

By contrast, in circumstances where the individual is under a more severe stress, the effects will be less easy to resist. This is particularly the case where conflict is involved, and there is perhaps no situation more productive of conflict than sexual molestation within the family. Patients' accounts of such traumatic experiences at first led Freud to the belief that middle-class Viennese children were continually involved in sexual dramas with close relatives, until he realised that much of the time he was dealing with fantasy, not reality — a realisation which led to some of his most fundamental insights into the way our minds work.

Sexual molestation in the family is the archetypal conflict situation, for the psychological factors involved in, say, a girl's sexual liaison with her father are very complex. The father's act both reinforces and conflicts with the natural tie of parental affection, and it is by no means sure that every child resents these attentions. However repulsive it may be to our moral scruples, the experience itself is not necessarily unpleasant, and it can be seen as an expression of love and favour — all the more so, if we go along with Freud and accept the existence of a subconscious mother–daughter rivalry for the father's affections. In receiving the father's attentions, the daughter has scored over her mother: in such a case, feelings of guilt are liable to enter into the picture and complicate it still further.

Of recent years there has been a flood of cases, particularly involving multiple personality, in which sexual molestation has been identified as the cause. With so many fundamental psychological factors involved, it is not surprising that this is the most frequently recurring trigger for the most traumatic of ASCs, and at the same time, the one most difficult to assess. It is by no means clear, however, that every one of these cases was founded on real events. If recent revelations of child abuse have alerted us to the very real existence of this happening, they also remind us that children possess a talent for improvised fantasy which tends not to be accompanied by a well developed reality-testing procedure.

A doctor who comes across indications of such an event when questioning a patient may feel that he has found the cause of her trouble; and so indeed he may have done. But he would do well to take warning from Freud's experience, and remember that it is often part of fantasy to masquerade as fact.

Just as a high proportion of crime occurs in the family setting, so the origin of a great many ASCs can probably be found in the intimacy of family relationships. Janet's Achille [#6], whose remorse for a brief extramarital escapade leads to hysterical illness and demon possession, is typical of many who are triggered into ASCs by emotional conflict in the domestic environment.

Fear, expectation, etc.
If we are expecting something, or dreading something, we are liable to be in a state of hyper-suggestibility — we mistake an approaching stranger for the person we are

expecting, or if we are sleeping in a room reputed to be haunted, we mistake any unusual noise for a ghostly footfall. At such times, we can easily be pushed over the edge into a hallucinatory state, whether our reason for being afraid is real or imaginary.

That persons in life-threatening situations are subject to hallucinations is well known, and this will be enhanced if they are also subjected to sensory deprivation — in an open boat on the open sea, isolated in the polar region and so on. In 1967 some American doctors were able to examine two miners who had been trapped in a mine. As a result of a cave-in they had to spend 14 days trapped 100m below the surface, in an area approximately three metres by five. Only after six days did they receive light, food and microphones.

> During the period of complete isolation, they experienced many kinds of hallucination. For one, these ranged from a belief that he could in fact see his surroundings, to fantasy scenes such as 'a doorway leading to marble steps, with people passing through it', 'a woman with long hair who was kneeling and praying', and the Pope (the man was in fact a protestant).
>
> The other was continually aware of other men working beside them. He too saw the door with people going through, and felt it was the doorway to death; he also saw a big garden with beautiful men and women, and felt he would like to go there, but that he wasn't ready yet; though he didn't think of it as religious, he agreed that it was some vision of heaven. He too saw the Pope — 'about 5000 times' — and both shared other visions, including other miners in normal clothing, and many lights. After contact was made with the surface and they received light and food, the second miner ceased to have hallucinations but the first continued.
>
> It is difficult to say to what extent the experience was shaped by their danger, to what extent by sensory deprivation. Both claimed not to have been particularly afraid, and confident of rescue, though this was clearly their dominant concern. (Comer *et al.*, 1967, p.164)

Fear had quite a different effect on the Strasbourg 'electric girl' [#4.1], but one of the symptoms was somnambulism — and this seems also to have been among the effects which fear had on another French girl, 22-year-old Marie, who in

1891 had been subject to hysterical attacks since the age of 12:

> One day she was advised by her doctor to report to the Hotel Dieu hospital in Paris for a surgical operation. That night she was found wandering in the streets with worn-out boots and lacerated feet, totally oblivious, and taken to a hospital where she recovered consciousness three days later. She had no memory of what had happened to her in the meantime, but under hypnosis she revealed that she had walked out of Paris to Versailles, in the belief that she might find a nurse who was keeping her baby, forgetting that the baby had in fact died some time before. Having failed in her quest, she returned to Paris on foot, insensible to fatigue or hunger, but now experiencing hallucinations of spectral surgeons who were trying to perform operations on her. It was in this state that she was found and taken to hospital where she woke two days later. (Myers, 1903, citing Boeteau, 1.318)

Clearly, the fear of the surgical operation was the trigger, operating on someone already prone to such attacks. The *ultimate* cause, therefore, was whatever had caused her to have her first such attack ten years earlier; we may well suppose it was something of the nature of a sexual attack. The pattern once created, she retraced it again in this later situation, a critical one as it seemed to her. Fear of surgery prompted the retreat into hysteria, in which she lost touch with reality, regressed to a period when her child was still alive, and lapsed into confusion when her long walk out to Versailles proved fruitless.

It seems that what fear does is to throw the subject into some sort of *undifferentiated* state — a trance of some sort — in which he is highly suggestible. Circumstances then dictate whether he starts to hallucinate, wanders about 'in a dream', or snaps into some more extreme behaviour such as amnesia or dissociated personality.

4.4 Cultural triggers

The build-up from individual behaviour to collective behaviour can come about in any of three ways. First, by *contagion* — one or two individuals set an example which others follow, perhaps in the process overcoming their own inclinations. Second, by *conformity* — the newcomer to a group behaves as he sees everyone else doing. And third, by *'emergent norm'* — the members of the group evolve a norm of behaviour which may not be precisely what any one on his own would have chosen, but is sufficiently close to it to be acceptable to each (refs in Colligan *et al.*, 1982).

Each of these processes involves a degree of *deindividuation*. This is not in itself an ASC, yet clearly it is similar, and perhaps equivalent, to the depersonalisation we have seen to be characteristic of so many ASCs, and the individual's subsequent participation in the collective behaviour can be seen as a kind of role-playing.

How does this fit in with the assertion, often made, that participation in group behaviour is equivalent to returning to primitive modes of behaviour?

The fact that in groups people 'let themselves go', resulting in football violence, lynching, gang rape, etc., seems to bear out the hypothesis that in the anonymity of a crowd inhibitions can be released, and the individuals are free to do the things they have always secretly wanted to do. But it is not quite as simple as that. An individual member of a crowd may have his own personal urge to rape a nun, say, but he would be unlikely to realise this urge in the context of a crowd unless, as might happen in a wartime context, he found himself in a crowd of potential nun-rapers. In an IRA funeral crowd, on the other hand, he would not be able to realise his urge, but he might have the opportunity to batter an 'enemy' soldier to death, as occurred in 1988.

So it is not so much what the individual wants to do, as what he shares with the other members of the group. Naturally, this tends to be simple, primitive feelings rather than the more subtle ones which he has developed as an individual:

> Men the most unlike in the matter of their intelligence possess instincts, passions, and feelings that are very similar. In the case of everything that belongs to the realm of sentiment — religion, politics, morality, etc. — the most eminent men seldom surpass the standard of the most ordinary individuals. From the intellectual point of view an abyss may exist between

a great mathematician and his bootmaker, but from the point of view of character the difference is most often slight or non-existent.

It is precisely these general qualities that in crowds become common property. By the mere fact that he forms part of an organised crowd, a man descends several rungs in the ladder of civilisation. Isolated, he may be a cultivated individual; in a crowd, he is a barbarian. The crowd is always intellectually inferior to the isolated individual, but from the point of view of feelings and of the acts these feelings provoke, it may, according to circumstances, be better or worse than the individual. (Le Bon, 1896, pp.31 f.)

This is confirmed by the fact that another basic emotion — panic — is far stronger when an individual is in a crowd; trapped, say, in the corridors of an underground station, he might alone be able to make a rational decision, but as part of a panicking mass he will probably not be able to think for himself and will 'go with the crowd'.

Collective fear

A shared fear — of 'The Bomb', say, or enemy invasion — provides an effective precondition in which hallucinations and other reality-denying experiences may be easily triggered. 'Phantom airships' were seen by many over Britain during the years immediately preceding the First World War, when the threat of war and the knowledge that Germany possessed a fleet of Zeppelins provided a plausible framework for fantasy. The fact that people's reality-testing procedure deserts them at such times suggests that they may be in a mild ASC; had the phantom airships presented more of a direct menace, no doubt panic and hysteria would have been reported, as they have on several occasions been reported when people have felt themselves menaced by flying saucers.

Nigel Watson, who has made a special study of 'airship scares', sees them as simply one manifestation of rumour-generated collective fears:

Since it seems that sightings of odd things in the sky are a periodic occurrence, why do they erupt into massive scares at certain specific times and places? One explanation is that they bring half-imagined fears into the open and as a consequence provide a vehicle for debate and action. At other times, or concurrently, scares about muggers, Hell's Angels, bombers, stranglers, pollution, atomic power, spies, inflation, unemployment, etc. can manifest themselves in the public consciousness and lead to decisions that are based on as much or as little evidence as the airship scares. (Watson, 1987, p.30)

The madness of crowds

Although outbreaks of collective hysteria (I give it this non-specific label simply for convenience) are a continually recurring phenomenon, the fiercest are those which are linked to a belief — sometimes political, but usually religious. Perhaps the fact that people seldom hold their ideological beliefs on rational grounds has something to do with their readiness to abandon rational behaviour when they feel those beliefs threatened.

No doubt for the same reason, it is difficult to achieve rational debate of what is involved in such outbreaks, owing to the fundamental difference of outlook between those who do and those who do not share the beliefs in question. What cannot be questioned is that the impulse is as strong and the resulting phenomena as remarkable, no matter what ideological banner they are carrying: the flagellation and dancing manias of the Middle Ages, the Jansenist convulsionaries of eighteenth century France or the voodoo devotees of twentieth century Haiti, the camp meeting convulsionaries of nineteenth century Kentucky and Tennessee or the Muslim devotees of present-day Algeria — all conform, more or less, to a behaviour pattern, of which J. Cornish's 1814 account of the 'Jumpers' in Cornwall provides as typical an account as any:

> In a Methodist chapel at Redruth, a man during divine service cried out with a loud voice, 'What shall I do to be saved?' at the same time manifesting the greatest uneasiness respecting the condition of his soul. Some other members of the congregation, following his example, cried out in the same form of words, and seemed shortly after to suffer the most excruciating bodily pain. This strange occurrence was soon publicly known, and hundreds of people who had come thither, either attracted by curiosity, or a desire from other motives to see the sufferers, fell into the same state . . . The disorder spread itself with the rapidity of lightning over the neighbouring

towns and villages, confining itself throughout to the Methodist chapels, and it seized none but the people of the lowest education. Those who were attacked betrayed the greatest anguish, and fell into convulsions . . . they remained during this condition so abstracted from every earthly thought that they staid two and sometimes three days and nights together in the chapels, agitated all the time by spasmodic movements, and taking neither repose nor nourishment. According to a moderate computation 4000 people were within a very short time affected with this convulsive malady.

The course and symptoms of the attacks were in general as follows: — There came on at first a feeling of faintness, with rigour and a sense of weight at the pit of the stomach, soon after which the patient cried out, as if in the agonies of death or the pains of labour. The convulsions then began, first shewing themselves in the muscles of the eyelids, though the eyes themselves were fixed and staring. The most frightful contorsions of the countenance followed, and the convulsions now took their course downwards, so that the muscles of the neck and trunk were affected, causing a sobbing respiration, which was performed with great effort. Tremors and agitation ensued, and the patients screamed out violently, and tossed their heads about from side to side. As the complaint increased it seized the arms, and its victims beat their breasts, clasped their hands, and made all sorts of strange gestures. In some cases exhaustion came on in a very few minutes, but the attack usually lasted much longer, and there were even cases in which it was known to continue for 60 or 70 hours. When exhaustion came on patients usually fainted, and remained in a stiff and motionless state till their recovery. The author once saw a woman who was seized with these convulsions resist the endeavours of four or five strong men to restrain her. Those patients who did not lose their consciousness were in general made more furious by every attempt to quiet them by force, on which account they were in general suffered to continue unmolested until nature herself brought on exhaustion.

Those affected complained more or less of debility after the attacks, and cases sometimes occurred in which they passed into other disorders: thus some fell into a state of melancholy, which however, in consequence of their religious ecstasy, was distinguished by the absence of fear and despair. No sex or age was exempt; children from five years old and octogenarians were alike affected by it, and even men of the most powerful frame were subject to its influence. Girls and young women, however, were its most frequent victims. (Madden, 1857, vol.1, p.488)

This account both illuminates the genesis of the phenomenon and shows how it is communicated. Some details are significant for our study; for instance, that it was clear to the observer (who I think must have been a medical man) that some of the 'patients' were conscious, and others not.

There seems no reason to think that the ASC itself is of a special kind, simply because it is collective rather than individual. There are plenty of accounts of solitary hysterical behaviour which match these. On the other hand, it is clear that a high degree of *conformity* is involved — in each outbreak, whether it be jumping, dancing, flagellation or convulsions, a pattern seems to be set early in the course of phenomenon, and late-comers comply with it — so that all three of the processes named earlier, contagion, conformity and emergent norm, seem to be involved. Lorenzo Dow, describing his experiences during the American religious revivals of 1805, mentions an illuminating incident:

> Yesterday whilst I was preaching some had the jerks, and a young man from North Carolina mimicked them out of derision, and soon was seized with them himself; he grew ashamed, and on attempting to mount his horse to go off, his foot jerked about so much that he could not put it into the stirrup; some youngsters seeing this assisted him on, but he jerked so that he could not sit alone, and one got up to hold him on, which was done with difficulty. Said he, 'I believe God sent it on me for my wickedness.' (Madden, 1857, vol.1, p.496)

We shall see, when we come to consider the question of motivation in #6, that there is much more to this kind of ASC than meets the eye: 'mass hysteria' is not only an inaccurate but a very inadequate label for what is occurring.

4.5 Do-it-yourself ASCs

Anyone who wishes to enter an ASC has a wide choice of triggers available to him, and can make his choice on the basis of whichever he finds congenial or convenient. Do-it-yourself ASCs range from the totally informal to the rigorously institutionalised, from the covert to the explicit.

At the most informal end of the spectrum are drinking intoxicating drinks and drug taking, whether solitary or social. Dance, music and religion all offer popular opportunities for depersonalisation; such dangerous activities as rock climbing and motor racing provide a euphoria which is close to an ASC.

Even these informal practices can be institutionalised to a degree — drinking societies and collective drug taking are features of many religious sects. In most depressed cultures there are opportunities for the individual to participate in social activities whose purpose, avowed or disguised, is fundamentally to give him the opportunity to escape momentarily from his wretched everyday existence. The reason why anyone would choose to enter an ASC, and which kind he would choose, are matters we will consider in #6.

Institutionalised ASC practices generally have the support of a strong belief-system; this provides a set of ready-made concepts so that when the individual has got, by whatever means, into his suggestible state, instead of floundering aimlessly he can grab hold of a suitable element from the communal store.

We can see this clearly in voodoo in Haiti: the individual joins in the dancing activity, and on reaching a critical point, believes himself to have been possessed by one of the cult's numerous deities. Maya Deren, (1953) speaking from first-hand participation in voodoo rituals, emphasises that 'possession is not a period of "self-expression". On the contrary, the individual's psyche is displaced by that of the loa [deity], whose character is constant and independent of that of the person in whose body he becomes manifest.' Since the participant is already familiar with the attributes of the deity, he can immediately switch to a role-playing process, and act as though he is possessed by Ghede, Baron Samedi or whoever, in the same way that a catholic Christian would have a pretty fair notion of how Jesus or Mary would behave.

But despite Deren's statement to the contrary, when someone loses himself in the role of a voodoo deity this may be no more and no less a form of self-expression than any other role-playing ASC. It is a question, ultimately, of what the subconscious finds useful and appropriate — and, of course, available. Even if our needs were the same as those of the voodoo participant, for you or I to indulge in voodoo practices would be inappropriate; instead, we would have to find our own equivalent in a form which is meaningful for us.

The anthropologist Eliade makes this point when writing of the shaman, for whom the do-it-yourself ASC is not an occasional diversion but a lifelong vocation. For him — 'there is no question of anarchical hallucinations and of a purely individual plot and dramatic personae; the hallucinations and the *mise en scène* follow traditional models that are perfectly consistent and possess an amazingly rich theoretical content' (1964, p.14).

Throughout the world, tribes and churches, cults and cultures, in their various ways provide the resources and the opportunity for do-it-yourself ASCs; some formally, others casually; some with drugs and drinks, some with drum and dance, some with steam or vapour baths accompanied or not by narcotics; some effectively, others on a hit-or-miss basis.

In all of them, what we are talking about is *means to an end*. It is no disparagement of these practices to point out that they have a down-to-earth material basis, just as even the wine which Catholics believe is converted into Jesus' blood had to be grown in someone's vineyard. European witches used drugs and ointments which led them to believe that they could soar through the air to the sabbat. Aztec priests would smear their bodies with a highly toxic ointment which they named *teotlacualli* — divine food — which was mixed with scorpions, spiders, centipedes and hairy black worms. Though we may suspect that these live ingredients were added largely for effect, they would in fact cause skin reactions which would stimulate the subject, while the vegetable ingredients induced the ASC in which he could believe himself in communication with his deity (Furst, 1977).

In all these cases, what is basically happening is that the individual is put into a suggestible state. What American author Francis Huxley says of LSD is probably true of any other DIY means:

> Its central action, psychologically, is to dissolve stable reference points in the outside world, an action whose other face is the dissolving of the usual self-image. What is left is the mind in a state of enormous suggestibility, receiving images both from the outside world and from its own unconscious. (PF, 1961)

In this state the particular beliefs of his community may impose themselves on him as hallucinations or dreams. Often, of course, there will be a combination of these triggers, and elaborate rituals will contribute to the effect by heightening the individual's emotional state.

These physical dimensions are present even in the most seemingly 'spiritual' of practices. This is quite explicit in practices like yoga, where physical exercises are specifically practised as a means to spiritual ends. Whether the technique is designed to attain its end by achieving total control of the body, as in yoga, or by treating it as something of so little importance that it should be ignored, as in asceticism, the process is fundamentally a physiological one, whatever spiritual benefits it may ultimately confer. Concentrated rhythmic breathing, for instance, may lead to a build-up of carbon dioxide; this can act on the brain cells to result in hallucination, feeling of expansiveness, and eventual unconsciousness (Puharich, 1962, p.135).

Similarly, the practices of religious mystics involve many of the triggers we have noted in this chapter — isolation, sensory deprivation, often augmented with fasting, lack of sleep and so on. Anyone who sticks himself up on the top of a pillar, or walls himself up in a cave, wearing few clothes or none, exposed to all weathers, with a minimum of nourishment and of communication with the rest of humankind, not to mention no sexual activity, and none of the other sensory stimuli that most of us take for granted — even if such a person doesn't do these things explicitly in order to enter ASCs, that is almost certainly what will happen to him.

The Oracle at Delphi provides an example of DIY ASC exploiting a natural trigger:

Classical writers agree that the place was discovered by shepherds from their first observing the effects on the nerves of their sheep and goats who, coming near a natural aperture that extended into the ground, began to have spasms, and caper and dance in a very strange and extraordinary manner. The shepherd approached to find out the cause; in attempting to inspect the aperture, he himself suddenly fell into a like state. Other persons became in a like manner affected, and it was found that many of them were suddenly gifted with an ability to foretell future events. When they came out of this state, which was precisely of the character of our modern so-called clairvoyance, they had no remembrance of what they had said and done.

After a number of persons had lost their lives in consequence of this strange influence, while imprudently tampering with it out of curiosity, a college of priests took possession of the place, and built over it a rude temple, which was dedicated to Apollo, and the oracle was consigned to the care of a female.

When the priests wished to consult the oracle, the priestess first spent three days in preparing herself, by fasting and bathing in the Castalian well. She then burnt on the altar laurel-leaves and flour of barley, after which she ascended and seated herself upon the tripod, or elevated seat erected over the aperture. So soon as the divine emanation from the earth struck her, she experienced violent convulsions, her face changed colour, her hair stood erect, her breast heaved amazingly, her mouth foamed, her voice altered, and she struggled like one endeavouring to escape until she had completely lost her consciousness, and became entranced. The effect upon her whole nervous system is said to have been so powerful, in some cases, as to sometimes cause the death of the priestess; in which case another female was in readiness to take the place of the first. Generally, however, the mundane agency threw her into a state of somnambulic or cataleptic trance. In this state the oracle was given. (Rogers, 1853, p.250)

The process of entering spirit trance is somewhat less dramatic, but then today's mediums are consulted not so much on the destinies of nations, as was the Delphic Oracle, as on the well-being of loved ones who have passed on . . . Just what are the triggers that induce the milder ASC of spirit trance is not easy to say, but this is how Maurice Barbanell (1959) had it described to him by medium Helen Hughes:

The process is akin to falling asleep. It is preceded by a welcome feeling of complete relaxation and resignation. As a preparation, she relaxes physically and mentally; she becomes aware of a gradual drugging of her consciousness which reminds her of the sensations accompanying the inhalation of chloroform.

And he adds:

The word 'trance' as applied to mediumship is really a misnomer. The number of mediums who are completely unconscious while under spirit control is comparatively small. There are degrees of 'trance' mediumship ranging from the elementary stages, which are really examples of overshadow-ing, to complete insensibility. In some of the lighter forms, the medium is aware of what is being said through her lips but has no control over the communication. Some say that they listen to the communication coming through them, but they seem to be standing some distance away from themselves. (p.77)

This sounds very like hypnosis, as Mrs Sidgwick thought, and it seems to me that the only thing which distinguishes spirit trance from auto-hypnosis is that it is directed to the specific end of making oneself available as a channel for otherworldly communicators. The medium himself evi-dently voluntarily dissociates himself from the outside world, and puts himself into a suggestible state, and that, more or less, is what happens in hypnosis, except that generally the subject invites someone he believes to be qualified — the hypnotist — to help him enter the state.

4.6   Interaction and combination

Speaking of the prophets of the Cevennes (#3) Calmeil (1845) quotes a contemporary commentator, Fléchier, who, though hostile to the protestants, was concerned to explain the phenomenon:

These poor folk heard no other discourse than devotions; their imagination was full of them; in their meetings they heard publicly presented the ideas they continually turned over in their minds privately. They would be instructed to fast for several days, which weakened their brain, and made them more susceptible to these empty visions and vain imaginings.

The travels they made from parish to parish, from mountain to mountain, spending days and nights on the way, taking no nourishment but apples and a few nuts; the public gatherings and the exhortations to give up everything if they wished to be numbered among the chosen faithful; the petty glory of standing on a platform, of being listened to as an oracle, making a thousand quake with a single word, making extravagances sacred and follies venerable by the stew of misinterpreted texts from scripture — so many causes combined to bring about this general corruption, so that by contagion all became either deceivers or deceived. (p.279)

The triggers which result in ASCs do so in one of two ways: some *cause* the ASC to occur, others simply *enable* it to occur. Taking drugs or anaesthetics, for instance, will *cause* someone to go into an ASC whether he likes it or not. On the other hand, fasting or sensory deprivation do not necessarily induce an ASC — they can be withstood by someone with the necessary willpower or who has had the necessary training or who, quite simply, is not susceptible to that particular trigger.

The triggers which can be classed in the 'causing' category will generally be able to effect the switch on their own. The 'enabling' triggers, on the other hand, will probably operate in conjunction with other triggers, or only when the subject is of a certain personality type, or is in a certain state.

Synergy is the action of two or more substances or processes to achieve an effect greater than the sum of what they would achieve individually. A great many ASCs come about synergetically. Among the tortures used by the inquisitors during the witch-mania was sleep deprivation, but that alone would probably not have induced a confession. The victim, however, was already suffering from the stress of being a prisoner facing a horrible death, away from home, family and friends, cold, underfed and probably weakened by the living conditions in a medieval goal, and who was probably there precisely because she was mentally sub-normal in the first place. For someone already so 'softened up', sleep deprivation — which can make even a healthy twentieth-century volunteer start to hallucinate — must often have been the last straw to tip the accused woman over the edge into an ASC where she would not only confess to unbelievable crimes, but, thanks to the adroit suggestions of her questioners, genuinely believe she had really committed them.

A predisposition to a particular explanation can blind a commentator to even the most obvious factors.

In 1550, in the convent of Yvertet, in the Netherlands, there was an outbreak of extraordinary phenomena, commencing with what seems to have been some kind of poltergeist manifestations, but leading to several of the nuns believing themselves possessed by demons, who sent them into convulsions, made them climb about in trees, and so on.

The events were reported by Johann Wier, doctor to the Duke of Cleves, and one of the few men of his day to take a public stand against the witch mania. Yet, for all his knowledge and good sense, he did not question that the devil was truly responsible, and failed to recognise the significance of a piece of information which he himself supplies:

> Since it was Lent, the nuns were fasting, and 'had for the space of fifty days eaten nothing but the juice of horseradish without bread'.

Add this to the fact that, like many nuns of the time, they were probably most of them young, healthy girls, deprived of the normal outlets and activities, and it is not hard to believe that they were in a condition when anything unusual might tip one of them into an ASC, who would in turn set off her more susceptible companions.

Finally, a contemporary example of synergy at work:

> A 52-year-old man and his 24-year-old son are driving across the Arizona desert when, about noon, they hear a strange 'mechanical' noise, stop to find out what it is, and see, hovering a few metres over their car, a UFO, which blinds and paralyses them with a brilliant flashing light; the father feels dizzy and hears 'voices' inside his head, but the son hears nothing. Both find themselves floating above the ground, and up through an opening into the UFO. Inside the UFO they float along a tunnel-like corridor to a brilliantly illuminated room peopled by vaguely discerned (because of the lights)

occupants. Neither sees the other while in the UFO, but each is shown a 'life review' of his past memories, right up to the stopping of their car in the desert, projected on a small screen. When they regain awareness, some 7 hours later, they are sitting in the car, it is night, and there is no sign of the UFO. (Siegel, 1984)

Connoisseurs of the genre will recognise a classic UFO-abduction report; but that does not make it any the less a fascinating psychological case. Additional factors came to light during investigation:

* ⋆ the two men had been driving non-stop for 35 hours;

* ⋆ the father's personality profile, confirmed by his medical records, indicates a tendency to paranoia, agitation and anxiety, though the son is normal;

* ⋆ father and son are both strong believers in paranormal phenomena, and — from what we know of popular beliefs about UFOs in the United States — may well have seen the UFO as life-threatening.

Add to these the fact that driving across a desert is apt to be monotonous, and that the incident occurred at noon when the heat was likely to be very great, and we have a potentially ASC-generating combination of physical circumstances and psychological predisposition, together with an appropriate mental set.

Further questions might have revealed information about the relationship between father and son which would enable us to be more specific about underlying motivations, but clearly there are good reasons not to go for the face-value interpretation, even apart from the question whether UFOs exist in the first place.

5 The process

Most alternate states are not static. We go into them for a purpose, conscious or subconscious; when that purpose is achieved, we generally come back out of them and revert to our usual state. Once in a while, things go wrong, and the state becomes chronic. This is when purposeful behaviour becomes purposeless disorder, requiring treatment.

We shall consider the purpose in #6, the achievement of the purpose in #7, the malfunctions in #8. First, it may be helpful if we gather together what we have learned about the ASC as *process*.

The most evident features of an ASC are (1) the body experiences loss of control, and/or (2) the mind experiences loss of sense of reality.

Over and over again we learn of people dancing until they are overtaken by convulsions, writhing on the ground, culminating in an orgasmic crisis which leaves them in a cataleptic trance-like state. It seems evident that such people have lost control of their physical bodies.

Similarly, we learn of people who experience a profound personality change, either changing their behaviour so much that they appear to be quite different persons; or becoming so detached or so distrustful that they refuse to communicate with the rest of the world; or being carried away in a rapture to what seems to be some private heaven.

It seems evident that such people have lost touch with reality.

But we see also that ASCs are not quite that simple. Some ASCs seem only or chiefly to affect the body, others only or chiefly the mind. And both body and mind may be affected in various degrees, so that while some are disabling, others are perfectly liveable with, and yet others positively enhance our capabilities.

When Ansel Bourne goes wandering off in his amnesia, no one realises it until he realises it himself. What could be further from the convulsionaries of Saint Médard or the Jumpers of Cornwall, whose behaviour is manifest to the point of exhibitionism? When spirit medium D.D. Home goes into trance, he gives every indication of being in touch with reality of a sort, even though it may not be our this-worldly reality. What a distance separates the genteel drawing rooms where he paraded his puzzling powers from the bare rooms at La Salpêtrière where Janet's Léonie and Berthe suffered their hardly less puzzling disorders. Each and every case, in one way or another, reminds us just what paradoxical things these ASCs are.

Indeed, any consideration of ASCs must start from the paradoxical fact that some of them commence with the body — like eating the wrong food, or not enough — and proceed to affect the mind — so ill-fed Guthlac (#4.1) sees visions of demons; while others start with the mind — straying husband Achille (#6) goes 'out of his mind' with remorse — and proceed to affect the body — his physical condition takes him first to bed and finally to the mental asylum.

Even when it seems that we can pinpoint the *modus operandi* of an ASC, we must beware of jumping to conclusions. Saint Philip Neri's biographer tells us that though he was extremely thin, his body heat was such that he had to keep his windows open even in the severest weather, and astonished those who touched his body. In particular, he said he felt intense heat in his throat, and had to bare his chest to obtain relief. Observers noted that when he was in ecstasy his eyes became extremely bright, his body trembled and he was liable to palpitations.

French researcher Aimé Michel points out that all these

signs are consistent with certain hyperthyroid conditions, which can increase the metabolic rate by 50 per cent and more, leading to extreme thinness and to just this array of symptoms.

But does that mean we can reduce Philip Neri's experiences to a physiological condition? Not necessarily. Michel wonders if perhaps the saint, in order to achieve his ecstatic experiences, employs whatever resources his body has to offer — which in his case happen to be those of a hyperthyroid condition. In other words, what Philip is experiencing is a self-induced ASC, which he achieves by making use of the same mechanism which, in a less spiritually developed person, might have been nothing more than an illness.

Personally, I find such explanations over-literal. I do not doubt that ASCs are ultimately definable in terms of physiological processes, because even a mental process has to work with the physical resources of the body and within their limitations. But I do not think we should fall over ourselves to explain them in terms of processes we already know and understand. Clearly, there is a great deal more to be learnt. In any case, no more than Michel do I suggest that *defining* an experience in terms of physiological processes is equivalent to *explaining* it by such means.

Sometimes it seems we can point confidently to a physical cause:

A Dr Bruce, in 1895, described a mental patient 'who not only showed two separate and distinct states of consciousness, but in whom also the right and left brain alternately exerted a preponderating influence over the motor functions. At one time he was ambidextrous and only understood English, at another he was left-handed and spoke Welsh! (Bramwell, 1903, p.380)

But even in this case, can we be sure which was cause and which effect? Can you not hear a psychoanalyst suggesting that the division of the brain was itself the consequence of a psychological conflict, perhaps associated with some hang-up about speaking the English or Welsh language?

Out of control?

Let us take a second look at those ASCs — and there are countless more of them — which display the kind of pattern we saw in the case of *pibloktoq* or the Cornish Jumpers: convulsions leading to collapse, with other symptoms. Those affected gave every sign of having lost physical control of their bodies.

Yet in fact they had done nothing of the sort, for the very fact that they conform to the stereotype — that *pibloktoq* subjects behave like other *pibloktoq* subjects, that one Jumper jumps like other Jumpers — implies that their behaviour is *controlled*.

True, no two people behave in *precisely* the same way: nevertheless, it is evident enough to an Eskimo when someone has *pibloktoq*, to a Malay when a woman has *látah*, and so on: the person's behaviour falls within the recognisable limits of the state. Yet if this is no more than a breakdown of the subject's control, why does he model his behaviour so closely on the stereotype?

We must conclude, then, that whatever may have happened to the individual's *conscious* self, his *subconscious* self is still very much in control, and sees to it that the *pibloktoq* sufferer behaves like a person afflicted by *pibloktoq*, the *látah* sufferer like someone with *látah*. When a voodoo dancer goes into a voodoo trance and is possessed by a deity, the subconscious self chooses which god it will be, and models the behaviour on that of that god and no other, basing it on what it has picked up from watching others, folklore, and so forth.

In short, here we are back again with *role-playing*. These people are being instructed by their subconscious producers in their performance. And this in turn is of the greatest significance for our study: for it tells us, yet again, that *the ASC is not arbitrary or accidental, but a controlled and consequently a purposeful event*.

Out of touch with reality?

The mental behaviour of people in ASCs is no less paradoxical. There are of course many ASCs in which the individual claims that if he has forsaken our everyday earthly reality, it is only to find a higher reality on another level — in the world of the spirits, for example.

Whether or not we accept such claims, we cannot deny that these people behave in a way which is consistent with such an idea, and logical and plausible within that framework. Perhaps there would be no reason for us to disbelieve them were it not that we have found reasons to disbelieve others who make comparable claims — those who tell us they have encountered extraterrestrials, or have been possessed by demons. So, since we have to find alternative explanations for *some* such claims, we should at least consider the possibility that *all* of them may be misinterpreting their experience.

Fortunately, for our immediate purpose that is neither here nor there. What concerns us is whether 'out of touch with reality' is a fair description of the condition of these people. And the moment we ask the question, we can see that the answer is no. It is manifestly evident that even in cases where the operation has gone wrong — in Janet's hysteria patients, in those whose personality has fragmented — there is indication of an intelligent mind which knows very well what it is doing and why it is doing it. And in the others, it really does not matter whether those who tell us their tales of encounters with spirits and extraterrestrials are telling us fact or fantasy — for either way, it is evident that behind the tale is the teller of the tale and that he knows very well what he is about.

It is this evidence that during the ASC there is some part of the mind which is very much aware of what is going on, and very capable of actively controlling the situation, that shows us that the ASC is not the uncontrolled accident it may seem at face value to be.

Awareness and activity during ASCs
Whether in our USC or an ASC, it seems we are always, to some degree, aware of what is going on around us. Even in sleep, the senses never leave off reporting external stimuli such as a child crying or a temperature change. We have seen that a witch who believes herself to be attending a sabbat, a person under hypnosis, a spirit medium in trance, a patient under anaesthetics, each in his own way gives an indication of being aware, at some level, of things happen-

ing and words spoken in his vicinity. These are noted and stored in the memory, and can frequently be retrieved under hypnosis.

In such passive states as sleep, of course, noting and storing is all the individual is able to do. But what about more active ASCs? Janet's Madeleine, in her 'consolation' state, would stand, sit or lie motionless, not eating, not drinking, not moving, for hours, sometimes days on end, seemingly totally deaf, blind and oblivious to everything around her. One day, she went into the state while she was in the middle of writing a private letter:

> At this moment, another patient allowed herself to behave most improperly; she picked up the pages, and since Madeleine didn't move, she began to read out passages from them, laughing aloud at the private confidences. Who d'you think reported the matter to me? Madeleine herself, who had seen everything in detail, and who felt humiliated and chagrined by the incident.
> — But this is absurd, I said, since you saw and heard it all, why didn't you protest, which would certainly have stopped her? — I can't understand it myself, she replied, today it seems abominable, but yesterday, at the time, it simply didn't seem to matter, so I made no objection. (1929, p.66)

This case warns us not to judge a person's awareness by his outward behaviour; for when someone is in an ASC, we must not expect him to react and respond as he would in the USC.

And that is just one of the ambiguities we must be prepared for. Here is another example: American researcher E. R. Hilgard told a hypnosis subject that when she woke she would find she had no hands, but this would not bother her. When she woke, not only could she not see them, but when Hilgard gave her (invisible, to her) hands an electric shock, she felt nothing. She said: 'Dr H told me that I didn't have any hands. He had a little shocking machine that kept floating around in the air. I was very interested in the fact that I didn't have any hands and I really felt I didn't . . . ' Yet she wasn't too anxious about the fact: 'Somewhere else I absolutely know I have hands. I know they're not cut off' (Marsh in Zinberg, 1977, p.140). Clearly, her mind was operating on two levels. One was playing the hypnosis game, accepting the hypnotist's suggestions and going along with them; but all the time, there was a part of her which was in touch with reality and knew that the hypnosis was only let's-pretend, like the girl lost in the department store in Hilgard's other case (#3.5).

Is this the same as a drunk who, if he is suddenly confronted with an emergency, can shake off his intoxication if not wholly, at least to a considerable extent? If so, we may speculate that what happens in such a situation is not that he suddenly ceases to be drunk, but that some part of him takes command and over-rides the worst effects of intoxication.

Quite a different kind of demonstration, but which likewise indicates that a supervising control is being maintained by the subconscious self, is instanced by a patient of Breuer's:

> One day Anna complains to Breuer that she is angry with him, though she can't think why; consulting a diary, he finds that on that day, precisely one year before, he made her angry. This was one of several incidents which showed him that, for psychological reasons, she was partially 'living in the past'; but this demonstration that her subconscious mind was keeping such precise track of the calendar shows that it was well aware what was going on. And indeed, we may suppose that her subconscious was responsible for the whole bizarre performance. (Freud and Breuer, 1895, p.33)

Apart from being evidence of continued awareness, the story of Anna demonstrates that even when it gives no sign of doing so, the subconscious mind is keeping precise track of the passage of time. This is shown clearly in one of Gurney's experiments:

> On March 26 the subject is instructed that on the 123rd day from that date he will post a sheet of blank paper to a specified stranger. On April 18 he is hypnotised and asked if he remembers anything in connection with this person. He at once repeats the instruction, adding 'This is the 23rd day: a hundred more.'
> — How do you know? Have you noted each day?
> — No, it seemed natural.
> — Have you thought of it often?
> — It generally strikes me in the morning, early. Something

seems to say to me, 'You've got to count' . . . I never think of it
during the day. I only know it's got to be done. (*PSPR* 4, p.290)

Robot behaviour

The most enigmatic displays of intelligent behaviour during
ASCs are the instances of 'robot behaviour', usually asso-
ciated with pathological ASCs. Canadian neurologist
Wilder Penfield had a patient who

> was subject to epileptic automatism that began with discharge
> in the temporal lobe. Sometimes the attack came on him while
> walking home from work. He would continue to walk and to
> thread his way through busy streets. He might realise later
> that he had had an attack because there was a blank in his
> memory for a part of the journey, as from Avenue X to Street
> Y. (1975, p.39)

The French doctor Martinet, a century and a half earlier,
had a patient in what was evidently a similar condition:

> A watchmaker's apprentice had an attack every fortnight.
> Though insensible to all external impressions, he would
> perform his work with his usual accuracy, and was always
> astonished, on awaking, at the progress he had made. The
> paroxysm began with a sense of heat in the epigastrium [a part
> of the abdomen] extending to the head, followed by confusion
> of ideas and complete insensibility, the eyes remaining open
> with a fixed and vacant stare. (Macnish, 1834, p.155)

Macnish, given the ideas prevailing in 1834, labels it a case
of somnambulism. Today, while recognising the similarity,
we would prefer to distinguish such attacks occurring to the
waking self from those occurring to the sleeping self; but he
is right, in so far as what occurs is pretty much the same in
both. He adds that the case 'undoubtedly originated in
some diseased state of the brain'. It is noteworthy that it
'terminated in epilepsy', which sugggests that it was of the
same nature as that of Penfield's patient.

H. C. Wood, an American doctor, provides a case in
which the robot behaviour *follows* epileptic attack:

> Not long ago I was consulted by a woman who had epilepsy,
> and who belonged to the lower walks of life, and was
> accustomed to do her own housework. Suddenly and without

warning she would at irregular intervals utter the terrible cry which so often ushers in the epileptic storm, and fall in a convulsion. After the fury of motion had passed, she would remain quiet for a short time and then rise and continue whatever work she had been doing when the attack came on, although she was entirely unconscious — at least she yielded no sign of recognition when spoken to or shaken — and afterwards had no recollection of events. Thus, if she had been setting the dinner-table when the epileptic paroxysm developed, she would go into the kitchen, get the dished-up food and arrange it on the table in the usual manner. By and by she would wake up, saying, 'Where am I? What am I doing?' There was no memory of the labour she had been performing. If in this condition she were spoken to, she gave no heed. If a hot iron were thrust into her flesh, she would not mark it. (1890, p.73)

It seems, though, there are limits to what subjects can do in these circumstances: the occupation has to be habitual or familiar. If they are confronted with a need to make a decision in a matter for which they have no precedent in their mental store, they are unlikely to be able to cope. Penfield had a patient who was subject to epileptic automatism: 'If Christopher was driving a car, he would continue to drive, although he might discover later that he had driven through one or more red lights' (1975, p.39).

Robot behaviour could account for some of the paradoxical aspects of ASCs; for instance, Bernadette holding out her candle to be re-lit while seemingly in an ecstasy in which she is not aware of what is going on around her. Could robot behaviour explain the skill and agility so often displayed by ASC subjects in trance and ecstasy, such as La Tourette's shoemaker in #3.2?

What a person can do when their conscious mind is 'switched off' probably varies from one individual to another, just as people vary in how they react to drink — some can 'hold their liquor' to such a degree that they function seemingly quite normally. I suppose I must be such a person, for twice in my life I have completely blacked out, to find myself in bed next morning with no recollection of getting there, yet seemingly — to judge by the lack of comment by my companions — not having behaved in any way out of the ordinary. If I did not attract notice with my brilliant wit, at least neither do I seem to have disgraced myself. Others, as we all know, are totally altered when they have a 'skin full', and become caricatures of their normal selves — usually, unfortunately, for the worse.

But it seems likely that robot behaviour, even at its best, falls a long way short of the adaptation to external reality displayed in, say, amnesia. The behaviour of the amnesia subject, like that of the multiple-personality subject when one of his 'other selves' is in command, is evidently directed by some kind of intelligence, and goes way beyond what is habitual and familiar. Consider Ansel Bourne again: even if we suppose that he was not as unfamiliar with Norristown as it seemed (we know he toured the country as an itinerant preacher, so perhaps he had visited the town without consciously recalling it), and if we add that perhaps the business of setting up in an unfamiliar trade was not so strange as it seemed (perhaps he had an acquaintance in just that line of business), none the less, there must have been hundreds of occasions, in the course of establishing himself in his new life, which called for intelligent decision-making outside his previous experience. It is difficult to see how he could have coped successfully unless some kind of *conscious* intelligence was being employed.

Robot behaviour is not confined to spontaneous ASCs; it — or something very like it — can occur also in voluntary states. Aldous Huxley, taking in a special delivery letter while in his 'deep reflection' state [#3], seems to have been using a similar ability to perform a familiar action. What would have happened if there had been some complication, or the visitor had been a robber masquerading as a postman? Would Huxley's 'robot' have coped as best it could, or would he have snapped out of his ASC?

Penfield (1975), who probably had more opportunity to study the human brain than anyone has had, comments on such cases: 'The behaviour of the automaton during an attack of epileptic automatism reveals what the brain without the mind and without the mind-mechanism can still do. It reveals what the moment-to-moment function of the normally active mind must be' (p.45). At the end of his career he concluded that, 'there is no good evidence . . .

that the brain alone can carry out the work that the mind does' (p.114).

These robot behaviours, then, represent the action of brain divorced from mind. If so, then they are no less divorced from the subconscious mind than they are from the conscious mind. Maybe we should think of them not as ASCs at all, but as malfunctioning USCs.

If so, the implications are crucial to our inquiry, for they offer us an alternative explanation for many types of behaviour. When we see a voodoo dancer, a possessed nun or a spirit medium in their characteristic states, we would have to ask: Is the performance being 'managed' by the subject's subconscious self, perhaps in the form of a secondary personality, capable of making intelligent decisions which may be just as sensible as those the conscious self would have made? Or is it being carried out by a robot-mechanism which is capable of performing basic functions of existence under almost any circumstances, like a loyal employee who can keep the business going while the boss is away, even though he cannot do any important decision making?

6   The motive

Gradually we are seeing the evidence accumulate that switching to an ASC is seldom accidental or arbitrary: what may seem at first sight to be uncontrolled behaviour turns out to be motivated. Even where it seems fairly clear that something has gone wrong, an initial intention can generally be discerned.

At the same time, it is becoming increasingly clear that the agency which possesses this sense of purpose is the subconscious self.

This is true even when the ASC is entered voluntarily, as when a medium or a shaman goes into trance. On the face of it, the process of depersonalisation, leading to the role-playing activities of the medium or the shaman, is a conscious and deliberate act; but it is an act which occurs only when behaviour or temperament have previously suggested, either to the individual or to those about him, that he is specially cut out for this kind of activity. In one form of words or another, mediums will refer to the impulses and intuitions which come to them from their 'hidden self'; the shaman, or course, will attribute it to the gods or to the spirit of a dead shaman, but for him too it is something other than a conscious choice.

But it is as the initiator of spontaneous ASCs that the activities of the subconscious self are most interesting. It may itself initiate an ASC, as seems to be the case in somnambulism or amnesia, or it may seize the opportunity of an accidental ASC, as when Mr Hanna falls off his horse and is concussed (discussed later in this chapter) or Mary Wood is afflicted with meningitis (#3.3).

The subconscious self also decides what *kind* of ASC we will have. For example, if it is to involve hallucination, it chooses that it will be of the Pope, as in the case of the trapped miners (#4.3), or if it is to be possession, that it will be by demons, like those who torment the Yvertet nuns (#4.5).

And finally it dictates how we behave during the ASC, for instance, that we will go into convulsions like the Cornish 'Jumpers' (#4.4), or compose a sermon like Diderot's priest (#3.5). We may suppose that each of these decisions — whether we have an ASC, what kind of ASC we have, and what form our ASC takes — is conceived of as a means to an end; so that to understand *what* is happening we must discover *why* it is happening, what the producer hopes to achieve.

Over-simplifying, it seems we can divide the individual's needs — and consequently the ASCs which are intended to resolve them — into two broad classes which can be labelled 'passive-protective' and 'active-assertive'.

The unself ASC : passive, protective, defensive, evasive

Often, the need is simply to enable the individual to duck out of a situation which he does not feel able to cope with. In such cases the producer may choose a passive, protective ASC. At its most extreme, this is a simple cop-out, the diminishing of the self into the unself. In sleep or catalepsy, the individual is incapable of action or outward response; it is the equivalent of 'lying possum' as many animals do in the face of danger, hoping the enemy will not notice. Or the person may take refuge in a psychosomatic illness — again, a common refuge: 'You can't blame me, I'm sick.'

But circumstances may not be appropriate for such total evasion, so that a more positive behaviour must be adopted. We can see this process taking place in one of Janet's patients:

Achille, a respectable family man of 33, returns from a short trip away from home, and behaves in a dour and preoccupied way, refusing to embrace or speak to his wife and daughter; then he takes to his bed, where he lies without movement, without eating, silent; next he reports seeing demons all around him; finally he is brought to the hospital, his face covered with blood from self-inflicted scratches, haggard and hardly able to walk, insisiting that he is himself possessed by a demon.

By questioning the alleged demon, Janet learns that while away from home the patient had permitted himself a momentary infidelity with another woman. This leads to remorse: he takes refuge in simple evasion, withdraws from his family, and becomes uncommunicative, as in many forms of hysteria.

Closed in on his thoughts, he starts to fear he may have contracted some disease: further evasion — he takes to his bed; here, his guilty conscience fosters the idea of punishment — hence the hallucinations of demons leading ultimately to the delusion that one of them has possessed him.

Once this is understood, Janet is able without too much difficulty to sort Achille's ideas out and restore his mental balance. (1911, p.408)

We can discern a similar process, occurring more subtly, in this 1897 case studied by Sidis and Goodhart:

While alighting from his carriage, the 24-year-old Reverend Thomas Carson Hanna falls head foremost to the ground and is rendered unconscious for some hours. When he comes to he is not only unable to speak, but even to understand; 'he was as a newly born infant opening his eyes for the first time upon the world.'

Over the ensuing months, under continual observation by doctors, he recovers his health but not his memory; 'like an infant, he did not know the meaning of the simplest words, nor did he understand the use of language.' He has to be painstakingly re-educated even in the most fundamental matters. However, this is not as laborious as was his original education, because 'although Mr Hanna was mentally blind and had lost all knowledge formerly possessed, although he was mentally reduced to a state of infancy, strange to say, his intelligence remained intact. His faculty of judgment, his power of reasoning were as sound and vigorous as ever.' As a result, he is soon able to communicate, and quickly regains a good working knowledge of the world.

In the course of this re-education, a new and totally different personality emerges. Hanna-2 is much more 'artistic' in his outlook: thus 'having had no familiarity with the banjo before the accident, he acquired the skill of playing it in but a few hours. A friend spent an afternoon teaching him, and was astonished at the remarkable aptitude of the pupil who in a few hours learned to handle the instrument with the facility of an experienced player . . . he showed the same remarkable aptitude in acquiring the technique of the piano.'

Eventually, Hanna comes to recognise that he possesses both these two personalities: 'I recognised that it was necessary to choose one or to take both . . . I decided to take both lives as mine, because of the fear and anxiety that the struggle would be repeated.' With some difficulty, the two personalities are ultimately combined to form a single healthy individual. (1904, pp.178–9)

The 'mechanics' of the case are fascinating, but it is not with them that we are presently concerned; what interests us here is the answer to a question which Sidis and Goodhart never once pose: *why* did Hanna go into this state?

After so many years, we can only speculate, and perhaps it will be thought that we do not even have the right to do that. Well, judge for yourself: here we have a young man of 24 who has been firmly brought up by his intensely religious father to follow in his footsteps as a preacher. During his amnesia, he takes on a new personality which, while by no means that of a wild debauchee, shows a distinct aversion for a religious career and a preference for the social life of New York. When Hanna-2 is taken to the theatre, his doctors comment : 'It was amusing as well as instructive to see the naturally austere and dignified young minister readily learning in his secondary state to applaud the 'highly' artistic, though somewhat ethically questionable, feats of the heel and toe.' (ibid., p.183).

Speaking for myself, I have no hesitation in diagnosing Hanna's fugue as an evasion; probably the fall itself was an accident (though I suppose we should consider the possibility that even this was subconsciously engineered), but I suggest that his subconscious self seized the opportunity to escape from his father's influence in this dramatic manner.

In the same way, Ansel Bourne's amnesia (#3.6) can be seen as a 'flight from reality', due to the conflict between, on the one hand, his wife's feeling that now he is into his sixties he should settle down and abandon his divine vocation as an itinerant preacher, and on the other, what he conceives to be God's wishes in the matter.

The otherself ASC : assertive, aggressive, goal-directed

The phenomenon of *pibloktoq* (#3.4) seems, superficially, to be an uncontrolled and meaningless outbreak. In the previous chapter we saw that it is far from being 'uncontrolled', and now, if we consider it within its social context, we can see that neither is it 'meaningless'. The Eskimos themselves seem to think that it is a way of getting something out of the system, a safety valve; and clearly this makes sense. Analysis might reveal what the 'something' is, but the fact that throwing off their clothes is generally part of the attack seems to be symbolic of a need for freedom. Women's liberation activists may interpret this as an expression of female frustration, and psychotherapist Robert Goldenson agrees:

> The basic reason why Eskimo women are subject to periods of brooding and anxiety appears to be their inferior status in society . . . The Eskimo wife is regarded as the property of her husband, and if he grows tired of her, all he has to do is to say 'There isn't room for you in my igloo', and she has to leave at once. This possibility hangs over her head all the time. But even during her normal, day-to-day life with her husband she is starved for love and affection and is likely to be subjected to constant abuse. She does not lack sexual satisfaction, or at least sexual activity, but her need for tenderness is rarely fulfilled and she lives in constant fear of being beaten . . . the sudden urge to run away is the culmination of a smouldering desire for release from servitude. It may also be a bid for sympathy and attention, for she undoubtedly wants to be caught and showered with sympathy and understanding. (1973, p.231)

It seems clear that *pibloktoq* is the result of several triggers working together — the physiological factor of defective diet, the environmental factor of the long polar night, and the psychological one of personal frustration. We have seen many of the characteristic behaviours in other ASCs: discarding clothes occurs time and time again, and evidently this exhibitionism is symbolic, as is the running away which is characteristic of somnambulism, amnesia and many other ASCs. We must therefore see *pibloktoq* as an ASC whose pattern is determined by local cultural factors, but which is fundamentally similar to many other varieties.

Such a view is supported when we find other ASCs which seem to be specific to a particular culture. *Látah* is a state which seems to be peculiar to the Malay race, in whom it is triggered when something startles them:

> They will then imitate actions which are painful, dangerous, or obscene. The Malays are a race particular to a fault about all matters of personal modesty; but a *látah* Malay woman will strip naked in a public place at the casual invitation of a passing stranger. (Bramwell, 1903, p.356)

Even if it were a fact that Malaysians, and Malaysians alone, possess an element in their DNA structure which makes them prone to such aberrant behviour, we would still question that this element could dictate the precise *form* of the outbreak. Once again, conformity is surely at work: a Malay knows from watching others how a *látah* person customarily acts, and when he becomes *látah* himself, he acts in that way. In short, he is *playing the role* of a *látah* person.

It is this compliance with a local stereotype which is the distinctive feature of these 'cultural' ASCs; in every other respect they resemble universal behaviours. Many of the resemblances are very striking. For instance, the *pibloktoq* victim's resentment at interference is matched by the Cornish Jumper's resistance when attempts are made to restrain her. The remorseless continuance until convulsions lead to collapse is matched at voodoo dances and religious revivals. Both the hyperactivity and the indifference to cold and pain are matched by possessed nuns in sixteenth century Catholic convents . . . and so on.

Beneath all these experiences we can trace a common pattern of depersonalisation — individuals cease to be their ordinary selves — and role-playing — they identify themselves with a culturally accepted stereotype. Their behaviour reflects a universal need, which is satisfied in pretty much the same kind of way, whether by frustrated Eskimo wife or frustrated Haitian shopgirl, by frustrated Cornish teenager or frustrated Flemish nun.

The 'need-based encounter'

On the face of it, ASCs which involve visionary encounters with otherworldly beings seem to fall into a quite different class. But if we go deeper, we find grounds for thinking that these experiences, too, are brought about by the individual's subconscious self, to enable him or her to resolve a personal crisis or satisfy a need (Evans, 1987).

If we study the people who have these experiences, we will invariably find such a need — but that is hardly surprising, for there is not one of us who does not have problems that are hard to solve, needs that we cannot satisfy. So it becomes a matter of examining why, for these people, the solution should take this particular form.

The answer probably relates to the kind of personality trait we considered in #2 when we answered 'Yes' to the question, Are some people ASC-prone? For some such people, an encounter experience may represent the best way out of their situation. Perhaps, in many cases, only psychiatric examination would establish why this should be so, but we have some general indications. For example, it cannot be just coincidence that Bernadette of Lourdes, the visionaries of la Salette, of Fatima, of Beauraing, of Garabandal, of Medjugorje, and many, many others, all come from one particular section of the community— adolescent children, predominantly girls, predominantly in peasant communities. Often they are poor, living close to the subsistence level, with future prospects no less bleak than their present circumstances.

Equally, it is significant that the visionary entity is invariably an authority figure — in western Europe, more often than not the Virgin Mary. To an underprivileged peasant girl, the visionary experience comes as the resolution of a kind of 'identity crisis' — look, here's Mary, come from heaven to assure Bernadette that she, too, is 'somebody' and has a place in the scheme of things. It is the same function as is effected when a voodoo dancer is possessed by a deity or an ecstatic is given a glimpse of heaven.

A second start

Of all the consequences of ASCs, by far the most dramatic are those which mark a turning-point in the individual's life — which incorporate an experience so overwhelming that he is never the same again. Significantly, Starbuck, in his classic study of religious conversion (1901), asks us to think of it as *'a process of unselfing'* (p.127). Here is a typical account from his study:

> A year before my conversion I had been to the altar, but felt no better; I wasn't ready to become a Christian. The following year, during revivals, I felt more in earnest than ever before. I went to the altar two nights in succession; I went in spite of my friends. A friend came and spoke to me, and it came over me like a flash of lightning that I was saved. (p.106)

Starbuck compares two attitudes towards such an experience: on the one hand, that of the alienist, who 'thinks in terms of psychiatry. He casts his pathological net, and anything sufficiently exaggerated above commonplaceness so that it cannot slip through the meshes he claims as his'; and on the other, that of the religionist who 'sees whatever happens in connection with the nominally religious as a divine manifestation. No excesses of excitement, no diseased imaginings, provided they have the cloak of religion, are too extreme to be regarded as normal and healthy' (p.164).

We, like Starbuck, see the need to steer a course between these two extremes, and to see the conversion-ASC as neither pathological nor, necessarily, quite as religious as it may appear. Most cases of conversion, despite their outwardly religious character, are probably best seen as a phase in the individual's personal development, religious only in the loosest sense; the specific trappings are incidental, the result of cultural conditioning.

Religious conversion provides us with a vivid example of how our interpretation of ASCs may be coloured by our cultural approach. The religious leaders who encourage it believe that it is a gift of divine grace, and consequently they see the process as a sudden rapture, in which the individual is swept off his feet by an overwhelming force. Wesley, adopting a more scientific attitude than we might expect of an eighteenth century revivalist, carried out a check on some of his re-born souls:

> In London alone I found 652 members of our Society [Methodists] who were exceedingly clear in their experience, and whose testimony I could see no reason to doubt. Every one of these (without a single exception) has declared that his deliverance from sin was instantaneous; that the change was wrought in a moment . . . I cannot but believe that sanctification is commonly, if not always, an instantaneous work. (in James, 1902, p.227)

But though religious conversion may *appear* to be a sudden blinding illumination, it is in fact the culmination of a subconscious process which may have been germinating for a long while. Starbuck's convert evidently underwent a period of 'courtship' before the 'flash of lightning' struck.

Although to be 'born again' has become something of an institutionalised ritual in some religious communities — notably the fundamentalist churches of the United States — it can also occur in an individual, subjective context. I have already suggested that something of this sort may have been true of Hanna's remarkable experience, and thanks to her visionary encounter Bernadette, from being a nobody, became a focus of attention, human as well as divine, and went on to achieve sainthood. This kind of experience can take many forms: those who encounter UFO occupants frequently proceed to have dramatic changes in their life-style; the Lives of the Saints are rich in pious stories of 'miraculous' conversions.

At the other extreme are those community practices in which re-birth is an essential rite of passage in personal development. All peoples to some extent mark the passage from childhood to adulthood, but while in highly-developed cultures only the shadow of the old rituals remains in primitive societies the initiation ceremonies continue to be practised and are given their force by a combination of ASC-inducing triggers — isolation, terror, drugs, pain, sensory overload, exhaustion, etc. — so that candidates for initiation are convinced that they have, in a literal sense, been born afresh.

Similarly, among the myths that accompany shamanism, a recurrent feature is the ritual dismemberment of the apprentice; the Yakut people of Siberia believe that

> the evil spirits carry the future shaman's soul to the underworld. Here he undergoes his initiation. The spirits cut off his head, which they set aside (for the candidate must watch his dismemberment with his own eyes), and cut him into small pieces, which are then distributed to the spirits of the various diseases. Only by undergoing such an ordeal will he gain the power to cure. His bones are then covered with new flesh, and in some cases he is also given new blood (Eliade, 1964 p.36)

Here we have, in explicit form, a symbolic account of the process of re-birth whereby an individual can re-fashion his life — a vivid example of the ASC as purposeful process.

The near-death experience : a special case?

Anecdotes telling what people experience on the threshold of death are among our oldest legends, and they are supplemented by the teachings of 'books of the dead' from cultures as far apart as Egypt and Tibet.

So long as people died at home or at any rate privately, these experiences remained little more than folklore, but as more and more people came to hospital to die, doctors and nurses found themselves confronted by claims, some made by patients who come close to death and others by those who watch people dying, of remarkable experiences at the threshold of death. It was clear that these were not rare one-of-a-kind anecdotes, but frequent and consistent features of the near-death state.

Eventually, more or less methodical studies of them were made, and their findings have been made public in a spate of more or less responsible books. Though not every researcher has interpreted the material in the same way, all confirm a pattern of experience so widespread as to cross all personal or cultural frontiers: it seems that anyone who comes close to death may undergo a visionary experience.

The evidence for these experiences is drawn either from the first-hand testimony of near-death experiences (NDEs) of people who did *not* die, or from second-hand reports of deathbed experiences (DBEs) of people who *did* die. There is no confirming evidence beyond what is contained within the stories: all the evidence is subjective, anecdotal and circumstantial.

A person who is, or seems to be, at the point of death, may have one or more of the following experiences, commonly but not necessarily in this order. Some may be experienced only by those who are actually dying, others only by people who are *not* dying:

* While still clinically alive they may be greeted by dead relatives or friends, who seem to be helping them to make the transition from this world to the next. Frequently the group of 'dead' includes persons they had no means of knowing to be dead, but who are found — by subsequent checking — to have indeed been dead at the time of the experience.

* They have the impression of leaving their body, which they may observe with some detachment as though it is no longer of great concern to them, but correctly noting details — for instance, regarding a surgical operation being carried out on the body — which could not be perceived from where the physical body is.

* They seem to travel down a tunnel and emerge into a non-earthly environment.

* They experience a 'life review' in which the whole or part of their life is visually recalled, rapidly yet often in meticulous detail, sometimes with detachment but frequently with the appropriate emotions.

* They have a glimpse of life in some non-earthly environment, usually pleasant but occasionally unpleasant, which may take the form of an ordinary human house in which their dead relatives are living; or a delightful garden, fields or meadows; or a gleaming city with spires and towers.

* In the case of people who return from death, they may
  have a moment in which they are rejected and forced
  to return to their earthly body; or they themselves may
  be asked to make the decision whether to remain or
  return; but either way they find themselves either
  rapidly returning to their body or actually back inside
  it with no recollection of the return. (If there are cases
  of a person choosing to remain and being allowed to
  do so, we do not know of them.)

* A number of physical sensations are consistently
  reported. Those who seem to leave their bodies report
  a 'click' as they return; some report a feeling of being
  connected to their bodies with a 'cord'; and so on.

Two factors in particular encourage us to believe that these
experiences are 'real': their almost universal overall similarity; and the evidential quality of the information, ostensibly
acquired paranormally, offered on the one hand by ND
subjects who report 'out-of-body' perceptions of things
they could not perceive in any normal manner; and on the
other by DB subjects who recognise people 'on the other
side' who, though in fact dead, are not at that time known
to be so either to the dying person or those with him.

The evidence for this 'paranormal' acquisition of
knowledge consists of a great mass of anecdotes which can
only sometimes, and not always completely, be confirmed.
Nevertheless, their quantity and quality is so overwhelming that I do not think it can reasonably be rejected, and I do
not propose to do so.

But it does not necessarily follow that the information is
supplied by the dead or by otherworldly beings: ESP of
some sort remains a viable alternative.

One obstacle to understanding these phenomena is the
assumption that the deathbed experiences (DBEs) of the
dying are related to the near-death experiences (NDEs) of
those who survive. Thus it is often supposed that the NDE
is the initial phase of the DBE, and would develop into one
if allowed to run its course.

Maybe so; but since we do not know whether the
prospect facing the individual is imminent extinction or

the commencement of a new and incorporeal mode of existence, we must consider the NDE not as an impending DBE, but as a distinct experience in its own right which should not necessarily be taken at face value.

We then see that the NDE embodies many elements which bear a different kind of interpretation:

★ Part of the NDE is pure fantasy. The visions of the next world, with its beautiful gardens and gleaming cities, embody a blend of personal beliefs and cultural imagery. Even if we are tempted to believe that some witnesses are vouchsafed a glimpse of the next world, the fact that each account differs from every other should make us hesitate to accept them at face value.

It has been suggested that the dying person is shown the heaven he expects to see in order to ease the shock of dying. Even if this is so, that does not alter the fact that a subjective fantasy is involved, whose elements derive from the person's own mind.

★ A feature which recurs so frequently that it has become a virtual symbol for the NDE is the feeling of travelling through a tunnel of light, which is seen as symbolising the journey from this world to the next. This image is depicted in works of art from the Middle Ages onwards, so it does indeed seem to represent something profound and universal.

However, it is *not* exclusive to the near-death situation. The same image recurs, just as regularly, in a very different experience: extraterrestrial abduction. Time and time again, abductees will describe being drawn up into the spacecraft through a gleaming tube or tunnel, describing their experience in terms which echo those of the NDE witness. So here, too, we find not objective fact but subjective fantasy.

★ Another recurrent feature of the NDE is the 'life review'. This is often equated with the 'day of judgement' of religious teaching, but in fact one of the features which emerges from the accounts is that *no* judgement takes place: the individual sees his past life, good deeds and bad, but is neither praised for the

one nor blamed for the other. True, he will often feel
remorse or regret for things he did or did not do, and
may wish he had his time over again to put them right,
but very rarely is any serious blame laid on him.

Instead, it is more in the nature of an amnesty than a
judgement; the individual is relieved of any intolerable
burden or guilt, though made to feel that he ought to
have done better. Again, it is a very *subjective* process.

★ People who return to life from the threshold of death
  are, understandably, very impressed by what has
  happened to them: almost all report a dramatic change
  in their outlook on life and death, their values and so
  on.

Fantasy heaven — symbolic re-birth — past life review —
new life-style: these elements *can* be seen as part of a real
visionary experience granted to persons who come close to
death. But I suggest they make far better sense if seen in a
context of *life*, not death. I suggest that, as in the case of the
Revd Hanna's fall, the subconscious self takes advantage of
the fact that the individual is in an eminently suggestible
state of mind, and by involving him in an appropriate
dramatic experience, gives him the chance to rethink his life
situation and make a second start. In short, the NDE is a
specific form of ASC, characterised — like so many other
ASC experiences — by a powerful and purposeful hallucinatory fantasy fabricated by the subject's own subconscious
self.

7   Reaping the benefits

Alberto Denti de Pirajno, an Italian doctor working in Tripoli, tells of the cure by a native healer of 'a girl suffering from what I suppose we would call extreme melancholia' but which was believed by the Arabs to be caused by 'some dark and evil spirit':

About seventy women were crouching in a wide circle, in the middle of which was a tub full of water. A voice was chanting, the women swayed to the rhythm of the drums, a continual murmur of prayers rose and at times swelled into groans and cries. This hellish din had continued for an hour or so when suddenly a girl sprang to her feet in a corner of the courtyard. Her eyes were open wide in an expression of stark tragedy. She stepped quickly over the women in front of her, flung herself into the open space and began to throw herself about in the most savage manner, stamping her feet, jerking her shoulders, agitating her arms and shaking her head violently. Gasping and panting, she took great leaps into the air; she drew her head into her shoulders, thrust it forward and then flung it back with such force that it seemed she must dislocate her neck. She progressively dispensed with her outer garment, bodice and trousers, and was now covered only in her shift, tied at the hip with a coloured scarf.

These contortions continued for an hour; the girl became soaking wet; her shift clung to her body, her hair stuck to her face and a stream of foam and sweat ran down from the corners of her mouth. Suddenly she stopped in front of the *faqih* and fixed her eyes on him, wrinkling her forehead as if trying to remember something. Then, with a piercing shriek, she flung herself on to the ground, writhing and twisting on her stomach. At this point two powerful negresses picked her up, removed the last remnants of the tattered shift which hung from her shoulders, carried her to the tub and plunged her repeatedly into the water. When I saw her again, she was wrapped in a blanket and her expression was completely altered. She smiled ecstatically and cast her eyes heaven-wards. (1956, p.45)

Here we have an ASC being put to a very practical use, doing deliberately and under social control what others achieve individually in *pibloktoq*, *látah* and suchlike states. We have seen enough of ASCs by now to realise that, by setting the individual free of the limits — or what he thinks are the limits – of his everyday self, they enable him to perform or function in ways which surpass his 'real' capability, or modify or transcend his 'real' personality.

Neither of these processes is, in itself, good or bad; each can lead to beneficial or to harmful consequences. In this chapter we consider some possible benefits, in the next, possible drawbacks.

7.1 Practical benefits

Useful suggestions

In an ASC, a person is markedly more suggestible than in the USC, and this can be exploited in various helpful ways — to help people give up smoking, overcome their fear of flying, and so on. A very practical application was used by Dr August Forel, of Switzerland. It was the practice in his hospital for night-nurses to watch over dangerous patients throughout the night, a tedious but necessary task. Forel would programme a nurse by post-hypnotic suggestion to sleep unless he was needed: 'I told him he would hear absolutely nothing of the greatest noise and knocking of the maniacal patients, but would sleep on quietly; but, on the other hand, he would awaken at once if a patient did anything unusual or dangerous' (1906, p.94). This worked successfully over a ten-year period, and we are led to wonder why the technique has not been used for other such applications such as night watchmen, security guards, etc? Maybe it is only in the milieu of a hospital that suitably willing subjects are to be found?

Problem solving

Many ASCs suggest that, when necessary, time can be overridden. We have evidence of this every night, in our dreams where epic sagas occur in a matter of seconds. The same is true of many hallucination experiences, in which the subject is taken on interplanetary voyages by friendly occupants of UFOs. True, in these cases the high speeds are often attributed to the superior technology of the spacecraft itself; but that does not explain how visitors are able to enjoy tours of alien planets in less time than they would spend on a High Street shopping expedition. Some visionary encounters also defy normal time limits; for instance, the Skilton case (#2.5). Madden (1857) reports this case:

> The celebrated Robert Hall was temporarily afflicted with mania. On his recovery he observed to a friend, 'You tell me I was only seven weeks in confinement, and the date of the year corresponds, so I am bound to believe you; but they have appeared to me like seven years. My mind was so excited, and my imagination so lively and acute, that more ideas passed through my mind during those seven weeks than in any seven years of my life.' (p.34)

American researcher Linn Cooper has shown that hypnotic subjects can put time distortion to practical use. In one experiment, he trained a subject to experience ten seconds as ten minutes, then asked her to sort out the difficult situation of a young couple whose wish to marry was complicated by the fact that the girl had an invalid mother, saying he would give her ten minutes to prepare her suggestions. After ten *seconds* of real time

> the subject reported that she saw and talked to a young man and a girl about their problem. She discussed the matter at length with them, asking the girl various questions and receiving answers. She suggested that the girl work after marriage in order to support her mother who, she felt, should not live with the young couple but rather with some friend her own age . . . etc.
> Her account was amazing in the fullness of detail and the

amount of reflection it apparently indicated. This was especially surprising in view of the fact that in waking life the subject is not prone to speculate on such matters. When told she had thought the problems through, not in ten minutes, but in ten seconds, she was astonished. (Estabrooks and Gross, 1961, p.112)

What is also noteworthy about this experiment is that the problem is worked out, not as an abstract problem, but as a real-life situation involving actual people — further evidence of the fondness of the subconscious self for casting all concerned in dramatic roles.

Enhanced physical abilities

In Newcastle, England, 15-year-old Michael Little saw a 140 kg gatepost fall on 3-year-old Susan Brown. He gave a mighty heave and single-handedly freed the girl. After she was driven to the hospital in an ambulance the slimly built boy tried to move the post to clear the path across which it had fallen. He was unable to budge it and had to call on two men for help. (*Fate*, May 1961, p.37)

Stories of temporarily increased physical powers are reported sufficiently often to show that in emergency many of us are able to call on reserves of strength we did not know we possessed.

Such feats also occur almost casually in other cases; thus while Skilton is experiencing his vision (# 2.5) he not only carries on with his work, but astonishes his workmates by lifting goods 'with the strength of a giant'. On the face of it, this performance seems to have been only incidental to his visionary experience; however, without it, it is unlikely that he would have been able to have the experience, for if he had not been able to do all the work by himself, interaction with his workmates would surely have brought him back to reality. So it looks rather as though this was part of the arrangements made by his subconscious self or whoever planned his experience.

Clearly there is no way we can test what state a person is in when he is in the process of rescuing a child from under a car or whatever; it is only from his subsequent description that we infer he must have been in an ASC. We are encouraged in this supposition by the many experiments which have been carried out, in which enhanced physical powers have been caused by hypnotic suggestion — improved vision, body-temperature control, blood-flow control, pain control, and many more. (Corliss, 1982, cites several cases.) Esdaile was able to perform hundreds of surgical operations by putting his Indian patients under hypnosis. The advantage of such a method, as against drugs with their high cost and uncertain side effects, is overwhelming, but doctors have generally resisted it, not altogether unreasonably, on account of its subjective nature which renders it out of their control.

The ability of someone in an ASC to obtain control over his autonomic nervous system is favoured by those religious systems which seek to develop the spirit by subjugating the body. But the feats achieved by yogis are surpassed by what must be the most remarkable demonstration ever recorded of physical feats surpassing normal limits in the ASC — those of the 'convulsionaries' of Saint Médard.

In eighteenth century Paris a bitter dispute arose between orthodox catholics and the partisans of the Jansenist 'heresy'; in 1727 there occurred the death of François de Paris, a deacon renowned for his ascetism and his good works, and a fervent Jansenist. Almost at once, his tomb in the churchyard of Saint Médard became a focus of pilgrimage for supporters of Jansenism, and before long, rumours began to circulate that miraculous cures and conversions were taking place in the churchyard; this attracted growing crowds of curious visitors, leading to yet greater wonders.

There seems no reason why we should question the truth of the reports, which were attested to by both Jansenists and catholics, though the former saw them as divine favours, the latter as diabolical tricks. Neither explanation satisfied the doctors who added the weight of their testimony — testimony which was the more valuable because often they had known the people concerned *before* their cures. Even though we may suspect that many of the 'cures' were superficial and short-lived, and that those which were effective were those which occurred to people suffering from nervous ailments of psychological origin, none the less the fact remains that the Deacon's tomb provided the trigger.

But even more extraordinary than the cures were the physical feats of the convulsionaries, which developed from the attacks which frequently preceded the miraculous cures and conversions. An observer who was involved at first hand, Carré de Montgeron (quoted in Calmeil, 1845, vol.2, pp.313ff.), has given us much relevant data, including this significant observation:

> Amongst the number of persons suddenly afflicted with convulsions were some very respectable persons, but it must be allowed that in general God has chosen the convulsionaries from the common people; that young children, principally girls, composed the greater part; that most of them up to that time had lived in ignorance and obscurity, that many were deformed by nature, and that there were many among them who, outside their supernatural state, appeared no better than fools.

— which sounds a familiar note. There is much in common between *pibloktoq* and other such states and, say, the experience of Mlle Fourcroy, who had previously visited the tomb but come away for fear of being overtaken by convulsions:

> On 20 March 1732, finding myself so ill as to consider I was at the point of rendering up my soul, the fear of death which I thought was so near prevailed over the fear of convulsions, and I begged them to bring me some of the earth from the tomb. On the 21st, at midnight, they made me take some wine, into which they had put some of the earth. Almost at the same moment I experienced a great shivering, and soon after a violent agitation in all my members, which caused me to fling my body up into the air, and which gave me a strength I had never before felt; so much so, that several persons together could with great difficulty hold me. In the course of these violent movements, which were truly convulsions, I lost all recollection. As soon as they were over and I had recovered my senses, I felt a tranquility and an interior peace that I had never before experienced, and which it would be exceedingly difficult to explain, though I have since then very frequently felt it after my convulsive fits.

That account is echoed over and over again by others, and can be taken as typical; yet hardly less frequent were the more extreme displays which make Mlle Fourcroy's experience seem mild:

> One convulsionary lay extended on her bed while two men held a cloth stretched behind her back, with which they raised her up and threw her forward 2400 times violently, while two other persons, placed in front, thrust her back no less violently upon the mattress . . .

> Gabrielle, a girl of 12 or 13, lying on her back on the floor, placed the blade of a shovel on her throat, just below the trachea artery, and insisted that one of those present should push down with all his strength against her throat; no matter how hard he pushed, she received nothing but a pleasant and soothing sensation, which made her ask for the operation to be repeated over and over again. Later, her chest and stomach were pounded with a rock weighing more than 20 kg, until those who gave her the relief were out of breath and exhausted.

> Jeanne Mouler insisted upon their administering to her a hundred blows on the stomach with an iron. Though Montgeron, who was administering the blows, did so with such violence as to make a breach in the wall; 'the convulsionary complained that the blows I was giving her were so slight that they did not bring her any relief, and she forced me to hand the iron to a large strong man who in no way spared her. Having seen that he could not administer too violent blows, he beat her in so frightful a manner, always in the hollow of the stomach, that they shook the wall against which she was leaning.

> 'A physician, hearing an account of these things, maintained that they could not be true, as according to him it was physically impossible. He objected, amongst other things, that the flexibility and the softness of the skin and flesh are incompatible with a force and resistance so extraordinary. . . In the end, for reply, they said to him, Come and verify the facts. He hastened to do so, and at the first sight was struck with astonishment. They put into his hands the iron instruments; he spared nothing, he beat with the greatest violence, he thrust into the flesh the instrument with which he was armed, penetrating far beyond the surface. . . . Notwithstanding which, the convulsionary laughed at his efforts; all the blows which he gave her only served to do her good, without leaving the slightest impression, the least trace, not only in the flesh, but even on the skin itself.'

We know that entertainers can train themselves, by years of practice, to perform such feats; but most of these convulsionaries were young girls, whose bodies, even the hardiest of them, could not have been 'prepared' for such ordeals, even if the will to carry out such deception were there.

The force which gave them this strength can only have been of mental origin, inspired by faith, nourished by example, fed by suggestion. How we classify their state is a problem which we do not have sufficient data to resolve; though many of the accounts refer to blackouts and amnesia, there are many — such as the last quoted — in which the 'victim' seems to have been fully conscious, and herself to have directed the operation. So though we need not doubt that she was in an ASC of some sort, it does not seem to have been one involving depersonalisation; if it resembles any other state, it is ecstasy. But it seems a long way from the pandemonium of Saint Médard to the quiet cell of Saint Teresa.

Not every 'convulsionary' went into convulsions. For some, the state was a profound contemplation, in which they would stare with wide-open eyes as if at some far-off vision. Some would maintain a death-like state for two or three days on end, lying with eyes open but giving no sign of life but a faint breathing; even though pricked in a cruel manner, they felt nothing.

The French doctor Calmeil, in his classic book on madness, says of one convulsionary: 'We find united in this pious woman, whose conduct had hitherto been irreproachable, indications of hysteria, of ecstasy, of nymphomania, of religious mania, and even some aspects of demonopathy.' As a clinical diagnosis that may well be valid, but it makes no attempt to face the paradox presented by the convulsionaries. A label is not an explanation. If we are to explain the experiences of the convulsionaries, we must face the paradox of the physical aspects of those experiences, aspects which were testified to by all observers, whether sympathetic, neutral or hostile.

Only two options are available to us. We may accept that some kind of supernatural forces were involved, enabling the convulsionaries to override the normal limits of physiological ability. Or, if we refuse to accept the intervention of the supernatural, we must accept that those supposed limits are not limits at all. Rather, just as in some ASCs we can step out of the restrictions of time, just as we can perform mental feats of calculation and creativity which are beyond our normal powers, so in some ASCs we can transcend, to a degree unrecognised by medicine, the normal physiological limits of what the human body is capable of doing and bearing.

We know from Esdaile's surgery under hypnosis, and from phenomena such as hysterical anaesthesia, that this is so. But the phenomena of the convulsionaries go beyond suspension of sense, and seem to involve modifications to body tissue, presumably at the bidding of the subconscious self. The implications are staggering, to say the least.

Memories, true and false

One way to help a person to resolve a personal problem is to get him to come to terms with whatever caused it. But often he has locked it away in the subconscious, deliberately hiding it from himself and throwing away the key. When Janet and his fellow doctors discovered that hypnosis offered a way of getting into the hiding place by a back entry, it was a major advance in psychotherapy.

For a while, it seemed that memories thus dredged from the subconscious, by hypnosis, 'truth' drugs and other means, were a sure way of getting at the truth. Only gradually was it realised that, in the favouring circumstances of hypnosis when the subject is abnormally suggestible, *paramnesia* may be occurring, and that what is offered as memory may be pseudo-memory. The conscious mind of the individual may sincerely believe he is recalling what actually happened, but in fact his subconscious mind is serving up a cunning blend of fact with fiction. The German psychologist Moll gives a simple example:

> I say to a subject, 'You remember that we went to Potsdam yesterday, and took a drive on the Havel?' The suggestion takes effect, and the gentleman at once begins to relate his experience in Potsdam. This is a retroactive positive hallucination. (1890, p.130)

Just as in any other ASC, the subconscious producer is using his creative powers to concoct a fantasy made up of role-playing and hallucination, which may be expressing significant wishes and fears, or may simply be created to oblige the hypnotist.

Fiction and fantasy can, of course, tell a doctor almost as much as does the truth; they are, no less than the truth, a guide to the contents of the patient's mind. But there are still many who are reluctant to settle for anything less than exact recall, for the reason that it is, at least in principle, a realisable aim.

The best-known application of this technique is, of course, in the currently fashionable early-life and previous-life recall.

That under hypnosis a person can recall submerged or suppressed details of his early life is well established:

> Janet: I suggest to Rose [under hypnosis] that we are no longer in 1888, but in April 1886, simply to establish what changes may have occurred in her personality. But a strange thing happens: she groans, she complains she's tired, she can't walk: — Why, what's the matter with you? — Oh, nothing, but in my condition. . . — What condition? She replies with her gesture, her belly has suddenly swollen and is held so by a hysteric access: without realising it, I have regressed her to a period when she was pregnant. (1889, p.160)

But subsequent experience has shown that not everything recalled in this way can be taken at face value: Martin Orne, professor of psychiatry and psychology at Pennsylvania University, was able to test the accuracy of ostensible age regression:

> I did the first study of this type back in 1951. For the first time, we actually got the drawings somebody did when he was six years old, which he hadn't seen since then. His father had saved everything the little boy did as he grew up: he had some drawings in the attic that his son had done at age six. So we age-regressed the individual. We asked him to draw a house, a tree, a man, and so forth. His drawings looked great. It seemed as if he actually relived it. Two weeks later we repeated it. He gave us a somewhat different drawing, but again it looked like a child's work. And then when we

compared it to the real thing, it became clear that it was totally different. If you didn't have the real thing, it would have looked as if it were an actual recollection and reliving. (1988, p.276)

What is true of early-life recall is presumably no less true of previous-life recall, though proving it is more difficult. Early in the twentieth century, Albert de Rochas alerted fellow researchers to the trap of pseudo past-life recall; but thousands in our own time are walking into the same trap, believing that when the subconscious mind purports to be offering memories of the past, it is doing precisely that.

I know of no case where evidence as good as Orne's childhood drawings is available: most recalled past lives contain little verifiable data. Either the information is too vague to be checked, or it is something the individual might be expected to know anyway. From time to time, however, specific but obscure names and dates are mentioned, and then it can be possible to check them:

Jane Evans, through regression hypnosis with Arnold Bloxham, claimed a past life as Livonia, living in second-century Roman Britain. Her account was rich in authentic-seeming detail. However, researcher Melvin Harris (1986) was able to demonstrate that her material came not from historical fact, but from historical fiction, which Jane must have read, forgetting it consciously but storing the details in her subconscious, whence they were retrieved by hypnotic recall. The characters and incidents she recalled were taken from the book, which was only loosely set in the context of the historical period.

By now, a sufficient number of such pseudo-memories have been exposed to convince all but the most determinedly gullible that we should at least be very cautious before accepting previous-life recall at face value.

Though it may not be much consolation for learning that we were not, after all, a Priestess of Atlantis in an earlier incarnation, the discovery that previous-life recall may not be what it seems is valuable as a further indication of the creative and improvisatory powers of our subconscious self. Jane Evans' life in Roman Britain, like Hélène Smith's invention of a Martian language, helps us to appreciate the hidden resources of our minds.

Recall of 'lost' memory is an ability which is not exclusive to hypnosis; it is also found in spontaneous ASCs, as is shown by this experience reported by Janet:

> Marguerite is a young girl of 23 who has been at the Salpêtrière hospital for more than a year and, in consequence, knows us all pretty well. She's had a number of hysterical attacks, and presents a good number of classic hysterical symptoms — more or less complete anaesthesia of the right side, muscular anaesthesia which prevents her moving her right arm unless she can see it, restricted field of vision, etc.
>
> Well, I said to her quite simply, 'Good morning, Margot.' She gave a little shiver and her expression changed. Since she was looking at me with astonishment, I asked what was upsetting her? — But I don't know you, Monsieur. — Why, you came to see me this morning. — No I didn't, this morning I was in class, doing my assignment. Surprised by this reply, I examined her more closely, and found she had quite forgotten the Salpêtrière, her illness, everything she'd done these past years, whereas she recalled her childhood in remarkable detail. Moreover, I found she had lost every one of her hysterical symptoms; she cried out when I pinched her right arm (normally paralysed), her field of vision was normal, and so on. What had happened? All was explained when I asked her how old she was? — I'm eight. 'Margot' was the name she'd been given at school when she was eight: my calling her by that name reawakened the whole store of memories, images and even feelings associated with it. (1911, p.204)

Besides giving us a vivid example of the suggestibility of the hysteric, this example demonstrates that *true* knowledge of the past does indeed exist, latent, within us, and can be recalled in other ASCs besides hypnosis. Well, of course we know that from our dreams; but our dreams also tell us that in none of these approaches can we be sure of obtaining the uncontaminated truth. Any state may reveal, interwoven with the true memories, the creative handiwork of the subconscious producer.

However, this leaves unanswered the question: *why* does the subconscious self create false memories? I don't think there is a single answer to this. I suspect it depends on individual circumstances. But what may be *part* of the answer is suggested by one of Sargant's discoveries when dealing with wartime mental casualties:

It was found that a patient could sometimes be restored to mental health not by his re-living a particular traumatic experience, but by stirring up in him, and helping him to discharge strong emotions not directly concerned with it. Thus, in some of the acute Normandy battle-neuroses, and those caused by V-bomb explosions, quite imaginary situations to abreact the emotions of fear or anger could be suggested to a patient under drugs; though as a rule these were in some way related to the experiences which he had undergone. *Much better results could often, indeed, be obtained by stirring up emotions about such imaginary happenings than by making the patient re-live actual happenings in detail.* (1957, p.xxi)

I have added emphasis to Sargant's words because of their potential value for our study; for they suggest that our subconscious self may be doing just the same thing — creating imaginary stories because they best suit his purpose. Just as seeing the Virgin was appropriate to Bernadette's situation, just as to make a fresh start with a new personality suited the Revd Hanna, so our previous-life fantasies and near-death visions may be scripted specifically to help us.

Sargant's approach is essentially pragmatic. He has a job to do, to get his wartime casualties back on an even keel after their shattering experience, and he uses whatever means prove effective. If pseudo-recall of false memories can initiate the release of the requisite chemicals into the system and thus restore his patient to mental balance, well and good. But we have reason to suspect that our subconscious self has a higher purpose in mind.

Enhanced mental abilites
ASC subjects may display enhanced mental powers of many kinds.

Calculating and estimating time
In 1922 Sydney Hooper carried out a series of experiments to test the appreciation of time under hypnosis. In one experiment, his subject (in her waking state, while working at her office) correctly drew a cross 2280 minutes after the suggestion had been made to her in the hypnotic state.

She explained (under hypnosis) that she had done it by 'counting until I had nothing left', working in one-second intervals. Hooper remarks on 'the unruffled patience of the subliminal level of the mind, which went on rhythmically counting 136,800 seconds without complaint or even boredom, showing a persistency of purpose worthy of a greater cause.' He concludes that though 'there is nothing in the experiments to suggest that the achievements were performed by any other powers than those which belong to the domain of the human mind', nevertheless such a feat 'reveals a supernormal faculty of measuring the passage of time'.

Musical composition

Rosemary Brown is only the most recent of a succession of people who, when in ASC, reveal a talent for composing music which far transcends their waking ability, which may be negligible. In Brown's case, she attributes the inspiration to the spirits of Liszt, Chopin and other dead composers, who dictate their new compositions to her. Though we are not here concerned with whether or not this is so, we should note that others have produced remarkable compositions *without* invoking the spirits. Whatever the origin of the material, it seems that the individual needs to be in some kind of ASC to be in the appropriate mood to receive it.

Mathematical calculation

In his fine study of mental calculators, Steven Smith presents many testimonies to the effect that their astonishing skills are in fact within the reach of all of us, the difference being basically one of *motivation*.

It is evident that the calculations are not carried out in the usual manner as taught in the classroom; nevertheless, they are carried out *logically*. There is nothing paranormal about them: though they are intuitive they are none the less intellectual. Manifestly, a mind is involved, and it would seem to be a mind other than the everyday conscious mind, or that mind in something other than the everyday conscious state.

I incline to think, therefore, that to perform these remarkable calculation feats the subject needs to be in a kind of ASC. In support of this view is what was said to Smith by the Indian Shyam Marathe (born 1931), who works for an insurance company:

When I concentrate and I do the work, I always have a feeling that I am having a different existence than what I have normally. It is a different state of my being, and I enjoy those moments. . . I become completely cut off from the rest of the things around me when I concentrate. . . I feel that someone in me, different from my usual self, is calculating, and I also feel that he is dependable. . . It would be a very bold statement to say that a different personality was at work there. I'm not that much different from the inner self which concentrates, but at the same time, there is a slight feeling that . . . it is some inner strength which is coming out and doing that work like an automatic process. (Smith, 1983, p.320, 326)

Marathe's comments are a valuable insight into the state of mind of someone as he deploys these unusual powers. Is what he does in a more or less conscious state the same as, say, we saw Gurney's subject doing in #5.2 under hypnosis? And if so, is Marathe employing a form of auto-hypnosis? Or is there such a thing as *direct* access to these subconscious powers?

Enhanced psychic abilities

The convulsionaries of Saint Médard (#7) and the possessed children of Morzine (#8.2) are just two instances of ASC subjects who display spontaneous extra-sensory perception, notably precognition, when temporarily in the ASC. Psychics such as Eileen Garrett (#3.5), on the other hand, voluntarily enter an ASC in order to use their psychic faculties. Though much of the evidence is only anecdotal, and much more has no doubt been exaggerated, so many instances have been reported by so many trustworthy people that I personally see little point in questioning that psychic abilities, whatever they may be, are enhanced in ASC states.

A typical case: a patient in a hospital casualty ward finds herself in the next bed to a girl who has been so badly injured in a car accident that there seems no hope for her:

For some inexplicable reason I became involved in this family, they treated me like one of them. One evening I prayed for this girl with a consuming force that I could not explain. I felt elevated in a horizontal position and filled with a strange power — a power in all my body which seemed to run out to

my hands, and a knowledge that if I put my hands towards
this girl I could cure her. It was a force that could bear no
argument or doubt, and as I pushed my hands towards this
girl, I could hear her say 'Mummy, mummy'. I then seemed to
be a spent force, but with the realisation that the girl would be
whole once again. . .

The following morning I was moved to another ward. That
evening the girl's mother came running in to say that her
daughter was speaking and had recovered consciousness. . .
[and so far as is known, the improvement was sustained].
(Cohen and Phipps, 1979, p.216)

When psychedelic drugs made their appearance, it was
widely conjectured that they might unlock the door to
controlled psychic functioning. In 1958, American researchers Fraser and Betty Nicol wondered: 'Do substances
which create the experience of depersonalisation and self-
transcendence facilitate psychic expression?' (PF, 1961)
Thirty years later, the question remains unanswered; certainly, the hoped-for breakthrough has not occurred, and
psychic powers remain as elusive as ever.

But this in itself tells us something about our ASCs, even
if it is something some of us would rather not know. It tells
us, yet again, that ASCs are not to be commanded or
controlled: that injecting this-or-that chemical or placing
the subject in such-and-such conditions can never do more
than encourage or inhibit the ASC. Ultimately, it is our
subconscious self who calls the tune.

Helpful visions

Tales of helpful visions have been part of popular folklore
throughout human history. This recent example is evidence
that the tradition persists:

One night in June 1986, 29-year-old Susan Arrance was
driving with her 5-year-old daughter Starlitt up a steep gravel
road in Oregon when her van went over the edge of the road
into a 30-metre ravine. Halfway down the slope Starlitt was
thrown free, but the mother went with the van and was
knocked unconscious.

Starlitt, barefoot, bruised and bleeding, managed to climb in
the darkness up the steep side of the ravine; halfway up, she
fell asleep for a while in a hole on the cliff's face. At 8 a.m. next

morning she was found at the top by a passer-by, and help was brought. The rescuers, bringing up the critically injured Susan, had to use rock-climbing gear to get to the top. Starlitt told her father she was helped in her climb by a young boy holding a black puppy, who came and comforted her. (*Fate*, November 1986, p.19)

We do not know what state Starlitt was in, but her extraordinary physical effort, not to mention the helpful vision, suggest an ASC of some sort.

It would be interesting to know what significance the 'boy with the puppy' had for Starlitt; possibly she was remembering an older boy at school who had befriended or protected her on a previous occasion.

Some light is thrown on the nature of Starlitt's ASC if we look at a very different story, but which also involves an extraordinary feat of climbing:

A boy dreamed that he got out of bed, and ascended to the summit of an enormous rock, where he found an eagle's nest, which he brought away with him, and placed beneath his bed. What he conceived, on awaking, to be a mere vision, was proved to have had an actual existence, by the nest being found in the precise spot where he imagined he had put it, and by the evidence of spectators who beheld his perilous adventure. The precipice which he ascended was of a nature that must have baffled the most expert mountaineer, and such as, at other times, he never could have scaled. (Macnish, 1834, p.154)

Macnish comments: 'The individual was as nearly as possible without actually being so, awake. All his bodily, and almost the whole of his mental powers, appear to have been in full activity.' We might say the same of Starlitt's feat. However, whereas Macnish, writing in 1834, attributed it to somnambulism, we today have a wider choice of explanations, and can speculate that the amazing climb, in each instance, was performed by what was in effect a dissociated personality, subconscious or secondary.

Certainly something of the sort is true of the Malay 'Monkey Dance':

The 'Monkey spirit' is caused to enter into a girl of some ten years of age by rocking her to and fro in a cot while being fed with areca-nut and salt. When she is sufficiently dizzy she performs a dance in the course of which she is said sometimes to achieve some extraordinary climbing feats which she could have never have performed unless 'possessed'. (Skeat, *Malay magic*, p.465)

Relevant, too, are the climbing feats performed by the possessed children of Morzine, discussed in the next chapter, and by the possessed nuns in many instances of convent hysteria, including one of the earliest reported outbreaks, at Cambrai in 1491: 'They could be seen running across the fields on all fours like dogs, throwing themselves into the air like birds, climbing trees and hanging from their branches like cats. . . ' (Görres, 1845, vol.5, p.267). It seems almost unbelievable that the children of the village of Morzine in the nineteenth century would know of the behaviour of the nuns of Cambrai nearly four centuries earlier — yet both are reported as taking to the trees in this way. Why? The case of a Paris architect adds to the strangeness of the phenomenon:

> While overlooking the erection of one of the many palaces for which that city is noted, suddenly, with a cry, the man would rush from scaffold to scaffold, up and down steep inclines, never falling, passing with a steady head over places where he dare not go when conscious. There was an apparently purposive action, and yet when the man came to himself he had no memory of what he had done, and during the time of the attack he did not respond to irritation. (cited by Wood, 1890, p.73, from Trousseau)

If children alone were involved, I would suggest that such manifestations represent a symbolic escape from adults, since a child knows, when it climbs a tree, that grown-ups are unlikely to follow. But the architect's case suggests something more. The best I can suggest is that it is some regression to our primeval ape ancestry, the Tarzan in us all !

7.2 Insights and ecstasies

The Jumpers of Cornwall (#4.4) and the voodoo dancers of Haiti (#4.5) are just two of thousands of communities who have sought, via ASCs, to participate in experiences which not only take them out of themselves but seemingly put them in contact with a higher level of spiritual existence. The fact that these experiences are structured into belief systems which not only conflict with one another, but are for the most part inherently absurd, should not lead us to conclude that the experiences themselves are valueless.

In his *Religions of the oppressed* (1963), Vittorio Lanternari surveys only a selection of the religious cults which have sprung up in ex-colonial cultures in the course of the last hundred years or so; yet he parades a staggering number of cults, from Latin America to the Pacific, from Indonesia to the American West, which indicates how universal is the scenario in which a millenarist prophet arises and promises to lead his people to a better future if they will do this or do that — kill the white man, placate the gods who send the cargo, renounce sex or take up vegetarianism.

His survey also shows that, however much the supra-structure of creed and doctrine may vary, at the popular participatory level the cults almost invariably incorporate ASC-inducing practices. In some, indeed, it is explicitly a central part of the cult's practices: for example, the peyote cult of the American Plains Indians.

Peyote is a carrot-shaped cactus whose round top, or button, eaten fresh or dried or drunk as an infusion, has non-narcotic, non-addictive hallucinogenic effects. As such it has been used in ritual since the sixteenth century, perhaps earlier. Lanternari tells us:

> Except for some tribal variations, the Peyote ritual takes place each week and lasts from Saturday evening to Sunday morning, in a special *tipi* reserved for this purpose. The faithful sit in a circle around a crescent-shaped mound of earth, which is their altar. The peyote buttons, which formerly were sought and gathered in pilgrimages but which today are purchased commercially, are placed on the crescent, and a fire is lighted. The faithful sing prayers to the accompaniment of drums, rattles, flutes and whistles, and finally they eat the peyote. The ceremony is conducted with great dignity and solemnity in an atmosphere of ever-rising exaltation until the worshippers go into trance and hallucinations and visions are produced, which often last through the night. In the morning they eat a ritual breakfast. (pp.63ff)

Lanternari's account of what is seen during the hallucinatory visions is pretty much what is reported by most participants in drug-induced ASCs:

> religious and secular experiences, drawn from aboriginal memory and combined with images and figures contributed by Christianity . . . monstrous creatures, the spirits of the dead appearing in heavenly beatitude, kaleidoscopic colours, hideous witches, magnificent landscapes, nude women of superhuman beauty, etc. (ibid.)

Other cultures do much the same thing in ways which differ only superficially: in Latin America, in New Zealand, in the Caribbean, there are dance-convulsions-trance practices which match those of the Jumpers and convulsionaries. Clearly, any evaluation of such practices has to be made within the social context, but apart from any spiritual benefits, there is no fundamental difference between them and, say, the English working man's traditional Saturday-night drinking sessions in the pub. We must suppose that all act as a safety valve for social frustrations. Sargant, talking to West Indians he had just seen in possession trance, reports:

> What was most impressive about the people we talked to was their normality, though they had been in states of full possession only an hour or two before. In our culture a person exhibiting repeated hysterical dissociative and trance phenomena would be considered nervously ill, but the same phenomena occurring in normal people in many African cultures leave very little nervous upset behind them; on the contrary, they help to relieve accumulated tension, as well as to create a deep conviction of being important, personally and individually, to the god or gods who are worshipped. (1973, p.160)

Such collective practices seem on the face of them to be very different from such private ecstasies as this:

> Rachel Baker was born in Massachusetts in 1794, into a very religious family. She herself, from the age of nine, was unusually given to religious contemplation, which culminated when she was 17 in a strong conviction of her own sinfulness.One November evening, sitting in a chair apparently asleep, she began to sigh and groan as if in excessive pain, and

started to talk incoherently but evidently on religious matters; this was repeated almost every night for two months, after which time she became calmer and her sleeping exercises became solemn and impressive. The eminent Dr Weir Mitchell described her trances:

These daily paroxysms recur with wonderful exactness, and from long prevalence have now become habitual. They invade her at early bed-time, and a fit usually lasts about three-quarters of an hour. The transition from the waking state to that of somnium is very rapid; frequently in a quarter of an hour, or even less. After she retires from company in the parlour, she is discovered to be praising God in a distinct and sonorous voice. Her discourses are usually pronounced in a private chamber, for the purpose of delivering them with more decorum. She has been advised to take the recumbent posture, her face being turned towards the heavens. Her body and limbs are motionless; the only motion the spectator perceives is that of her organs of speech, and an oratorical inclination of the head and neck. She commences and ends with prayer; between these is her sermon or exhortation. She proceeds with an even course to the end, embellishing it sometimes with fine metaphors, vivid descriptions, and poetical quotations. There is a state of body like groaning, sobbing, or moaning, and the distressful sound continues from two minutes to a quarter of an hour. This agitation, however, does not wake her; it gradually subsides, and she passes into a sound and natural sleep. In the morning she wakes as if nothing had happened, and entirely ignorant of the scenes in which she has been an actor. She declares that she knows nothing of the nightly exercises, except from the information of others. (Ennemoser, 1854, pp.442ff.)

But the differences between this and the instances cited previously may be only superficial. Each may be, within the social parameters in which individuals are confined, an appropriate way for them to meet their personal needs.

Spiritual experiences

Most voluntary ASCs are sought because they are thought to confer spiritual benefits of some kind. Thousands of people have tried to describe their experience of the ineffable, gained as the result of an ASC, spontaneous or sought. Teresa de Avila's 'Interior Castle', Juan de la Cruz's

'Dark Night of the Soul', the anonymous 'Cloud of Unknowing' — these titles show how those who have such
experiences look for metaphors to describe the process by
which they attain to the insights, the enlightenment, the
enhanced perception of one's place in the scheme of things.
Some are linked to a specific religious belief-system, but
many are not.

It is possible that these practices, some of which have
been studied and performed for thousands of years, are
truly the path we should *all* seek to tread, not only the
monks, hermits and other devotees who have forsaken the
High Street of daily life in order to follow them. At the same
time, the states in which these mystic communions occur
show many signs of being much the same as other ASCs,
and we should note how they relate to *pibloktoq*, spirit
trance and hallucinogenic drug taking, even if we end by
deciding that they occur on a quite different spiritual level.

Apart from the physical features — the indifference to
external reality during ecstasy, the narrowed focus of
attention, the anaesthesia — what is striking about many of
these mystical experiences is their marked role-playing
character. Many a devout nun who renounced human
sexual love saw herself instead as 'the bride of Christ' and
as such went through the stages of betrothal, espousal and
even lovers' quarrels. A particularly dramatic example is
the fifteenth-century Florentine nun Domenica del Para-
diso, who

> complained to our Lord that her heart was indifferent and cold
> and could not love him properly. Jesus replied: 'I, O my
> spouse, will bestow upon thee a new heart and fresh blood.'
> Domenica was then in great agony of body and mind and had
> taken no food for eight days. On 18 October, 1501, she seemed
> at the point of death. Then suddenly she felt her bosom
> opened and realised by some interior conviction that her
> heart had been withdrawn from her breast by the Mother
> of God herself. . . The ring, invisible to all but herself, with
> which her heavenly Bridegroom had espoused her, slipped
> from her finger. . . Her soul was conducted to paradise while
> her guardian angel was instructed to animate the body.
> Suddenly the almost lifeless hand moved and, pointing, drew
> her Confessor's attention to the left breast, while the lips

whispered, 'I no longer have any heart.' The good Father, laying his hand upon the place indicated, found only a hollow and empty space between the ribs. . . Meanwhile, the soul of Domenica in paradise had been offered the choice of two hearts, one large, very splendid and luminous, the other smaller and less beautiful. . . When she had chosen the larger, our Lord told her this was the new heart, while the other was that which had belonged to her hitherto. Then our Lady descended to earth and put the new heart in its place. Domenica assured her confessor that inasmuch as the new heart was bigger, it occasioned her great discomfort at first and produced a marked swelling in her breast. (Thurston, 1955, p.106)

Unless we are prepared to take Domenica's story at face value, it is best seen as dramatic fantasy: Domenica, in her role as bride of Christ, has the sort of adventure which, extravagant as it may seem to others, is typical of the sort of experience recounted by many such visionaries, to whom Jesus would continually reveal his wounds, open his breast to display his heart, pierce *their* hearts with swords, place rings on their fingers and so on. To describe this as 'role-playing' is not to pass judgement on the spiritual quality of the experience. Just as the authors of mystical books call on clouds, castles and dark nights to express their feelings, so *the mystical experience itself is dramatised metaphor*.

Some oriental teachings hold that all paths lead to enlightement. Though I await the publication of *Zen in the art of stockbroking* or *How football hooliganism brought me to God*, we are certainly confronted with an astonishing choice of paths to self-transcendence — see the advertisement pages of magazines like *Fate*. A Japanese researcher tells us:

Numerous activities such as the game of nô, ken-do (a martial art using bamboo swords), judo, sado (tea ceremony), kado (flower arrangement) and kyudo (archery) have been raised to the level of disciplines (Mishi or Do) intended to achieve the control of the self, the realisation of the self, and even satori (= enlightenment). 'Do' signifies the path one must follow to reach enlightenment.

In the tea ceremony, for example, the participants can attain a sort of ASC by controlling sensory stimuli by fixed positions, the gracefulness of the movements, the regulation of breathing, the scent of incense, the monotonous but peaceful sound of the water boiling in the iron kettle, and all the tranquillising aspects of a special room dedicated to the ceremony. Dr Ishikawa has established that the autoregulation of breathing during the practice of yoga and the tea ceremony can lead to autoregulation of blood pressure and pulse. So, training in the tea ceremony has a psychophysiological intention, succinctly summarised by the words *Ichigo Ichie*, which mean literally 'an occasion, a meeting'. The ceremony is perceived as being perhaps the first and last opportunity to meet and prepare tea for some of those present. It is with the awareness that each of us is destined to die sooner or later, a lucid conception of the true nature of existence, that one does one's best to prepare, with a deep affection, the little bowl of tea intended for each participant. Thus the tea ceremony, like zen, is seen as a way of approaching enlightenment, not simply as a pastime. (Ikemi, 1980, p.136)

We have already noted the controversy that bubbles round the question, Can we attain spiritual enlightenment via psychedelic drugs? Many who use them report that the experience gives them 'a sense of belonging, a group empathy' and Eugene Exman, an editor of religious books, insists: 'It is easy to say that this experience is a kind of joy-ride, a kind of selfish, self-satisfying experience. It isn't at all. As we all know, at its height the experience carries with it this aspect of sharing' (PF, 1961).

Conversion

The Cornish Jumpers (#4.4) were inspired by a recruiting campaign on the part of the local Methodists. Those who went into convulsions at the American religious revivals were equally on the receiving end of attempts to persuade them to 'convert', either from another religion or from no religion at all. Wesley's preaching, in the eighteenth century, directed at the same ends, played on the emotions rather than the reasoning powers of his audiences:

Some sunk down, and there remained no strength in them; others exceedingly trembled and quaked; some were torn with a kind of convulsive motion in every part of their bodies, and that so violently that often four or five persons could not hold one of them. I have seen many hysterical and many epileptic fits, but none of them were like these in many respects. (Wesley's journal, cited by Sargant, 1957, p.82)

The fact that Wesley explicitly distinguishes the effects of his preaching from hysteria is an indication that he was uncomfortably aware of a similarity. An important difference, of course, is that the preaching effect occurred in a crowd situation, where one person's response would be likely to conform to another's. It is precisely this point which has made many question whether recruitment to religion by playing on the emotions is ultimately beneficial to the indvidual. (We shall see, in #9, that it is not even always effective.)

What is happening in these as in many other ASCs is that the normal functioning of the brain is disturbed by fear (of hell-fire, damnation and whatever other horrors the evangelist dangles over his hearers' heads) coupled with the excitement of participating in group activity. This leads to a suspension of normal reality testing, and to heightened suggestibility. The same effects could have been induced in any number of ways; but of course it was essential for Wesley's purpose that he, as the personal representative of God, should be seen as the agent, since it is from him that the new ideas, which are to replace the old, must be seen to come.

But perhaps Wesley's greatest feat was to convince his converts that their convulsions were of divine, not diabolic origin. Nothing distinguished their behaviour from that of the Samoyed victims of *ikóta* (#3.3) or the German peasants who succumbed to the dancing mania (#9), which in both cases was attributed to evil spirits. Only Wesley's authority gave him the power to suggest to his converts that their convulsions were of God.

Accounts of conversion by observers are suspect because the narrator is not a participant; accounts by those concerned are suspect because the narrator *is* one. How far can we trust a subjective account? For what it is worth, here is (a small part of) American revivalist Charles Grandison Finney's account of his spiritual rebirth. Realising that, though intellectually persuaded, he had not made the necessary commitment of faith, Finney 'withdrew to the woods to

wrestle with his spirit'. He was overwhelmed with a sense
of his own wickedness and so discouraged that he was
almost too weak to stand. He addressed himself directly to
God and, what with inward voices and passages of Scripture dropping into his mind with a flood of light, we are
assured that God directly answered him:

> Without any expectation of it, without ever having the
> thought in my mind that there was such a thing for me,
> without any recollection that I had ever heard the thing
> mentioned by any person in the world, the Holy Spirit
> descended upon me in a manner that seemed to go right
> through me, body and soul. I could feel the impression, like a
> wave of electricity, going through and through me. Indeed, it
> seemed to come in waves and waves of liquid love; for I could
> not express it in any other way. It seemed like the very breath
> of God. I can recollect distinctly that it seemed to fan me, like
> immense wings.
>   No words can express the wonderful love that was shed
> abroad in my heart. I wept aloud with joy and love: and I do
> not know but I should say, I literally bellowed out the
> unutterable gushings of my heart. These waves came over me,
> and over me, and over me, one after the other, until I recollect
> I cried out, 'I shall die if these waves continue to pass over me'
> I said, 'Lord, I cannot bear any more,' yet I had no fear of
> death. (quoted in Seldes, 1928, p.103)

Some of us will be bothered by the fact that we have this
account at all, that Finney is willing to reveal — some would
say flaunt — in public his intimate encounter with the
divine. He would no doubt answer that it was no more than
his duty to do so, and thereby help other sinners to undergo
the same process of re-birth.

Maybe he was right: certainly he became one of the
foremost preachers of his day, to whom many thousands
owed the joy of being born again. But how many enjoy such
experiences and keep them to themselves?

Everyday ecstasy

Many of our witnesses, in many different kinds of ASC,
have reported experiences which have something of the
mystical about them. Even a high-altitude balloonist (# 4)
may feel a detachment from 'the trials and tribulations of
earthly existence' which is pretty much what those who

take drugs are hoping to achieve. But it is not only what such experiences promise escape *from*, there is also what one escapes *to* — and that can be positive insight and enlightenment which constitute positive rewards in themselves.

Sometimes, what seems at the time to be a wonderful insight, turns out in the cold aftermath to be something less. Oliver Wendell Holmes' experience with nitrous oxide illustrates this well:

> The veil of eternity was lifted. The one great truth, that which underlies all human experience, and is the key to all the mysteries that philosophy has sought in vain to solve, flashed upon me in a sudden revelation. Henceforth all was clear; a few words had lifted my intelligence to the level of the knowledge of the cherubim. Staggering to my desk, I wrote, in ill-shaped, straggling characters, the all embracing truth still glimmering in my consciousness. The words were (children may smile; the wise will ponder): 'A strong smell of turpentine prevails throughout.' (cited by Hyslop, 1913, p.91)

Hardly more helpful is this reported experience:

> Whilst under the anaesthetic for a short operation, I had a complete revelation about the ultimate truth of everything. I understood the 'entire works'. It was a tremendous illumination. I was filled with unspeakable joy. . . When I came round I told the doctor I understood the meaning of everything. He said, 'Well, what is it?' and I faltered out, 'Well, it's a sort of green light.' (in Laski, 1961, p.261)

Even though they tend to be so subjective that they cannot be shared with others, genuine insights have been received by many while in ASCs. They are not always visions of cosmic understanding, but may simply be useful snippets of thought. One helpful idea embodied in this study came to me quite clearly in a dream, proof that my subconscious self is working on this book along with my conscious self. Unfortunately, whether the subconscious self is very capricious, or whether the conditions need to be very precise, we seem unable to formalise our relations with it. Insights and guidance may come — or they may not.

Eileen Garrett, a sensitive who devoted her life to exploring her own and other people's alternate states, recognised 'euphoric states' distinct from the trances she entered during her activities as a sensitive:

> This euphoric state, which appears to resemble certain psychedelic experiences, may be touched off by a musical fragment, or even by a passage in a book. The private domain of such a state is often filled with colour, but lacking in symbolism, dogmatic content, or even activity as such. One does not, at such a time, concern oneself with body or material element of any kind. There is, on the other hand, a fundamental oneness with everything, and an overwhelming timelessness. (PF, 1961)

She also speaks of another state which she feels may be a 'cleansing' state:

> Perceptions are intense. Everything in a room takes relation to its own shape or nature. Furniture and other objects appear to shimmer and breathe, but distinctly in harmony with breathing. One is outside of time. There is an imagined essence to everything. The tree in the furniture may actually be smelled; even a curtain may become like a forest of pines.
>
> At one time, these special states caused me some concern, particularly as I could not easily communicate their essence. They may relate to the burning fever of delirium, yet one remains in possession of one's heightened hearing and observation. Sometimes music of a strange, bell-like quality attends these euphoric states. Street noises may become intensified, but these noises do not seem discordant. The tick of a clock becomes a child's trumpet. The sense of smell becomes highly acute. Above all, one wants to sing and move in rhythm with the dancing movement of the room. (*ibid.*)

Perhaps more than any other type of ASC, these 'peak experiences' force us to confront the question, to what extent they are the consequence of purely physical factors of physiology, environment, etc. Canadian psychologist Barry Beyerstein (1988) wonders what we are to make of the correlation which has been shown to exist between, on the one hand, epilepsy and epileptic events in the brain, and on the other, 'mystical' experiences:

> While it cannot be proved retrospectively that any experience of possession, conversion, revelation or divine ecstasy was merely an epileptic discharge, we must ask how one differen-

tiates 'real transcendence' from neuropathies that produce the same extreme realness, profundity, ineffability, and sense of cosmic unity. When accounts of sudden religious conversions in temporal-lobe epileptics are laid alongside the epiphanous revelations of the religious tradition, the parallels are striking. The same is true of the recent spate of alleged UFO abductees. Parsimony alone argues against invoking spirits, demons, or extraterrestrials when natural causes will suffice. (p.255)

While our inquiry confirms Beyerstein's feeling that we can manage quite well without otherworldly beings, it also suggests that his 'natural causes' must be interpreted very broadly. For while he, like Persinger, pinpoints epileptic discharge as the *means* whereby the event occurs, this simply pushes the initial cause one step further back, to the question, What causes the epileptic discharge?

I see no reason to question that this can occur spontaneously as the result of all manner of causes, from inadequate diet to atmospheric conditions: but while those causes may bring about the release of the material which give the experience its individual character, they clearly do not dictate the *content* of that material. If the experience is a meaningful one, it must have acquired that meaning somehow: and here , it seems to me, is the *ultimate* source of the experience.

Whether that same source — which we may suppose to be our subconscious self — is ever responsible for bringing about the experience, or whether it simply takes advantage of experiences spontaneously occurring by the means suggested by Persinger, Beyerstein and others, is a matter we can only speculate about. Indeed, we could logically go even further, and ask whether the same mechanism may be being used by opportunist spirits and extraterrestrials, manipulating our brains. (Just such a hypothesis has been proposed by French researcher Pierre Guérin, who suggests that extraterrestrials may be responsible for creating hallucinations of UFO sightings and encounters.)

What is certain is that we can put ourselves into a condition where these experiences are more likely to occur. Persinger (1983) has included this suggestion in his hypothesis:

There is no doubt that TLTs (temporal lobe transients) can be conditioned since they are intrinsically rewarding experiences; they can be considered learned microseizures provoked by precipitating stimuli and followed by anxiety reduction. People whose brains are prone to self-stimulation would be characterised by multiple conversions and protracted periods of religious/mystical experiences.(p.1260)

If so, we can look for a physiological basis for those spiritual Don Juans who seem to spend their lives shopping around from one new cult to the next, trying each path to cosmic understanding in turn. The bookstores are full of books offering every reader the possibility of inner-life enhancement; but if ecstasy-proneness has a physical basis, some of us will find it easier than others to achieve a man-made spiritual experience.

7.3   Inter-state data-sharing

Janet, when he was trying to track down his patients' *idées fixes*, found that he might obtain access to them through their dreams, through hypnosis, or through dissociation in the form of automatic writing or crystal gazing (1911, p.241). Other ASCs might have been no less revealing. Perhaps the most practical benefit offered by ASCs results from the fact that through one we can obtain access to another. Without the aid of hypnosis, for example, few mutliple personality cases would even have been discovered, let alone healed.

Hypnosis is not the only way of using one ASC to gain access to another. Drugs can be used not only to remedy chemical imbalances in the system, but also as social agents, to overcome the mutism of schizophrenics who resist all our attempts to communicate with them and the hostility they frequently display to those who seek to help them:

Mlle Pascal, Médecin-chef of the Asiles de la Seine, proposes a method which relies at the same time on the use of pharmacodynamic agents — alcohol, ether, chlorohydrate of cocaine, strychnine sulphate, hashish, peyotl, etc. — and on certain psychoanalytic techniques, verbal exploration, use of evocative words, sensory excitation by the use of music, etc. . . Her findings show that in a majority of cases the barriers of mutism and, negativitism can be broken down by these methods, and sociability reawakened. (Félice, 1936, p.237)

The question whether a person in one state will recall what happened to him in another state, or in his usual state, is one whose complexities fascinated Janet, who never tired of testing what his subjects would or would not remember in any given state. After getting Léonie to hallucinate wearing a black velvet dress (#3.1), he notes:

> When the hallucination is over, when she stops being a princess, Léonie reverts to her habitual hypnotic state without passing through any intermediary state of lethargy or catalepsy. Generally, but not always, Léonie-2 remembers the change of personality — 'What a funny dream I've had! I had a velvet dress and I was talking with a marquis in a posh drawing room. . . you weren't there.' If by any chance we can't find any such memory in Léonie-2, we're sure to find it in the other hypnotic state. Léonie-3, who remembers all the rest of her life, remembers also her hallucinations: 'Is she really that stupid, that poor Léonie? Did she really believe she was a princess? It's you who made her think so.' (1889, p.164)

So while we can state, as a general principle, that what we experience in one ASC we can recall in another, it is far from being an absolute rule: nor does there seem to be a supplementary rule to cover the exceptions. Equally puzzling is what is or isn't recalled in the USC. A visionary like Bernadette will recall what happens during her ecstasies, but spirit mediums do not recall what happens in their trances; some selves in multiple-personality cases know what happens to the others, some do not.

Surely there is rhyme and reason behind what seems to be a more-or-less arbitrary decision on the part of the subconscious self; but if so, we have yet to discover it. What this uncertainty does give us, though, is further cause for doubting the efficacy of 'truth drugs', 'lie detectors' and other devices for obtaining information which for one reason or another an individual is reluctant to disclose. More and more, it seems our subconscious self makes its own decision what we will and what we will not recall.

8 Paying the price

Maya Deren, speaking of the moment when 'possession' overtakes the voodoo dancer, refers to 'the state of helpless vulnerability' which the subject reaches in his progressive submission to the drums which dictate the pace and pattern of the ritual.

Anyone who exchanges his USC for an ASC makes himself vulnerable. The world is full enough of dangers as it is; all the more so, when a person loses the reality-testing defence which enables him to identify what is happening to him.

The trouble is that just about anything can happen — or seem to happen — in an ASC. A person who enters an ASC lays himself open to experiences which may be supremely life-enhancing or may drag him down to a life-evading depersonalisation; he may be given a chance to talk with God, or he may be reduced to a convulsive robot who will not communicate with anyone.

Nor is it always obvious when an ASC is positive and purposeful, when it is accidental and arbitrary, when it is negative and dangerous.

If he enters his ASC voluntarily, within the supportive protection of the community, as does the voodoo dancer or the volunteer in a sensory deprivation experiment, the risk he runs is relatively small. He can rely on the accumulated wisdom of his companions — the priests, the scientists — to protect him should the need arise.

Those who have studied ASCs most seriously are most aware of the pitfalls. Zen teachers acknowledge the concept of *makyo*, a phase which the initiate has to traverse in order to attain enlightenment, and which corresponds to the ordeals faced by the Christian mystics, the temptations of Jesus and Saint Antony, the danger of pride for the mystic who thinks he is getting somewhere, and so on. Zen teachers have a word for it — *zen-byo* — which means, literally, the zen-disease.

The danger arises when things get out of control — when the practitioner's behaviour is not recognised for what it is, or takes an unpredicted turn — when a revival participant in the ecstasy of being re-born throws herself into a river and is drowned, when someone's secondary personality commits a crime , when the person who has retreated from reality into a private ASC can't get back again.

The 'saved'

If *using* the ASC were the same as *understanding* the ASC, the world's leading experts would be religious revivalists. In the course of this inquiry we have seen how many such religious leaders, in all sincerity, have encouraged their followers to experience ASCs in the course of which they achieve re-birth and qualify for heavenly grace.

Whether or not we think that religious revivals do any good, it is arguable that they do not do very much harm. The popularity of the American revivals in the early nineteenth century, and indeed to this day among deprived populations, shows that they have a social value if no other. But how do we determine what is and what is not morally permissible? Should we approve of a Wesley using mind control to induce others to embrace what he thinks best for them? If so, where do we draw the line as regards the methods we allow him to use? And where do we draw the line between those whom we allow to use these methods and those we do not? If it is all right for Methodists is it for Scientologists?

The questions become even more acute when it is a matter of political ideologies — the 'mind control' used explicitly by totalitarian regimes in our own time, and more covertly by politicians and ideologues throughout human history, convinced that in the cause of converting others to their point of view, since it is for their own good, such means are legitimate. Sargant describes the process:

> For conversion to be effective, the subject may first have to have his emotions worked upon until he reaches an abnormal condition of anger, fear or exaltation. If this condition be maintained or intensified by one means or another, hysteria may supervene, whereupon the subject can become more open to suggestions which in normal circumstances he would have summarily rejected. . . All the different phases of brain activity, from an increased excitement to emotional exhaustion and collapse in a terminal stupor, can be induced either by psychological means; or by drugs; or by shock treatments, produced electrically; or by simply lowering the sugar content of the patient's blood with insulin injections. (1957, p.16)

Sargant is speaking of processes which can be used for good or for ill; the same basic strategy is used, whether it is to help a mentally disordered patient to shed his *idée fixe* or to persuade a person to change his beliefs. As with all our ASCs, they are neutral in themselves: the danger is in the vulnerability of the subject, once the natural defence system is knocked out by drugs or by psychological means.

Though they excused their practices on the ground that the ends justified the means, and that all was to the greater glory of God, the fact remains that Wesley and his kind were manipulating the minds of their hearers — with all that entails in self-surrender and suggestibility.

Any such process involves depersonalisation. A Wesley would say, yes indeed, by this means I am helping the individual to reject his old sinful persona and find a new and better one. The same no doubt might be said by those who administer the initiation rites of primitive tribes, the entry procedures of religious institutions, or the practices of military training. In all such processes, a number of stress-inducing elements — isolation from the outside 'real' world, stereotyped activities, etc. — are combined with depersonalising practices — shaving the head, for example, features in all three; monks take new names, soldiers are known by numbers — together with fatigue, reduced or interrupted sleep, fasting or reduced diet, celibacy and so on, all of which add up to make the individual more vulnerable to suggestion which, while it may be for his benefit, may also be used to achieve more sinister ends.

The 'anointed'

The history of mankind is full of people who claim to receive divine commands, whether it be to lead a nation, to head a revolt, or simply to go forth and murder prostitutes. Understandably, such people rarely present themselves for medical examination, so that it is only at a distance, and in retrospect, that any kind of diagnosis can be made, and it will always be a matter of argument whether the fanatical cult leaders of the Middle Ages, or Adolf Hitler, or the Reverend Jim Jones of Jonestown and other cult leaders of our own time, should be considered as mentally disordered, and if so, what form of mental disorder afflicted them.

However, such cases do from time to time become available for psychological observation:

Bernard, who was aged 33 when he came to Janet as a patient, was a man of limited intelligence, who had been brought up by priests in a strongly religious atmosphere. At age 14, he had been sent to guard animals in the mountains, spending days on his own: here, he discovered the pleasures of masturbation, and this came to take a central role in his life, leading to extraordinary fantasies. This in turn developed to the point where he began to have fits; at the moment of ejaculation he would lose consciousness and fall into convulsions, after which, echoing his first teachers, he would declaim against the vices of our times and the catastrophes predicted by the prophets to the impious masses; the crisis would terminate in a long sleep.

On at least one occasion, Bernard saw an angel during his delirium, who charged him to save mankind, and to protect it from women. By the time Janet met him, these fantasies had systematised into a formal structure. He no longer masturbated, and his hysterical symptoms had been replaced by a systematic delirium in which he evidently believed himself to be Jesus Christ, who had returned to Earth at this time of great corruption which is predicted by the scriptures.

The way in which such an individual will interpret outward circumstances to fit with his view of things is illustrated by his pointing out to Janet that the predictions speak of a time when darkness will cover the face of the Earth, and indeed, this year, the weather has been dark and gloomy. Jesus must go from Jericho to Jerusalem; this is a metaphor for Bernard's journey from Châlons to Paris. . . and so on. (Janet, 1911, p.229)

Safe in the hands of doctors, it is unlikely that Bernard will have the opportunity to disturb humankind; but how many of the fanatical leaders of history drew their inspiration from similar fantasies?

A secondary aspect of the self-anointed bearers of revelation is the effect they have on their followers. In a sense, these sometimes seem to be in a permanent ASC, in that they have surrendered their own personality, their own judgement, their own reality-testing procedures, in order to abide by those of their leader. When Charles Manson's 'family' appeared in court after murdering Sharon Tate and others, Prosecutor Vincent Bugliosi described them: 'Same expression, same patterned responses, same tone of voice, same lack of distinct personality. The realisation came with a shock: they reminded me less of human beings than of Barbie dolls' (1974, p.133). Like nuns who take new names along with the veil, Manson's followers changed their identities, symbolically cutting themselves off from their own families and joining 'the family'. The corollary of their leader promoting himself to 'superself' status was the voluntary adoption by his followers of 'unself' roles.

The 'message bearers'

Outbursts of spontaneous utterance, surpassing everyday eloquence, occur in many cases noted in this study, and have generally been interpreted according to the prevalent belief system. When the convulsionaries of Saint Médard (#7) or the 'preaching children' of Sweden (#3.4) treat those about them to pious discourses, or when fundamentalist Christians start 'speaking in tongues', this is seen as a divine manifestation. On the other hand the spirit medium, when he utters messages whose content surprises him as much as it does everyone else, is presumed to be in communication with the spirits in the beyond.

Given the evident sincerity of the speakers, and the remarkable quality of their delivery, it is not surprising that a divine origin was presumed. However, uncontrolled utterance is a symptom of other ASCs; 'possessed' subjects will hurl abuse at their friends and relatives, doctors and officials, claiming that it is the Devil that speaks, not they, and the same phenomenon occurs in hysteria: 'Renée will suddenly come out with all manner of abuse, and every now and then take advantage of a pause to say, with a groan, "It's not my fault, it isn't me, I myself don't even know these digusting words." ' (Janet, 1911, p.364). In Renée's case, we are in no doubt that the material is welling up from her subconscious; could all our other instances of extraordinary eloquence have so down-to-earth an explanation?

Perhaps the most characteristic feature of extraterrestrial encounters is the claim of the witnesses to have been entrusted with messages for humankind. Here is a characteristic sample, from a Space Man named (characteristically) Orlon:

> My brothers, my sisters in Light, I, Orlon, communicate to you from the craft stationed above your locality. WE COME IN PEACE. As the midnight hour approaches for change upon your planet, our mission is one of enlightenment, is indeed one of rescue from the morasses of the lower mind of Earthman: Rescue in the sense of bringing that enlightenment which gives release, which gives evolvement into that greater self which Man, in essence, IS.
>
> We who come in craft your peoples have called Flying Saucers, come in the One Light of the One Creator, our All-Knowing One, come with concepts of brotherhood, of Light, enlightenment beyond the wildest dreams of your people as they walk their daily lives. Our craft are massed in areas outside of your planet awaiting the time for descent to the surface that they may assist your people at the time of these changes. Those who are in tune with the things of their own infinite being will respond with love and understanding

to our coming. . . *and so on.* (Orlon, channelling telepathically to Aleuti Francesca, Doctor of Spiritual Science, Director of the Solar Light Retreat, 7700 Avenue of the Sun, Central Point, Oregon. Cited in Brownell, 1980, p.74)

While it is by no means impossible that otherworldly beings may be concerned for Earth's welfare, and choose this somewhat improbable way of making their intentions known, what ultimately fosters skepticism is the fact that I must have at least a hundred such collections of messages here on my shelves, each purporting to come from a *different* entity from a *different* part of the cosmos; and though their messages tend to be remarkably similar in their 'philosophy', they show a distressing tendency to contradict one another in matters of fact.

It should be added that there is not a scrap of convincing evidence for the extraterrestrial origin of any of these communications.

Does all this do any harm? It can be argued that man has always incorporated his hopes and fears in myths and legends, and that the myth of extraterrestrial contact does no more harm than the beliefs of former ages.

Certainly it is unlikely that the current phase of extraterrestrial revelation will lead to anything as widespread and devastating as the witch mania of the Middle Ages; but it is certainly not altogether harmless. When, in 1949, a Mrs Martin began to receive messages similar to the above, she gathered around her a group of believers who shared her conviction that catastrophe was about to strike Earth, but that they would be rescued in time and taken away to another planet. So convinced were they, that they abandoned careers and families, sold their homes and committed themselves to preparing for the great day — which, of course, never arrived (Festinger *et al.*, 1956. *passim*).

I dare say no real harm was done, and perhaps the process was ultimately beneficial in some cases. But such things can turn out worse: in 1986 a 57-year-old Englishwoman killed her two grandchildren because she was afraid they were in danger of being abducted on board an alien spacecraft (cited in Evans, 1987).

The 'possessed'

When reality-testing is abandoned, the sense of proportion tends to go with it. For many an ASC-subject, this has the result of making him forget he is just one among millions. George King is not unduly surprised when the extraterrestrials choose him from all humanity to be the Voice of Interplanetary Parliament; nor Teresa de Avila that Jesus gives her so much of his attention; nor Bernadette Soubirous that the Virgin Mary will come down from Heaven for no other purpose than to meet her.

Vianney, the Curé of Ars, whatever his private virtues, emerges even from the pages of his sympathetic biographer Trochu (1926) as not only a tiresome bore to his neighbours, whom he eventually succeeds in convincing that dancing is a mortal sin and should be banned from the village, but also extraordinarily egocentric, obsessed with the notion that the Devil has singled him out from other men as a special target. For years on end he is harassed by a personal demon, the *grappin*, who seems to have no other duties to attend to but to play childish tricks on Vianney in the naive hope that this will persuade him to sell out on his Christian beliefs. Even if we accept the existence of the *grappin*, we feel it might have occurred to the Curé that the soul of any of his fellow-villagers was worth as much as his own; but no, he and he alone is Satan's target. . .

The difficulty is magnified when the delusion is *collective*: In 1857 there was an outbreak in Morzine, a small (pop. 2200) town in the mountains near Lac Léman, so isolated that for much of the year it was virtually inaccessible.

One day in March my neighbour's little girl, 10-year-old Perronne T., who was then preparing for her first communion, was coming out of church when she saw a little girl fished out of the river almost drowned. A few hours later, in class, she suddenly fell as if dead on her schoolbench. She was carried home, and remained in this state for several hours; it was followed by several other such attacks.

Then in May my second daughter, who was the same age as her and also preparing for her first communion, went with Perronne to mind the goats; she fell into the same state; they were found stretched on the ground, side by side, and were carried home without seeming to know what was going on. After about an hour, my daughter awoke. . . The next day the same thing happened and from then on the ailment seized her five or six times a day, and her friend likewise, but now it took a different form. They remained motionless, turned their eyes towards the heavens, stretched their arms as if to receive something, made the movements of opening and reading a letter; this supposed letter seemed sometimes to give them great pleasure, sometimes great disgust; after that, they made as if to fold the letter and give it back to the messenger. Afterwards, back to their normal selves, they told how they had received a letter from the Virgin, who said nice things to them; that on her invitation they had visited paradise, which was very beautiful. When the letter was displeasing, it was because it came from hell.

The townsfolk remembered the case of a young girl of a nearby village who had a similar attack two or three years previously; maybe, too, the currently fashionable craze for table-turning had something to do with it. At all events, the malady spread, mostly to children, but soon to people of all ages. By 1861 there were 120 victims.

By now the outbreaks were taking a different form, displaying many symptoms we have seen in other cases. There were convulsions, accompanied by hallucinations, insults and blasphemies shouted at relatives, doctors, priests; there were reports of ESP and precognition, and tests showed that during the fits the subjects were anaesthetic; some performed extraordinary athletic feats, such as climbing 25-metre trees and leaping from one tree to another. They exhibited such strength that it took three or four strong men to hold a 10-year-old girl.

Many aspects of the victims' behaviour parallel other cases. As in preaching epidemics, the children speak perfect French, not patois; as in many depersonalisation ASCs, children who are normally gentle and timid behave with great familiarity, even insolence. Jeanne P. had fits which lasted three minutes. When asked 'Do you know, poor child, that you said terrible things to us?' she replied, 'Oh no, sirs, you're mistaken, it wasn't me.'

The illness was persistent: Angélique Baud, though physically in good health, was afflicted over a four-year period with fits during which, for about three minutes, she would be twisted with convulsions, foam at the mouth, shout the filthiest obscenities . . . and then the fit would end as suddenly as it began. She had been knitting before, now she was knitting again, feeling no fatigue and with no recollection that anything had happened.

Because it was assumed that only the Devil could be responsible, recourse was had to exorcism, but the civil authorities intervened and forbade this. A few parents found their own ways of dealing with the matter; Juliette Lavaud was cured when her father grabbed her by the hair, waved a hatchet, and told her that he would cut her neck if her crisis did not stop on the spot or if she ever had another one. It stopped and was never repeated. M. Marolaz cured his daughter the first time by promising her a new dress, but when she had another fit he put a stop to it by threatening to chain her in the cellar. A highly respectable man, finding himself alone with a possessed girl at the moment of her crisis, made a gesture which seemed to be an attack on her modesty — and checked the fit on the spot.

But not everyone was as resourceful, and soon the exorcisms began again by public demand, with the predictable effect of giving a new impetus to the epidemic — in the words of one commentator, 'it was adding oil to the fire'. More and more the epidemic came to resemble the witch mania, with inhabitants being accused of being magicians and witches and persecuted. But this was too much for the authorities, who stepped in with firmer measures: the parish priest was replaced, the sick were isolated, the worst cases were sent to distant hospitals, and in a little while Morzine's ordeal was over (Blanc, 1865; Cauzons, 1901–12; Mirville, 1863).

Hippolyte Blanc, from whose contemporary account I chiefly quote, finds the conclusion of Calmeil and other doctors, that the 'possessed' of Morzine are mentally ill, less than adequate. 'The scientific explanation has yet to be found', he declares, and in the face of such an incident as the following we must surely agree. Even though we do not have to take it at face value as demonic possession, it nevertheless indicates an extraordinarily complex interaction between the conscious and the subconscious self:

Twelve-year-old Joseph T. has already shown himself subject to attacks, and is overtaken by one while returning from the funeral of his father. Suddenly he climbs an enormous pine-tree; reaching the top, he breaks off the topmost branch, bends it over, and stands head down on the summit, singing and waving. His brother calls to him to shut up and come down, this is no time to be playing games when they have just buried their father. This reminder seems to bring the boy to himself; but then, realising where he is, he becomes horribly scared and calls for help. His brother, seeing how things are, cries out, Devil, go back into this child so that he can climb down! The boy reverts to his 'possessed' state and at once loses his fear, descending the tree, head downwards, with the speed of a squirrel. (Blanc, 1865, pp.291ff.)

The 'ASC-addicts'

As Charcot has often pointed out, most hysterical states are almost voluntary to start with. You start to dream because you want to; you could stop — but it's so enjoyable. You cut down on your food, it's because you want to be slim, to have an attractive figure and not to look like mum; you have an argument, a little flare-up, well, but that was because you were provoked. In every case — and the patients will freely admit it — it could be halted right at the outset. But the activity continues, becomes more and more automatic, until the patient is no longer able to stop of her own accord, it's become a delirium, an anorexia, an attack. 'When I've started something.' a patient said, 'I have to continue despite everything, I would break windows, I would kill myself rather than stop' (Janet, 1911, p.131).

ASCs often become chronic simply by becoming a habit. Just as many people take drugs because of the 'high' and the release they give, so other ASCs are sought for similar gratification. Participation in such activities as religious revivals, pop music concerts, ritual dancing and the like can become an end in itself which many people find gratifying; generally there is little harm in such indulgence, any more than in occasional over-drinking. But just as the occasional drink can, for some unfortunate individuals, lead to alcohol-dependence, just as others become addicted to drugs, so there are 'cult junkies' who move from one religious cult to another, seeking new sensations when the current one loses its power to stimulate.

The American camp-meeting revivals of the early nine-teenth century are perhaps the most sensational example of collective hysteria recorded in relatively recent times. Sel-des quotes a typical account:

> A more tremendous sight never struck the eyes of mortal man. The very clouds seemed to separate and give way to the praises of the people of God ascending to the heavens; while thousands of tongues with the sound of hallelujah seemed to roll through infinite space; while hundreds of people lay prostrate on the ground crying for mercy. Oh! my dear brother, had you been there to have seen the convulsed limbs, the apparently lifeless bodies, the distorted features. (p.60)

— all of which the writer interprets as signs of grace. A French observer was less sanguine:

> On the one hand there was preaching and singing, on the other, the confused noise as the new arrivals settled their belongings and pitched their tents. Soon a good number of those present had begun to tremble, to enter into convulsions, to agitate themselves like maniacs, rolling on the ground, foaming at the mouth, uttering piercing shrieks and cries. The enthusiasm grew daily, as the numbers grew to some four thousand. The chaos of the Tower of Babel would have been a model of harmony and order by comparison; it is impossible to imagine the extravagances — one young woman, in a pious ecstasy, threw off her clothes and plunged into the river and was drowned; another was so penetrated with the joy of being born again that she miscarried. (Calmeil, 1845, p.305)

Most of us shed our early reality-substitutes when the need for them fades away. The teenager who once craved the mind-blowing excitement of the pop concert discovers maturer pleasures. The man who got drunk to drown his sorrows when his girlfriend walked out on him, doesn't need this escape when he regains his sense of proportion — or meets another girl. It is the person who clings to his lifebelt when the danger is past who is in trouble.

We have seen that the ASC is often adopted as the best way of dealing with a specific situation. This kind of ASC is not — or should not be — so much a state as a *process*, which should run its course and then cease.

Trouble occurs when what starts as a beneficial temporary

expedient becomes a chronic state. This can often lead to mental illness, and is the primary reason why ASCs are so often supposed to *be* mental illness. Doctors have assumed that because a patient is in a pathological condition, his state was pathological from the outset; often, of course, this is the case, but often it is not. It is certainly a mistake to assume it, and to treat the symptoms as a disorder in themselves.

Multiple-personality cases

This is particularly true of multiple-personality cases such as the following, reported by Italian psychiatrist Enrico Morselli in 1925:

> Elena, a 25-year-old piano teacher, came to Morselli complaining of strange feelings, including that people were reading her thoughts and uttering terrible accusations against her. She spoke to him in perfect French, and when he asked why, as an Italian like himself, she didn't speak in Italian, she insisted that she *was* doing so.
>
> Examination revealed that she had two personalities: Elena-1 was Italian, Elena-2 was French. Elena-2 knew about Elena-1, but not the other way about.
>
> Morselli learnt that her home life was terrible because of quarrels between her father, an industrialist, and her mother, a neurotic alcoholic. Elena had a strong aversion for sexual matters; at times she believed her father was dead; there were gaps in her childhood memory relating to weeks spent with her father in a place whose name she could not recall.
>
> Eventually he established that Elena's father had made incestuous attacks on her. (in Ellenberger, 1970, p.138)

This case clearly illustrates the way in which dissociation of the personality initially serves a purpose — in this case, to escape from the reality of an intolerable family situation. Incest is the most common cause of personality multiplication for the simple reason that no other situation generates such emotional conflict, particularly for an adolescent inexperienced in personal relations.

Once the problem has been resolved, the personality should in principle be able to reintegrate. The doctor's first task, if he finds a patient in a dissociated state, is to ascertain what caused it; there is little point in attempting to resolve the disorder so long as the situation which brought it about remains unresolved.

Schizophrenia

Perhaps the most serious situation of all comes about when the ASC turns to schizophrenia. It is possible, indeed, that schizophrenia should be seen as no more and no less than a chronic ASC.

Such a view is supported by the comments on her own schizophrenia experience recounted by Barbara O'Brien in her remarkable book *Operators and things* (1958). I had not read her account when I wrote my book *Gods, spirits, cosmic guardians*, so it was a rewarding discovery to find that the 'psychodrama' concept I proposed there (and which I have briefly stated in #1) is very close to what O'Brien thought was happening to her.

No summary can do justice to the richness of O'Brien's experience, but this brief account demonstrates its affinity with many of our ASCs. Following on personal troubles involving a life-style conflict, Barbara starts to hallucinate a number of entities, who identify themselves as part of what amounts to a parallel world of 'operators', some benevolent, some malevolent. They persuade her to leave home and wander for several months, during which she lives, as it were, on two levels, that of the real world — where apart from occasional breakdowns she manages pretty well to cope — and that of her hallucinated world in which a succession of bizarre events gradually steer her towards resolving her situation in her own way. She says:

> There is an amazing lack of accurate knowledge among laymen concerning the effects of schizophrenia. The most prevalent notion is that the individual becomes two people, two distinct personalities, or even multiple personalities. . . In infrequent cases, this appears to be just what does happen. The unconscious has rebelled, assumed control, created the person it wishes to be, forced the conscious controller into a small, tightly closed box where it cannot even see what is going on, and then taken over the floor of the conscious mind.
>
> In most cases of schizophrenia, however, the unconscious appears to prefer not the techniques of the actor, but those of the director. It does not create a new personality but, instead,

stages a play. The major difference is that the conscious mind is permitted to remain, an audience of one, watching a drama on which it cannot walk out.

Even though the circumstances which induce or permit the unconscious mind to rise and take over are still a mystery, the fact that in schizophrenia it rises to do just that is strikingly clear. As you sit watching your Martian, it is your unconscious mind which is flashing the picture before your eyes, sounding the Man's voice in your ears. More than this, it is blowing a fog of hypnosis over your conscious mind so that consciously you are convinced that the hallucinations you see and hear, and the delusions that accompany the hallucinations, are real. (p.5)

Whether we choose to think of the ASC as a momentary schizophrenia from which the mind is able to recover without too much trouble, or of schizophrenia as an ASC from which the mind is unable (or unwilling) to recover, the parallels are manifest. Moreover, they provide further confirmation — if it is needed — that ASCs are fundamentally purposeful. O'Brien never doubts that there is a rationale behind the seemingly irrational events in which she is involved, and eventually she is able to track down the cause, a personal conflict exacerbated by work stress. We have seen enough instances to recognise that many ASCs result from just such a state of affairs.

The question remains, was it necessary for O'Brien's life to be quite so disrupted? Remember, too, that she was not simply one of the lucky people who recover from their schizophrenia, she was also one of the very rare people who do so by themselves, without help from the professionals. (Indeed, the professionals whom she consulted make a poor showing in her story: if she had taken their advice, it is likely her condition would be worse today rather than better.)

Ultimately, O'Brien triumphed over her ordeal, and in doing so, resolved her personal conflict: her story has a happy ending. Nevertheless, the price she paid was a high one.

Indifference to danger and death

We have seen many examples of ASCs in which the

secondary self is prepared to take extraordinary risks. Sleepwalkers seem to feel an urge to walk along narrow parapets high above the ground. The children of Morzine take to the trees and perform perilous acrobatics. The Self-2 in the Beauchamp (#3.4) and other multiple-personality cases like to live dangerously, doing things which Self-1 would never dare.

It seems reasonable to relate this to the reversion to childish behaviour we have noted. But there are other indications of such indifference. Lanternari (1963) tells us about the Guarani of southern Brazil:

> In the village of Araribà, inhabited by more than one hundred Nandeva-Guarani, there has recently been found a wide-spread psychosis that expresses itself in the form of dis-couragement and tedium, so serious as to border on suicidal mania. These Indians devote themselves intensively to rituals which enable them to escape from life into a state of mystical beatitude and personal perfection. Some cannot resist the yearning for death. (p.177)

Ultimately, there are the ASCs which get so skewed that the customary instinct to survive is eliminated. Many religious sects have gone in for self-mutilation; some have gone so far as suicide. But these are not necessarily signs of despair. The motive can be a strongly positive one. The French sociologist Le Bon (1896) reminds us:

> Doubtless a crowd is often criminal, but also it is often heroic. It is crowds rather than isolated individuals that may be induced to run the risk of death to secure the triumph of a creed or an idea, that may be fired with enthusiasm for glory and honour, that are led on — almost without bread and without arms, as in the age of the Crusades — to deliver the tomb of Christ from the infidel, or, as in 1793, to defend the Fatherland of France against its foes. Such heroism is without doubt somewhat unconscious, but it is of such heroism that history is made (p.37)

The need for understanding
Often the problem arises from the fact that people do not realise an ASC is involved at all.

When in 1977 Billy Milligan, arrested for rape, was found

to be a multiple personality subject, only one of whose secondary personalities was involved in the incidents, society was baffled as to how to treat the matter. Milligan eventually revealed a total of 24 secondary personalities, ranging from a pathetic lesbian to a Yugoslav of phenomenal strength. It is a sign that awareness of these states is spreading, that his lawyers' plea of not guilty on the grounds of insanity in the form of multiple personality was accepted; but equally it is a sign that society has a long way to go, that his subsequent history has been one of being passed from one mental hospital to another, the victim of constant disagreement between the doctors. And if the doctors cannot agree, it is not surprising that the rest of society is confused about what to do about people like Milligan (Keyes, 1981).

Patanjali, the legendary philosopher of yoga, says there are many ways whereby man may possess the gift of performing *siddhis* (extraordinary feats). He may be born with such a gift; he may acquire it by taking drugs; he may recite mantras (sacred formulas); he may practise austerities; or he may attain it through enlightenment. So far as Patanjali was concerned, only the last of these ways was advisable, because it was the only one in which the practitioner *understands* his powers and is able to control them.

As this inquiry makes only too clear, we are still a long way off understanding ASCs. While a good many people *use* ASCs to help them communicate with gods and spirits, achieve personal enlightenment or escape from their present condition, few *understand* what is happening.

There is no better instance of this confusion than the use of hallucinogenic drugs as a path to enlightenment. It is clear that for many drug takers, their experiences are paths which lead not *toward* a higher reality, but simply *away from* the present reality. Masters and Houston, in their *Varieties of psychedelic experience*, recognise this delusion:

> It is frequent and funny, if also unfortunate, to encounter young members of the Drug Movement who claim to have achieved a personal apotheosis when, in fact, their experience appears to have consisted mainly of depersonalisation, disso-

> ciation, and similar phenomena. Such individuals seek their beatitude in regular drug-taking, continuing to avoid the fact that their psychedelic 'illumination' is not the sign of divine or cosmic approval they suppose it to be, but rather a flight from reality. . . (1966, p.259)

To make matters worse, the experience is liable to be wrapped up in a half-understood belief-system derived from eastern mysticism:

> Armed with such terminology and ideation, depersonalisation is mistranslated into the Body of Bliss, empathy or pseudo-empathy becomes a Mystic Union, and spectacular visual effects are hailed as the Clear Light of the Void. (*ibid.*)

As Gita Mehta reminds us in her *Karma Cola* (1979) — a splendidly sane perspective on gurumania — the Indian sacred books, the *Upanishads*, themselves warn us: 'Sacred knowledge in the hands of fools destroys.'

9 Self, unself, or otherself?

Even this brief and superficial study has shown us that ASCs are complex and multiform in themselves, and that their interactions with our 'normal' life are more complex and multiform still. However, though we need to learn so much more before we can hope to understand them fully, by adopting this comparative approach we have been able to identify some recurring features, and they in turn help us to answer some basic questions about what ASCs are and why they happen.

Are ASCs 'real'?

> This amnesia is real enough and painful enough for the person concerned: it may be only a little psychological lesion, but it's none the less an infirmity. Berthe's moments of forgetfulness, which happen every moment of the day and which I can reproduce at will and seemingly so easily — these were what got her sacked from the shop where she worked and reduced her to misery. Mme D-'s amnesias forced her to come to Paris, to stay in hospital for months on end, far from her husband and children who had to manage without her. . . Such things may be 'all in the mind' but they're none the less real for all that; a question of personality may lead to someone spending his entire life in an asylum. (Janet, 1911, p.93)

Anything that gets you sacked from a job must be real in some sense. So yes, the *condition* unquestionably exists. But there are those who claim that such conditions are no more than combinations of interpersonal factors, with no existence *per se*. ASCs as such, *as states* of hypnosis, trance, etc. they say do not exist.

To me this seems merely playing with words, like saying a cocktail doesn't exist because it's no more than a combination of other liquids. The fact remains that a Manhattan is a unique combination with its own particular characteristics, and if you wish to enjoy precisely that combination, it is helpful to be able to order it by name instead of spelling out the recipe to the bartender.

So, surely, it is with hypnosis or hysteria, ecstasy or trance. Each shares characteristics with other ASCs, and could be dissected into those parts; but the whole is, none the less, specific, something in its own right. The condition of a person in hypnosis is not altogether the same as his condition in trance, despite the similarities and the overlap.

Are ASCs distinct from the USC?
Though USCs vary from one individual to another, and though ASCs come in all shapes and sizes, there are sound reasons for believing there is a difference in kind between the USC on the one hand, no matter whose, and each and every ASC on the other, no matter what form it takes.

★ When people come to themselves, after being in an ASC — out of hypnosis, say, or spirit trance — it is virtually always to their USC that they return: it seems to be an equilibrium to which the system reverts after an ASC. Occasionally, they switch first to sleep: but when they wake, they will usually be in their USC, not back in their ASC again.

   The exceptions are multiple-personality and amnesia subjects, who may go to sleep and awake in their secondary personality. But this actually confirms the point; for the very question posed by these particular kinds of ASC is, which is the 'real' personality of the individual?

★ Only the USC is characterised by a high degree of self-control and sense of identity; whereas *all* ASCs are to some extent characterised by a loss of these qualities. Admittedly, this difference is only relative; even in the USC, none of us is wholly in control of ourselves, entirely able to perceive things as they are, and equally, control and awareness by no means altogether disappear in the ASC. None the less it *is* felt to be a real difference by those many subjects for whom it is a sense of 'not being their usual self' that tells them they are in an ASC.

Are ASCs distinct one from another?

Miss Beauchamp's doctor, Morton Prince, wrote:

> We may lay it down as a general law that during any dissociated state, no matter how extensive or how intense the amnesia, all the experiences that can be recalled in any other state, whether the normal one or another dissociated state, are conserved and, theoretically at least, can be made to manifest themselves. (1924, p.78)

Such research as has been done in this direction confirms Prince's hypothesis, but I think he may be premature in laying it down as a law: as with all questions relating to ASCs, much further research is needed. Do we know, for instance, if when someone who has taken an LSD-trip is later hypnotised, he will be able to recall his psychedelic experiences?

Here, however, is one example of inter-ASC continuity — in this case, from hypnosis to dreaming — which dramatically supports Prince's claim:

> Dr Voisin suggested to a hypnotised patient that he should stab a patient in a neighbouring bed (actually a stuffed figure): this he did, but retained no conscious memory of doing so. Three days later he reported dreaming that he was haunted by the figure of a woman who accused him of having stabbed her to death. Dr Voisin had to hypnotise him again to erase the pseudo-memory. (Myers, 1903, vol.1, p.129)

We have seen that many characteristics are shared by several different ASCs. A hypnotist can make his subject hallucinate, or this may happen to a person spontaneously. Amnesia-and-recall are characteristic of intoxication as much as of hypnosis; anaesthesia is symptomatic of *piblok-toq*, of vision-seeing, of somnambulism and of many hysterical behaviours. Selective blindness and deafness are common to many ASCs; hysterics share with geniuses the ability to pursue their activities in a state of abstraction.

Clearly, it would be naïve to suppose that a different process is involved in each of these instances. But it would be equally naive to infer that all these states are really no more than variations of one another.

Manifestly there is more to it than that. To take just one instance: Janet found that his hysterical patients, if forced to concentrate on something, would lapse into somnambulism. This was a distinct shift from one behaviour to another, implying two distinct states.

What happens if we rephrase the question and ask, is there a 'basic state' of which all the others are really only modifications, the differences being imposed by where and when they happen, to whom they happen, in what cultural milieu or environment, and by any other local circumstances which might affect the matter? Let us consider some possible candidates.

'Auto-hypnosis'?

If we look back over the experiences described in this inquiry and ask is there any one factor which recurs sufficiently often for us to consider that it might be the common basis of all ASCs, the one that suggests itself is hypnosis, induced either consciously or subconsciously.

We saw in #3.5 that Mrs Sidgwick considered self-hypnosis to be the basis of Mrs Piper's 'spirit trance', and it is easy to believe that this is equally true of shamanic trance. Breuer was not alone in thinking that hysteria too is, at bottom, self-hypnosis. It could be argued that self-hypnosis underlies all those ASCs which involve role-playing — whether it takes the form of dissociation of the personality, or possession fantasy, or a visionary encounter.

But though some sort of auto-hypnotic process may be involved in all these behaviours, it is only one of the elements, and the differences between the states are at least as distinctive as what they have in common. No useful purpose would be served by defining them all as variants of hypnosis.

'Dissociation' and 'role-playing'?

Every ASC involves a shift away from the everyday self, so that dissociation is, to some degree, implicit in every ASC. Similarly, it could be argued that every ASC is a kind of performance, in which the individual plays a more or less stereotyped role — The Drunk, The Visionary, The Ecstatic.

Both dissociation and role-playing are necessary elements of the ASC, but they do not define it: they are simply the means by which the subconscious self achieves what it wants to achieve. To see either as the essence of the ASC is to confuse the process with the *purpose*.

To use the cocktail analogy again, there is nothing to be gained by lumping together all the drinks that use a gin base as if they are one and the same; it is not the fact of containing gin which gives them their character, but the way the gin is combined with other ingredients. So, too, the fact that many ASCs display hypnosis, or role-playing, or have other features in common, does not entitle us to lump them all together so long as they also display unique features, or features in a unique combination.

Are ASCs 'better' than the USC?

The French mathematician Henri Poincaré had been struggling to resolve a mathematical problem for a fortnight, until one day the solution came to him during a sleepless night. Understandably, he commented, 'Is not the subliminal self superior to the conscious self?'

Janet's colleague Despine had a patient, Estelle, who in her waking state suffered from anaesthesia and paraplegia, but when in hypnotic trance would run about the hills: 'Her one idea is to pick flowers and run about in an entranced state from 10 in the morning till 9 at night'. (1911, p.369)

A housewife went for a walk in the wood behind her house after taking a hallucinogenic drug:

I felt I was there with God on the day of the Creation. Everything was so fresh and new. I continued to wander through this wood in a state of puzzled rapture, wondering how it could have been that I lived only a few steps from this place, walked in it several times a week, and yet had never really seen it before. . . I saw there and I knew then that there were dimensions to life and harmonies and deeps which had been for me unseen, unheard and untapped. Now that I know they are there, now that I have awakened to the glorious complexity of it all, I shall seek, and perhaps some day I shall find. (Masters and Houston, 1966, p.261)

When Eileen Garrett came back to reality after the euphoric states she describes in #7.4, she found 'once the experience has come to an end, everything looks brown or grey, or even coarse as materials assume their original shape'.

OBE subjects tend to look on their earthly bodies with 'a cold contempt'. Not surprisingly, they treasure the 'peak experiences' which their ASCs bestow. Mr Skilton, the American engineer who had a vision while loading a railway truck (#2.5) said of his experience: 'This I count the brightest day of my life, and what I saw is worth a lifetime of hardship and toil.'

Almost everyone, at some time of their life, has had an experience which seems to indicate that the ASC is superior to the USC, which is why bookstores are full of books, and our magazines full of advertisements, encouraging us to seek life-enhancement by consciousness-raising techniques which generally involve ASCs of some sort.

But there is a world of difference between Poincaré's ASC and Estelle's, a difference which relates to them as individuals, and their individual needs. It was nice and convenient for Poincaré to have his problem sorted out for him, just as it was kind of my subconscious self to help me with the ideas for this book, but these are matters altogether trivial when set beside the life crisis in which Estelle was involved.

ASCs, at their best, give us a glimpse of higher possibilities, but in doing so they are liable to make us dissatisfied with the here-and-now, and that is a very mixed blessing. Perhaps those who approach their experience with as much wisdom as Garrett did can enjoy the benefits without suffering the drawbacks; perhaps one day we shall all learn to enjoy the promised blessings of psychedelic drugs. In a famous poem, Housman speculated that 'could man be drunk for ever', he might enjoy unalloyed happiness: but as things are, we have to come back to reality.

Starbuck, in his sociological analysis of conversion, compares the results of revival meetings conducted by a professional evangelist, of the kind we have quoted in the course of this study, with a much less dramatic revival effort made in the course of regular church activity by a pastor. He found that though the evangelist's dramatic methods initially attracted 92 converts, 62 had 'dropped' in less than six weeks, and eventually only 12 remained church members in good standing. The pastor's relatively low-key effort, though it initially attracted only 68, suffered only 16 early drop-outs and ended with 41 church members.

Some people, perhaps, may manage to live in what amounts to a permanent ASC without causing too much trouble to themselves or those around them — people such as Blake, Swedenborg and other 'god-intoxicated' persons. But we have only to study the lives of the great majority of those who live permanently in their ASCs — the mental patients in our hospitals, the chronic drug-takers, etc. — to realise that reality with all its shortcomings, like Starbuck's pastor, wins in the long run. Janet says of his own patients:

> It is clear that Lucie 3, Rose 4 or Léonie 3 are superior, by a long way, to Lucie 1, Rose 1, Léonie 1. But in these cases we are talking of hysterical women, and this superior existence which we bestow on them is simply a normal existence, which they would be enjoying anyway if they weren't ill. It is so far from being superior to their everyday selves that it is in fact indistinguishable from the state of these women in their rare moments of health. (1889, p.136)

There is perhaps no more striking illustration of an ASC providing a short-term benefit than the dancing mania which afflicted Europe in the Middle Ages, first described in detail at Aachen in 1374:

> Assemblages of men and women formed circles hand in hand, and appearing to have lost control over their senses, continued dancing, regardless of the bystanders, for hours together, in wild delirium. While dancing they neither saw nor heard, being insensible to external impressions through the senses, but were haunted by visions, their fancies conjuring up spirits whose names they shrieked out; and some of them afterwards asserted that they felt as if they had been immersed

in a stream of blood, which obliged them to leap so high, until at length they fell to the ground in a state of exhaustion. They then complained of extreme oppression, and groaned as if in the agonies of death, until they were swathed in cloths bound tightly round their waists, upon which they again recovered, and remained free from complaint until the next attack. The bystanders frequently relieved patients in a less artificial manner, by thumping and trampling upon the parts affected.

When the disease was completely developed, the attack commenced with epileptic convulsions. Those affected fell to the ground senseless, panting and labouring for breath. They foamed at the mouth, and suddenly springing up began their dance amidst strange contortions. (Hecker, 1854, p.87)

Though at first the outbreaks occurred in a more-or-less haphazard manner, they gradually became more formalised; it became usual for musicians to accompany the dancers, and for dancing to take place at certain locations associated with either St John or St Vitus, who were believed to be the most effective saints when it came to combatting the Devil, who was held by the Germans to be responsible. In Italy, on the other hand, the mania was attributed to the bite of the tarantula spider, an intriguing parallel to the 'June bug' which was one of the alleged cause of multiple psychogenic illnesses (#4.3).

As for the behaviour of the afflicted, it matches closely several others, from *pibloktoq* to the Cornish Jumpers. However Hecker, the nineteenth-century professor of medicine whose account I quote, goes beneath the surface aspect of what seems at first to be a wild delirium, and recognises that the mania *served a purpose*.

Crucial, in his view, are the social circumstances. The European peasantry at that time lived appallingly wretched lives, oppressed by feuding barons, roving bands of robbers, constant hunger and bad food, an underlying sense of instability whether from human predators and uncertain harvests — all adding up to what we have seen to be appropriate conditions for ASCs. In addition, there was 'the influence of the Roman Catholic religion, connected as this was in the Middle Ages with innumerable practices which strongly excited the imaginations of its votaries, and certainly brought the mind to a very favourable state for the reception of a nervous disorder. In such circumstances the dancing mania served the function of a much-needed outlet:

> Most of those affected were only annually visited by attacks. Throughout the whole of June, prior to the Festival of St John, patients felt a disquietude and restlessness which they were unable to overcome. They were dejected, timid and anxious, wandered about in an unsettled state, and eagerly expected the eve of St John's day. This hope was not disappointed, and they remained, for the rest of the year, exempt from any further attack, after having thus, by dancing and raving for three hours, satisfied an irresistible demand of nature.
>
> Such was their faith in the protecting power of the saint, that one of them visited the shrine more than 20 times, another 32. The cure effected was in many cases so perfect, that some patients returned to the factory or the plow as if nothing had happened. Medical men were astonished to observe that women in an advanced state of pregnancy were capable of going through an attack of the disease, without the slightest injury to their offspring, which they protected merely by a bandage passed round the waist. (ibid., p,105)

This brief account does not do justice to the complexity of this fascinating outbreak, but it is sufficient to provide us with a splendid illustration of *how* the ASC is superior to the USC: in the dance, these wretched folk found a relief which their everyday life could not have given them; equally, it is quite unthinkable that it could be anything but an occasional indulgence.

If I press down hard on my car's accelerator, I force it to change down to a lower gear giving a terrifying surge of power — wonderfully useful if I have to get rapidly out of an emergency traffic situation. I could well conclude that such 'peak performance' is superior to my car's normal running; but of course it would be disastrous to run it so on a permanent basis.

So it is with our ASCs: many are indeed superior to the USC — but only as a short-term expedient.

Are some ASCs 'better' than others?
Many different kinds of ASC are felt by those who expe-

rience them to be of immense and unique value. Do the 'everyday ecstasies', obtained by everyday people as diverse as high-altitude balloonists and near-death patients differ in kind or in degree from those bestowed upon the great mystics — or is it simply that the latter are able to analyse their feelings more deeply and express them more articulately? Is all this 'cloud of unknowing' and 'dark night of the soul' stuff no more than the result of being better educated?

In these democratic days it is tempting to think so, and to feel a kind of resentment against privileged souls secure in their cloisters whose experiences are considered to be so much more refined than those of lesser mortals.

Perhaps fortunately, we have no means of judging between one subjective experience and another. We can evaluate the experiences only by their consequences, which is only a partially valid yardstick. If it could be said that those who have these experiences live noticeably better lives as a result, this would be some kind of estimate of the value of their experience.

But the disconcerting fact is that people can be made better and happier not only by experiences which are thoroughly banal, but also by ones which are manifestly delusory! Many of those who report encounters with the occupants of flying saucers are notably the better for the experience; their life-styles are transformed, their values enhanced, their consciousness raised at least as effectively as by a religious conversion or a course of meditation.

Can a lifetime of yoga and zen do more? An evangelist would say that life-styles are all very well, but what matters is the immortal soul. It may be so. It may be that those who dedicate their entire lives to preparing themselves for the next phase of existence are going to have a better time in their future lives, like the schoolboy who refuses to join his friends on the football field because he is studying for university entrance. But if so, it is an act of faith. It is by no means certain that there *exists* a world to come, nor that if it turns out that there is, those who have spent their lives in this world in preparing for the next will get a pat on the head for doing so; nor do we have any assurance that they are going about it in the right way.

It is even arguable that, whatever the obscure purposes of the universe, the fact that we have been given this earthly life implies an implicit instruction to live it as best we may, and that to seek to escape or transcend it is to miss the point of existence.

Are we in control of our ASCs?

If we have no control over our ASCs, if they are imposed on us without our say-so, then it is hard to refute the traditional view of ASCs, that they are morbid and pathological states, best avoided, but if unavoidable, then best treated by whatever means may be available.

The exceptions would be those ASCs which are not really ASCs at all, but celestial privileges bestowed by the divine powers, or malevolent machinations of the powers of evil. So the question, Are we in control of our ASCs?, is the ultimate key to understanding the ASC.

In 1966, at the height of the drug euphoria in the United States, Pahnke and Richards described their experiments with drug-induced ASCs and concluded: 'It now appears possible to select almost any normal, healthy person and, combining a sufficient dose of a psychedelic substance with a supportive set and setting, enable that person to experience various altered forms of consciousness' (in Tart, 1969, p.416). Their claim, as worded, is probably justifiable; but at this stage of our inquiry we can see that it is a very limited claim. In the first place, no guarantee is offered that the person will experience one *kind* of ASC rather than another; and in the second place, there is no control over the *content* of his experience.

Pahnke and Richards would doubtless reply that, while they could offer no guarantees, they could be fairly sure of guiding their subject into the ASC of his choice, and while they could not control the content in detail, they could direct it into general areas — erotic, religious, etc.

So, in so far as artificial states are concerned, we can claim to be in control of our ASCs within broad limits. But artificial ASCs are only one part of the spectrum.

Spontaneous ASCs, as we have seen, may be induced in us by external triggers, perhaps even imposed on us by external agents, or they may be the result of physiological processes within us.

That external agents may be responsible for our ASCs is something we must accept as possible, but we must at the same time acknowledge that the evidence for them is less than convincing. In 1853 the American writer E.C. Rogers, who has supplied several of our most interesting cases, wrote: 'This easy method of accounting for anomalous phenomena, by referring them to spirits, is that which has been the characteristic of ignorance or intellectual apathy in every age.' It seems to be no less true of our own age than of his, but today's believers, like those of Roger's day, have nothing better than circumstantial evidence to justify their belief. Even if we allow that in some cases — communication by the spirits of the dead, say — external intervention is the best explanation we have, that is still a long way short of *proving* that it occurs.

If external agencies do exist and are responsible for some ASCs, you might think they must be so powerful that we could not hope to have any control over what happens. This, however, is not the case. The churches offer guidance as to how the wiles of Satan, at least, may be thwarted. Dealing with extraterrestrials may not be so easy.

That external forces induce some ASCs is beyond question, and it is equally clear that many of them are clearly beyond our control. We can refuse alcohol and drugs; we can refrain from mountain-climbing, or marriage, or playing the stock market — activities liable to lead to stressful situations; by not meditating, by not becoming a shaman, by abstaining from voodoo or ritual dancing, by not putting our hands up when a stage hypnotist ask for volunteers, by refusing invitations to revival meetings, we can avoid many more ASC-inducing circumstances. If we suffer from allergy, we can protect ourselves; we can control our diet, our food intake, our exposure to toxic substances. If Schmeing is right in saying that second sight can be inhibited by adding calcium to our organism, a visit to the chemist will enable us to strike that danger off our list. But when we have taken every precaution, there remain circumstances we cannot avoid, and when they arise we are ultimately unable to control them. The air we breathe, the weather, the environment, will always impose limitations on our ability to control our ASCs.

However, a discovery such as Schmeing's simply raises further and larger questions — *Why* does calcium deficiency have this effect? *Why* should a negative factor of a purely *chemical* nature result in a positive improvement in performance of a *psychological* nature?

This is where the purely behaviourist scheme breaks down. It is not simply that we all *feel* that our bodies are not simply closed systems, the sum of a vast complex of electro and chemical reactions, responses and processes. It is that such a model is simply not adequate to explain the fact of interaction between physical process and psychological process, such as has been displayed on every page of our inquiry, and which a finding such as Schmeing's demonstrates in simple clarity.

That Mary Wood's meningitis (#3.3) led to her multiple-personality ASC is self-evident: what is not evident is *why* it did, and why it took the form it did. It is as though, once the physical process had been started, the psychological processs took over. I do not see how her doctors could possibly have anticipated that her physical state would lead to the fragmentation of her personality into 'Good thing' and 'Persuader'.

Throughout the course of our inquiry, underlying the complex subject-matter we have tried to compose into a coherent structure, two concepts have recurred over and over again: *depersonalisation* and *role-playing*.

Time and time again, we have found that the ultimate source of the ASC is a deliberate act, which we may suppose to be initiated by the subconscious self, which involves detaching the individual from the close contact with reality he has in his USC, and giving him freedom to transcend the limits of his everyday self in an ASC.

This state of detachment, we label *depersonalisation*; the process by which we redefine our behaviour, we may loosely label *role-playing*. I am not sure that these are the best terms, because each of them is associated with specific activities, whereas I am trying to give them a wider relevance. But they are familiar terms, and so help us to relate the process to the ASCs we are familiar with.

Role-playing, which we have found occurring in ASCs ranging from Janet's games with Léonie to Barbara O'Brien's schizophrenic fantasies, can be simply a performance — as it was for Léonie — or it may lead to the emergence of a second self — as it did for O'Brien. Which it will be, who we will be, not our conscious but our subconscious self will decide. With Pahnke and Richards' help, we can force our way into an ASC of a sort, but when we get there, we are in the Wonderland where our subconscious self may know its way around, but our conscious self is hopelessly lost.

So before we answer the question, are we in control of our ASCs, we must ask: Who do we mean by 'we'? If we mean: Is our conscious self in control? the answer is certainly No. But if we accept that we have, built into us, a subconscious self, and accept that subconscious self as part of ourselves, then we have not relinquished control so much as it may appear.

Throughout this study, we have been skating over the surface of ASCs — but aware, thanks to numerous glimpses, of hidden depths and rarely realised potentials beneath. A woman who is moved to 'heal' the sick girl in the next bed by exerting some hitherto unrecognised potential within herself; the visionary whose life is changed for the better by an experience which objectively is downright delusion; the man who while loading a railway wagon has a glimpse of a higher plane of existence — these and many other experiences point to our possession of personalities more rich and more powerful than those we think we know. Thanks to the ASC, we can escape from our everyday selves and take temporary refuge in an unself or an otherself; or we may for a moment rise above our usual selves to discover our superselves.

The experiences we have looked at in the course of this inquiry demonstrate, first, that despite appearances the great majority of ASCs have a purpose which is ultimately beneficial; and second, that the way to benefit from them is to adopt a prudently pragmatic attitude. ASCs are short-term means to immediate ends; once that end is achieved, we should come back to reality where we belong — just as nature, in her wisdom, sees to it that we do.

Some people can bear more ASCs than others, but I don't see why we should regard this as anything more than a pattern of temperament, similar to the fact that some people can live alone more happily than others: we cannot say that one is better than the other. Those people who seem to thrive on prolonged or continual ASCs — the Teresas and the Swedenborgs — come naturally to their condition: it is unlikely that anyone who deliberately exposes himself to massive doses of ASC will by so doing become a Teresa or a Swedenborg. It is far from certain that he will even add one centimetre to his spiritual stature.

Most of us, once the trance or the dance or the ecstasy or the dream is over, come back to our USC: our subconscious self sees to that. And though it may have been exciting out there in Wonderland, it's just as well to be back home where we belong, in our usual state of consciousness.

References

The literature of ASCs is vast, and I am indebted to a vast number of other researchers in arriving at what is written here. It seems more helpful to the reader to divide my list of references into (A) those writings which I have found continuously helpful, or which the reader too may find helpful as general commentaries or references; and (B) sources to which specific reference is made in the text, often only for a single observation or case.

SPR = *Society for Psychical Research, London*
JSPR = *Journal of the Society for Psychical Research*
PSPR = *Proceedings of the Society for Psychical Research*
PF = *Parapsychology Foundation, New York*

A General sources

Bramwell, J. Milne, *Hypnotism*, 1903.

Calmeil, L.-F., *De la folie*, Baillière, 1845.

Corliss, William R. (ed.), *The unfathomed mind: a handbook of unusual mental phenomena*, Sourcebook Project, 1982.

Ellenberger, Henri F., *The discovery of the unconscious*, Basic Books, 1970.

Evans, Hilary, *Visions, apparitions, alien visitors*, Aquarian, 1984.

___ *Gods, spirits, cosmic guardians*, Aquarian, 1987.

Hilgard, Ernest R., *The divided consciousness*, Wiley, 1977.
___ (with Josephine H.), *Hypnotic susceptibility*, Harcourt, Brace, 1965.
James, William, *Principles of psychology*, Macmillan, 1890.
___ *The varieties of religious experience*, Longmans Green, 1902.
Janet, Pierre, *L'automatisme psychologique*, Alcan, 1889.
___ *L'Etat mental des hysteriques*, Alcan, 1911.
___ *De l'angoisse à l'extase*, Alcan, 1926.
Laski, Marghanita, *Ecstasy*, Cresset, 1961.
___ *Everyday ecstasy*, Thames & Hudson, 1980.
Madden, R.R., *Phantasmata*, Newby, 1857.
Myers, F.W.H., *Human personality*, Longmans, Green, 1903.
Oesterreich, T.K., *Possession*, Kegan Paul, 1930 (from German).
Parapsychology Foundation, New York, *Proceedings of two conferences on parapsychology and pharmacology*, 1961.
Parker, Adrian, *States of mind*, Malaby, 1975.
Penfield, Wilder, *The mystery of the mind*, Princeton University Press, 1975.
Rogers, E.C., *Philosophy of mysterious agents*, Jewett, 1853.
Sargant, William, *Battle for the mind*, Heinemann, 1957.
___ *The mind possessed*, Heinemann, 1973.
Society for Psychical Research, London, *Proceedings (PSPR); Journal (JSPR)*.
Tart, Charles T. (ed.) *Altered states of consciousness*, Wiley, 1969.
Wolman, Benjamin B. and Ullman, Montague (eds), *Handbook of states of consciousness*, Van Nostrand Reinhold, 1986.
World Health Organization, *Mental disorders: glossary & guide to their classification*, Geneva, 1978.
Zinberg, Norman E. (ed.), *Alternate states of consciousness*, Free Press, 1977.

B Specific sources

Alacoque, Marguerite-Marie, *Entretiens mystiques*, Spes, 1947 [orig. circa 1680].
Allison, Ralph, *Minds in many pieces*, Rawson Wade, 1980.

Barbanell, Maurice, *This is spiritualism*, Herbert Jenkins, 1959.

Barthélemy, Toussaint, *Etude sur le dermographisme*, Société d'Editions Scientifiques, 1893.

Beyerstein, Barry L, 'Neuropathology and the legacy of spiritual possession' in *Skeptical Inquirer*, Spring 1988.

Blanc, Hippolyte, *Le merveilleux dans le Jansénisme etc.*, Plon, 1865.

Bord, Janet, *Astral projection*, Aquarian, 1973.

Bourgaux, Jacques, *Possessions et simulacres*, Epi, 1973.

Bourneville, Dr, *Louise Lateau*, Paris, 1875.

Brownell, Winfield S. (ed.), *UFOs, key to Earth's destiny!*, Legion of Light, 1980.

Bugliosi, Vincent, *Helter skelter: the true story of the Manson murders*, Horton, 1974.

Calmet, Dom Augustine, *Dissertations sur les apparitions*, De Bure, 1746.

Cauzons, Th. de, *La magie et la sorcellerie en France*, Dorbon-Ainé, 1901–12.

Cohen, J.M. and Phipps, J.-F., *The common experience*, Rider, 1979.

Colligan, M.J., Pennebaker J.W. and Murphy, L.R. (eds), *Mass psychogenic illness*, Erlbaum, 1982.

Comer, N.L., Madow L. and Dixon J.J., 'Observations of sensory deprivation in a life-threatening situation' in *American Journal of Psychiatry*, August 1967.

Crookall, Robert, *The supreme adventure*, James Clarke, 1961.

Davis, J.M., McCourt W.F. and Solomon, P., 'The effect of visual stimulation on hallucinations and other mental experiences during sensory deprivation', in *American Journal of Psychiatry*, 1960.

Deleuze, J.P.F., *Historie critique du magnetisme animal*, Mame, 1813.

Denti di Pirajno Alberto, *A cure for serpents*, Deutsch, 1956.

Deren, Maya, *Divine horsemen*, Thames & Hudson, 1953.

Diderot, *Encyclopédie*, Paris, c. 1760.

Eliade, Mircea, *Shamanism*, Princeton University Press, 1964.

Ennemoser, Joseph, *The history of magic*, Bohn, 1854 (from German).

Esdaile, James, *Natural and mesmeric clairvoyance*, Bailliere, 1852.

Estabrooks G.H. and Gross, N.E., *The future of the human mind*, Dutton, 1961.

Félice, Philippe de, *Poisons sacrés, ivresses divines*, Albin Michel, 1936.

____ *Foules en délire*, Albin Michel, 1947.

Festinger, L., Riecken, H.W., and Schachter, S., *When prophecy fails*, University of Minnesota Press, 1956.

Fiore, Edith, *The unquiet dead*, Doubleday, 1987.

Flournoy, Théodore, *Des Indes à la Planète Mars*, Atar, 1899.

Forel, August, *Hypnotism*, Rebman, 1906 (from German).

Freud, S., and Breuer, J., 'On the psychical mechanism of hysterical phenomena' in Freud, *Collected papers*, Vol. 1, 1892.

Freud, S. and Breuer, J., 'The case of Anna 'O', *Studies in Hysteria*, 1895, in Freud, *Collected Works*, Vol. II, Hogarth Press, 1964.

Furst, Peter T., '"High states" in culture-historical perspective' in Zimberg, N.E. (ed.), *Alternate states of consciousness*, Free Press, 1977.

Goldenson, Robert M., *Mysteries of the mind*, Doubleday, 1973.

Görres, Johann Joseph von, *La mystique divine, naturelle et diabolique*, Poussielgue-Rusand, 1845 (from German).

Gregory, William, *Letters to a candid inquirer on animal magnetism*, Taylor, Walton & Maberly, 1851.

Guérin, Pierre, 'Le problème de la preuve en ufologie' in J.C. Bourret, *Le nouveau défi des OVNI*, France-Empire, 1976.

Guilleminault, C., Billiard, M., Montplaisir, J. and Dement, W.C., 'Altered states of consciousness in disorders of daytime sleepiness', in *Journal of the neurological sciences*, vol. 26, no. 3, November 1975, pp. 377–93.

Guilleminault, C., Phillips, R. and Dement, W.C., 'A syndrome of hypersomnia with automatic behavior', in *Electroencephalography and clinical neurophysiology*, vol. 38, 1975, pp. 403–13.

Gurney, E., Myers, F.W.H. and Podmore, F., *Phantasms of the living*, SPR, 1886.

Harris, Melvin, *Sorry, you've been duped!*, Weidenfeld & Nicolson, 1986.

Hecker, J.F.C., *The epidemics of the Middle Ages*, Sydenham Society, 1854.

Herschel, Sir John, *Familiar lectures on scientific subjects*, London, 1816.

Hooper, Sydney E., 'The appreciation of time by somnambules' in *PSPR*, July 1923.

Horowitz, Mardi J., 'The imagery of visual hallucinations' in *Journal of Nervous and Mental Disorders*, Vol. 138, no. 6, June 1964.

Hufford, David J., *The terror that comes in the night*, University of Pennsylvania, 1982.

Hyslop, James H., 'The subconscious and its functions', in, *Proceedings of the American Society for Psychical Research*, vol. VII, Part 1, 1913.

Ikemi, Yujiro, 'Les états modifiés de conscience' in *Science et conscience*, 1980.

Jones, Ernest, *On the nightmare*, Hogarth Press, 1931.

Joyeux, H. and Laurentin, René, *Etudes médicales et scientifiques sur les apparitions de Medjugorje*, OEIL, 1985.

Kenny, Michael G., *The passion of Ansel Bourne*, Smithsonian, 1986.

Kerner, Justinus, *The seeress of Prevorst*, Moore, 1845 (from German).

Keyes, Daniel, *The minds of Billy Milligan*, Random House, 1981.

Kroll, J. and Bachrach, B., 'Visions and psychopathology in the Middle Ages' in *Journal of nervous and mental disease*, vol. 170: 1, 1982.

Lanternari, Vittorio, *The religions of the oppressed*, Macgibbon & Kee, 1963 (from Italian).

La Tourette, Gilles de, *L'hypnotisme et les états analogues au point de vue médico-légal*, Plon, 1887.

Laurentin, René, *Lourder histoire authentique*, Lethielleux, 1962, p. 89.

Laurentin, René and Billet, Bernard, *Lourdes, documents authentiques*, Lethielleux, 1958.

Lawson, Alvin H., 'The birth trauma hypothesis' in *Magonia*, 10, 1982.

___ 'The hypnosis of imaginary UFO abductees', in *Journal of UFO studies*, no. 1, c. 1983.

Leaning, F.E., 'An introductory study of hypnagogic phenomena' in *PSPR*, vol. 35, 1925.

Leary, Timothy, 'The religious experience: its production and interpretation', in Heenan, E.F. (ed.), *Mystery, magic and miracle*, Prentice Hall, 1973.

Le Bon, Gustave, *La psychologie des foules*, Flammarion, 1896.

LeShan , Lawrence, *The medium, the mystic and the physicist*, Turnstone, 1974.

Lignières, Jean, *Les messes noires*, Paris, c.1928.

Lindley, J.H., Bryan, S. and Conley, B., 'Near-death experiences in a Pacific Northwest American population: the Evergreen study' in *Anabiosis*, 1981.

Luce, Gay Gaer, *Body time*, Random House, 1971.

___ (with Julius Segal), *Sleep*, Heinemann, 1967.

Macnish, Robert, *The philosophy of sleep* (2nd edn), Appleton, 1834.

Masters, R.E.L. and Houston, J., *The varieties of psychedelic experience*, Blond, 1966.

Mathieu, P.-F., *Histoire des convulsionnaires de Saint-Médard*, Didier, 1864.

Mehta, Gita, *Karma Cola: marketing the mystic east*, Simon & Schuster, 1979.

Michel, Aimé, 'Une autopsie de l'amour divin', in *Planète* 17, 1964.

Michel, Frère, de la Ste Trinité, *Apparitions à Medjugorje?*, Contre-Réforme Catholique, 1988.

Mirville, J.E. de, *Des Esprits*, De Surcy, 1863.

Moll, Albert, *Hypnotism*, Scott, 1890 (from German).

O'Brien, Barbara, *Operators and things*, A.S. Barnes, 1958.

Orne, Martin, 'Alien-abduction claims' in *Skeptical Inquirer*, XII:3, 1988.

Paul, Saint, *Second epistle to the Corinthians*, Authorised Version, 1611.

Persinger, Michael A., 'Religious and mystical experiences as artifacts of temporal lobe function' in *Perceptual and Motor Skills*, vol. 57, 1983.

Podmore, Frank, *The newer spiritualism*, Fisher Unwin, 1910.

Prince, Morton, *The dissociation of a personality*, Longmans Green, 1905.

___ *The unconscious*, revised edn, Macmillan NY, 1924.

Puharich, Andrija, *Beyond telepathy*, Darton, Longman & Todd, 1962.

Rhine, J.B., *The reach of the mind*, Faber & Faber, 1949.

Rochas, Albert de, *L'extériorisation de la motricité*, Chamuel, 1896.

_____ *Les vies successives*, Leymarie, 1924.

Rogo, Scott, 'Ketamine and the NDE' in *Anabiosis*, Spring 1984.

Romains, Jules, *Eyeless sight*, Putnam 1924.

Saint Denys, Hervey de, *Les rêves et les moyens de les diriger*, 1867.

Salverte, Eusèbe, *Des sciences occultes* Baillière, 1856.

Sedman, G., 'A phenomenological study of pseudohallucinations and related experiences' in *Acta Psychiatrica Scandinavia*, vol. 42, no. 1, 1966.

Seldes, Gilbert, *The stammering century*, The John Day Company, 1928.

Sidis, Boris and Goodhart, Simon P., *Multiple personality*, Appleton, 1904.

Siegel, Ronald K., 'Hostage hallucinations' in *Journal of nervous and mental disease*, vol. 172, no. 5, 1984.

Skeat, W.W., *Malay magic*, Macmillan, 1900.

Smith, Steven B., *The great mental calculators*, Columbia University Press, 1983.

Soyka, Fred, *The ion effect*, Dutton, 1977.

Starbuck, Edwin Diller, *The psychology of religion*, Scott, 1901.

Stevens, E.W., *The Watseka wonder*, Religio-Philosophical Publishing House, 1887.

Sulman, Felix Gad, *The effect of air ionization, electric fields, atmospherics and other electric phenomena on man and animal*, Thomas, 1980.

Szasz, Thomas S., *The myth of mental illness*, Secker & Warburg, 1962.

Taylor, Gordon Rattray, *The natural history of the mind*, Secker & Warburg, 1979.

Thigpen, C.H., and Cleckley, H.M., *The three faces of Eve*, Secker and Warburg, 1957.

Thulié, H., *La mystique des théologiens*, Vigot, 1912.

Thurston, Herbert, *Surprising mystics*, Burns & Oates, 1955.

Trochu, Francis, *Le curé d'Ars*, Vitte, 1926.

_____ *Sainte Bernadette Soubirous*, Vitte 1953.

Tromp, Solco W., 'Effects of weather and climate on mental processes in man' in *Parapsychology and the sciences*, Parapsychology Foundation, 1972.

Twemlow, S.W., Gabbard, G.V. and Jones, F.C., 'The out-of-body experience' in *American Journal of Psychiatry*, April 1982.

Watson, Nigel, 'Before the "flying saucers" came' in Evans, H. and Spencer, J., *UFOs 1947–1987*, Fortean Tomes, 1987.

Wier, Jean, *Histoires des illusions et impostures des diables*, 1560 (from German).

Wilson, S.C. and Barber, T.X., 'Vivid fantasy and hallucinatory abilities in the life histories of excellent hypnotic subjects' in Klinger, E. (ed.), *Imagery: concepts, results and applications*, Plenum, 1981.

Wood, H.C., 'A study of consciousness' in *Century Magazine*, May 1890.

Index